YOU are not YOUR ANXIETY

Dr. Carly Crewe breaks down from start to finish how anxiety works, attacks, and takes over your mind, body, and soul. As a therapist who works daily with clients, she explains and understands what is actually happening when we suffer with anxiety. Her writing and knowledge are so insightful and digestible to help normalize mental health in such an approachable, caring, and supportive way. If you're struggling with anxiety, this is the book for you!"

– *Eli Weinstein, LCSW / Host of The Dude Therapist Podcast / Creator of ELIvation*

As a physician, mother, and CEO dealing with anxiety, I am pleased to say that this manual has helped me understand that anxiety doesn't define me, and that I am in control. We are constantly working to harmonize all parts of our life—work, business, marriage, motherhood . . . and the list goes on. Dr. Crewe lends her personal experience and professional expertise in helping us understand how to navigate it all. I recommend that every woman add this book to her bookshelf—it will change your life!

– *Abha Sharma, MD / Founder of Health Has No Finish Line / Precision Certified Health Coach / Writer / Podcaster / Mom of one*

As a disabled mom navigating the ups and downs of multiple autoimmune conditions, anxiety is something I struggle with daily. If you can relate to that feeling of perpetual uncertainty and are looking for a book to ground and center you, this is it. Carly's thoughtful and diverse tips on creating boundaries and self-care strategies to truly understand and explore anxiety are so in depth that you will be able to immediately access new skills no matter who you are and no matter where you are on your health journey. This book is an invaluable resource.

– *Kat Inokai, Writer / Host / Content Creator*

I have danced with anxiety my entire life. When I was younger, I didn't know what to call it, but now that I'm a full-blown adult, I know exactly what it is when it rears its ugly head. Sometimes the tools I've gathered along my life journey just aren't enough to help me rise above a bout of it. If you're like me and you struggle with anxiety, I strongly urge you to pick up this book by Dr. Carly Crewe. She calls it like she sees it. This book is straight to the point with no BS, while still being gentle and supportive. It's like having your own personal anxiety specialist on speed dial without the price tag; I instantly felt my shoulders drop and my mind calm after only one chapter in.

– Shantelle Bisson, Amazon best-selling author of
Parenting Your Teen Without Losing Your Cool

I didn't experience anxiety until suffering a traumatic event at twenty and then spent two years trapped in my mind. In *You Are Not Your Anxiety*, there are so many explanations of what's happening inside your brain that are broken down into bite-sized, impactful, and easy-to-implement concepts. If I had this book ten years ago, it could've saved me a lot of stress. No matter the severity of your anxiety, the explanations and suggestions in this book will help you rewire it.

– Felly Day, CEO of FellyDay VA / Mentor and Speaker

YOU are not YOUR ANXIETY

HOW TO STOP BEING AN ANXIOUS, PEOPLE-PLEASING MESS

CARLY CREWE, MD
Women's Mental Health Expert

You Are Not Your Anxiety: How to Stop Being an Anxious, People-Pleasing Mess

Copyright @ 2021 Carly Crewe, MD

YGTMedia Co. Press Trade Paperback Edition

ISBN trade paperback: 978-1-989716-19-9

eBook: 978-1-989716-20-5

Audio Book: 978-1-989716-24-3

All Rights Reserved. No part of this book can be scanned, distributed, or copied without permission. This book or any portion thereof may not be reproduced or used in any manner whatsoever without the express written permission of the publisher at publishing@ygtmama.com—except for the use of brief quotations in a book review.

The author has made every effort to ensure the accuracy of the information within this book was correct at time of publication. The author does not assume and hereby disclaims any liability to any party for any loss, damage, or disruption caused by errors or omissions, whether such errors or omissions result from accident, negligence, or any other cause. The advice contained within this book does not constitute—or serve as a substitute for—professional psychological treatment, therapy, or other types of professional advice or intervention.

The reader should consult with their doctor in any matters relating to their health.

Published in Canada, for Global Distribution by YGTMedia Co.
www.ygtmama.com/publishing
To order additional copies of this book: publishing@ygtmama.com

Developmental Editing by Kelly Lamb

Edited by Christine Stock

Book design by Doris Chung

Cover design by Michelle Fairbanks

ePub & Kindle editions by Ellie Silpa

Author Photo by Meghan Unger

Cover image: © Shutterstock/Astafjeva

Printed in North America

This book is dedicated to all the women who have trusted me with their hearts and minds. May you always remember that you are not alone and that the impact you have on the world is limitless.

table of contents

introduction	This Book Is Going to Change Your Life	1
chapter 1	What We'll Cover in This Book	13
chapter 2	The Shapeshifter: My Story	17
part 1	**The Beast That Is Anxiety**	**37**
chapter 3	Anxiety Is a Universal Human Experience	39
chapter 4	It Makes No Sense to Resist Your Anxiety	49
chapter 5	Only You Can Decide How to Move Forward from Here	59
chapter 6	The Anxiety Recovery Process	65
chapter 7	Anxiety's Last Stand	83
chapter 8	It's Normal to Feel Overwhelmed	89
part 2	**Let's Get Down to Business**	**95**
chapter 9	The Eunoia Approach	99
chapter 10	Your Experience and Your Suffering	125
chapter 11	You Are Not Your Thoughts	139
chapter 12	You Are the Subject of a Science Experiment—Get Curious	149
chapter 13	Your Anxiety Is Separate from You	153
chapter 14	Your Anxiety Is More Predictable Than You Realize	159
chapter 15	Almost All of Your Anxious Thoughts Are Cognitive Distortions	163

chapter 16	You Can't Just "Stop Thinking" Something	171
chapter 17	Avoiding What Triggers Your Anxiety Will Only Make You More Anxious	177
chapter 18	Survival of the Busiest: You Can't Busy Yourself Better	183
chapter 19	Cognogens: False Beliefs	195
chapter 20	Perfectionism: When Good Enough Is Never Good Enough	203
chapter 21	Habit Creation for the Recovering Perfectionist	213

part 3	**Interpersonal Relationships and Communication**	**219**
chapter 22	Let's Talk About Your Personal Power	225
chapter 23	The Connection Between Anxiety and Passivity	231
chapter 24	Assertiveness Means Speaking from Your Personal Power	237
chapter 25	You Need to Stop Being So Invested in the Lives of Others	247
chapter 26	You Don't Own That	255
chapter 27	You Need Better Boundaries	271
chapter 28	An Unhealthy Relationship Is Not a Relationship You Need	287

part 4	**Self-Care Is Mental Health Care**	299
chapter 29	Self-Care Is Not Massages and Bubble Baths	301
chapter 30	Behavioral Activation: Sometimes You Have to Fake It to Make It	317
chapter 31	Let's Do This Thing: Creating a Self-Care Ritual	321
chapter 32	The Three Components of a Self-Care Routine	331
chapter 33	Tracking and Monitoring Your Anxiety: The Easy Way	343
chapter 34	Let's Go Deeper: Anxiety, Alignment, and Trust	349

acknowledgements	363
resources, works cited, and next steps	366

introduction

THIS BOOK IS GOING TO CHANGE YOUR LIFE

Seriously, it is.

Every single day, I work with women who feel like their lives have been taken over by their anxiety. They often ask me if there is a book or books I can recommend for them to learn more. I recommend countless resources, none of which have been a perfect match for my approach and teachings, until now.

Now, when I'm asked for resources, I can literally say: I actually wrote the book on this shit, and here it is.

In your hands is what I consider to be your coach, best friend, therapist, and doctor in one neat package (minus the prescription pad and plus an additional degree of sass). It's the majority of my strategy, approaches, and insights on anxiety management for women in written form, complete with my honest and sarcastic personality (you know I couldn't leave that part out, right?). I'm so excited to share it with you.

This book is designed to be a manual for you to learn how to manage your anxiety and reclaim control over your mind and life, once and for all. This book is my manifesto for a new generation of women—a generation that is done feeling overstretched, anxious, guilty, resentful, and overwhelmed all the time. It's designed to open your eyes and show you things about your life as a woman, your behavior, and your mind that will help you finally step into your power. It will help you shed the shitty self-limiting beliefs that continue to keep you stuck and hold you back from being the powerful, independent, and confident woman you've always wanted to be. The woman you know you're meant to be. Think of it like a good kick in the ass, a good shake of your head, or a good come-to-Jesus talk with your brutally honest best friend. If you're someone who is offended easily, I advise you to put down this book and to pick up something a bit more polite or a bit more fluffy.

Why did I write this book? First of all, women's mental health is my passion, so it follows that I have lots of insights to share. However, there's a deeper purpose to this book and all of my work. I believe helping women heal is truly legacy work. As women, whether we're mothers or not, we are influencers. No, I'm not referring to social media influencers, and no, you don't need a certain number of followers. When I refer to being an influencer, I mean a real-life, flesh-and-blood influencer. Whether at our homes in our own families, at our workplaces with colleagues, in our churches and spiritual centers, or in our wider communities at large, women influence people in their lives every single day. We are role models for one another and for our partners. We are role models for our children, and we are constantly striving to improve how we raise them, so they can be kind, authentic, and loving. When we are taking care of ourselves well, we inspire those around us to take care of themselves too. I can't tell you how many times a woman has asked me if I could see her husband or sister because the changes she is making have inspired them to heal themselves as well. We influence others in the way we care about them, the passions we pursue, the businesses we build, and the ideas we manifest. I believe the potential of women to heal the world by simply being ourselves is infinite. However, I also believe that to heal the world, we must first heal ourselves. We must first be well within ourselves.

As someone who has been intimately involved in the field of mental health care for some time as both a provider and a patient, I bring a unique perspective to this issue. I believe that our current mental health system is outdated and fragmented. It has not been designed to support women in the ways that women's brains need to be supported. Our system is strained, and despite best efforts from mental health practitioners, many women struggle to get the support they need in the time they need it. Many of the women I've worked with also find it a challenge to find someone they can connect with or who truly understands what they're going through. It's time for a new revolution in how we care for our mental health as women, and I hope this book will be the first introduction to a new way where women are central to their own healing.

This book is going to teach you everything you should have been taught about how your mind works and how anxiety works in your mind. This book is written to teach you how to think about your anxiety in a different and more empowering way than you likely have before. I believe that the way we think about our mental health, our stressors, and our anxiety is also very important, which is why we will review some mindset shifts that you will need to make to manage your anxiety for life. If you are diligent about reading and following the steps and strategies I outline in this book, I believe you will learn how to accept your anxiety as part of you, you will shift your mindset to a more empowered one, and you will reclaim your sense of agency in your life.

After you have read this book, it's my intention that you will have learned how the health of your body is integral to the health of your mind. I'm confident you will learn to recognize your anxious thoughts and have strategies to work through them in the moment and during quiet reflection. By employing the self-care strategies in this book, you will bolster your sense in your own self-worth so that you'll no longer struggle to find the time to take care of yourself or feel guilty if you do. It's my hope that through reading this book, you'll learn how to recover control of your mind, gain self-confidence, and take solid steps toward creating the life that you really yearn for and deserve. I have very high expectations for this book—and I hope you do too.

I'm not saying this venture is going to be easy. This book is going to call on you to shine light into the areas of your life that you've either been avoiding or have felt too anxious to explore. You will be challenged to examine the subconscious behavior of your mind and consider some strategies and mindsets that may counter what you have considered true in the past. This book will challenge you to examine your beliefs in your own self-worth and honestly look at how you consider your worth in comparison to those you love and care for. It's going to ask you to look at relationships that make you feel depleted and be honest with yourself about whether these are really serving you. It's going to ask you to dig down into the layers of your onion (sometimes tears included) and get crystal clear about what you really want in your life. You will need to identify your most important values and honestly ask if you treat the woman in the mirror like she is worthy of everything she wants. It's going to ask you whether you're living a life that is genuinely authentic to you rather than some version of your life that you have created to feel "acceptable" to others. And finally, I'm going to challenge you to bring light to all of those dreams you have for yourself that have been hidden away under the excuse of "too busy" or "not deserving."

So, buckle up, sister. This will be the start of a new chapter of your life, one in which you are empowered and calm. One where you no longer feel like you are an unwilling passenger on the emotional roller coaster that is anxiety.

To get started, I'm going to share a few somewhat harsh truths to make sure we're on the same page.

Harsh Truth #1: YOU NEED THIS BOOK.

This book is my love letter to anxious, overwhelmed, and passive women everywhere who are sick of feeling this way and are ready to reclaim their power and finally become the leading lady of their own lives. I suspect this description fits you, otherwise you probably wouldn't have picked up this book. It's intended for the woman who struggles with anxiety more than her friends or family members, who sometimes feels like her anxiety makes her feel out of control and wants more than anything to *feel like herself again*. It is written for the woman who has a brain that doesn't know when to stop, that goes around in thought spirals, making her feel like she needs to give her own head a shake. It's for the woman who wants to be empowered and inspired to learn about her mind and how it works so she can harness it as the superpower it is. It's written for both mothers and non-mothers, for although who we are before and after motherhood are often strikingly different versions of ourselves, the strategies I share in this book apply to both seasons. Therefore, this book is also written for the mother who believes that there is a better, calmer, and more enjoyable version of motherhood available to her, and this book will provide the strategies to find that. Finally, if you identify as a "people-pleaser" who struggles to advocate for your own needs, who avoids conflict like the plague, and who feels more like an employee than the boss of her own life, this book is going to be your new best friend. It's for the woman who has put others' needs before her own for so long that she may not even be aware of her own needs anymore. It's for the woman who was taught to be a "good girl," avoids disappointing others at all costs, and feels like she "can't possibly say no" in certain relationships (you know the ones).

Most of all, this book is designed for the woman who is genuinely committed to making changes in her life so that her life is truly her own. So she can take back control of the thoughts that circle her mind night and day and finally feel like herself again. I know what it is like to feel trapped in your own mind. To second-guess and doubt your own thoughts because you're not sure if they are your anxiety or reality. To constantly battle with irritability and overwhelm. To feel tired all the time from fighting the battle in your own head. I see you, and we've got this.

Whether you would consider yourself someone who struggles with anxiety or not, I believe that some version of anxiety is present in all of us. In my work with women, in both my clinical and coaching practices, I have found that anxiety plays a part in almost every experience we have. More often than not, the "normal worry" that we have come to believe is just "part of who we are" or "part of being a mother" plays a bigger role in our lives and experiences than we realize.

If you struggle with anxiety regularly or have been diagnosed with a clinical anxiety disorder, to you I say: You are in the right place. As an anxiety warrior myself and a clinician who helps women manage their minds regularly, I want you to know that this book will provide you with a new perspective on managing your anxiety and learning skills to keep it under control for your lifetime. There are no quick fixes here, but I assure you the slow, steady, and intentional approach will pay off. Whether your anxiety stems from "always being this way" or from a specific situation or event in your life, the teaching and strategies provided in this book will help you. If you have previously worked with a counselor or have engaged with cognitive behavioral therapy, you may find some overlap between the strategies in this book and those previous experiences.

Harsh Truth #2: YOU ARE NOT SPECIAL.

There is a particular group of women I hope this book will be very helpful for, and these are the ones who have a "special" version of anxiety. In my experience, there are women who seem to be unconsciously committed to their anxiety, to their being "a mess," and to their anxiety being "unfixable." They believe they are a "special" case for some reason or another and that no one can possibly understand them completely, and that's why traditional therapy or research-based strategies "just won't work" for them. Their anxiety is just "different." In some cases, despite being provided many different options and solutions, they refuse to give them a solid effort or even acknowledge their anxiety at all.

If this is you, friend, I'm here for you. I see that you're struggling and don't know which way is up some days. However, this mindset won't serve you, so here's a little straight talk:

There is no denying that you are indeed unique.

There is no denying that you have special qualities about you and have gone through experiences unique to you.

Your struggle with anxiety and your battle for happiness and mental health is valid and real. Life's been hard; you've been through some incredibly tough shit. I get it. *I see you.*

However, at the risk of making you angry this early in our time together, I'm also going to tell you that believing you are "a special case" that is unfixable is bullshit. Your commitment to this belief that you are chronically misunderstood or beyond help is a barrier preventing you from feeling better and becoming the woman you want to be.

The reality is that anxiety is anxiety. No matter where it comes from or how special you think your version of anxiety is, it behaves just like everyone else's anxiety. (I can already hear you arguing with me in your brain, so just cut it out.)

First of all, your anxiety being *just like everyone else's* is a good thing because once you learn about how anxiety works (in general), it becomes very predictable and manageable. I would hazard a guess that you can easily identify what triggers your anxiety and can predict with a high level of certainty about when your anxiety will flare and how it will feel. Your anxiety is very treatable and manageable, but you've got to get your mindset right about it. I can give you all the strategies in the world on how to manage your anxious thoughts, how to cut toxic relationships, and how to rid yourself of unnecessary guilt, but if you're subconsciously carrying beliefs about being unfixable, it won't matter. You have to ask yourself whether there's a part of you that refuses to give up your anxiety because it's become part of your identity; it allows you some sort of "brokenness" that provides special treatment in your life.

If you come to me and claim your anxiety is "different," I typically hear that claim as "It's part of me and I'm not giving it up; I'm attached to it and the suffering it brings me." I also hear, "I'm too scared to get rid of it because I actually might have to chase my dreams and live up to my full potential if I don't have it."

Many women who say these things to me view their anxiety as being part of their personality. They're not sure who they would be if it didn't exist.

If you're identifying with this section or if my statements here are triggering you, let it come. Don't sweat it. Embrace it. This message isn't intended to shame you because shame is not my game. This truth is intended to encourage you to question whether there could be some subconscious value that you have assigned to your anxiety. It's asking you to question whether there is perhaps a secondary gain you are receiving from your anxiety, some sort of benefit that your anxiety is giving you. Truthfully, why you are so committed to keeping your anxiety around may be something you can't explain, and that is okay. In my clinical work as well as in this book, I talk a LOT about what our minds do without us realizing it or being consciously aware of it. To truly overcome anxiety, it's my job to challenge you into considering what your brain has been unconsciously doing (or even consciously doing) that is limiting your ability to get well.

It is likely that if you're feeling triggered by this section, then perhaps you need to hear this more than ever right now.

> *Self-Check:*
> Take this opportunity right now to ask yourself:
> 1. Am I genuinely willing to commit to this process and learn how to change my thinking so I can truly be free of my struggles?
> 2. Am I willing to consider that I may be wrong about certain aspects of my anxiety and my mental health and that there may be things I don't know that could help me?
> 3. Is this moment of self-righteousness worth me never getting my anxiety under control?
> 4. Am I genuinely and authentically ready to show up for myself, ask the hard questions, and push myself out of my own comfort zone?
> 5. Am I willing to examine all the ways that my anxiety and "brokenness" have been serving me and learn new ways of interacting with my mind and the world?
> 6. Am I ready to stop getting in my own way? Am I ready to stop putting up with my own shit?

Harsh Truth #3: Trauma changes your brain.

Now, in saying this, I am in NO way referring to those of you who are reading this book with severe and intractable mental health disorders or who have experienced trauma. This book is not intended to replace formal psychotherapy or be an exhaustive treatment for severe mental illness. If you are someone who has experienced trauma in your life and have developed powerful negative coping and defense mechanisms in response to that trauma, you are possibly reading the wrong book. I am not an expert in trauma-focused approaches to mental illness (yet), and this book is not intended to be an exhaustive approach to trauma. These situations are much more appropriately handled by highly specialized and experienced professionals in the realm of working with the traumatized brain. There is no doubt that the brain that has experienced trauma works in different and complicated ways. That being said, depending on where you are in your healing journey, I believe the concepts outlined in this book will still help you, even if you have experienced trauma in the past.

Harsh Truth #4: THIS BOOK WILL NOT FIX YOU.

No matter who you are, there is one critical point that must be made regarding this book and your mental health: This book will not fix you. In my work, far too often I have patients and clients who come to me hoping that I will "fix them." To be "fixed" is a completely human thing to want—to find someone or something that will completely remove all distress (defined as extreme anxiety, sorrow, or pain) and suffering once and for all, in one swoop. I want to make it clear right here and now that there is no substance, therapist, or self-help book that will take away all your struggles without significant effort and commitment on your part. There is no magic pill or fix to get your anxiety under control and make your life easier.

Will this book help you? Yes, very much. But first you have to commit to releasing all of your preconceptions about yourself and the ways that your anxiety is serving you. You have to adopt brave and uncomfortable new beliefs about yourself, your self-worth, and your fears to overcome perfectionism and chronic people-pleasing. Therefore, this book is meant for the woman who is genuinely ready to take an active role in her own life. It is designed to provide you with the information, new perspectives, and mindset shifts you need to make to finally get control of your anxiety and to keep working at it for the rest of your life. It will introduce you to a new lifestyle and a new system of thinking and behaving in relation to your own mind so you can free yourself of unnecessary struggle and become the joyful, calm, and present person you want to be. That you and your family deserve you to be.

Ready? Let's do this.

chapter 1

WHAT WE'LL COVER IN THIS BOOK

In my work with women and mental health, I use a very comprehensive and holistic approach, which can sometimes feel overwhelming to anxious people. The beautiful thing about you reading this book is that you can take it at your own pace, choosing one or two areas to focus on in your life at one time. The challenging thing about you reading this book is that it is easy enough to put on your bedside table or bookshelf, then conveniently "forget" about it. As you read this book, you will be challenged to examine certain areas of your life that you have been avoiding. It's possible that you may feel some increased anxiety or discomfort while reading it. If that happens, please know that it is normal and expected. Be gentle with yourself. And keep reading.

In fact, I'd go so far as to say that these feelings of discomfort are signals that you are on the right track. That being said, if you find yourself feeling overwhelmed or not sure where to begin, I recommend starting with the chapter on biology and the body (Chapter 9). This content is usually the least intimidating, the easiest to implement, and it can provide simple, quick wins with your anxiety early on. Focus on one or two areas of each section at a time rather than attempting to dive into every area of your life, making massive changes all at once. When I work with women in my virtual clinic, I often say that although it feels like things are going slowly and we are making very small changes, those small changes will create amazing results over time with consistency and support. As in all areas of behavioral change, the guiding principle to improving your anxiety and mental health is to take it slow and steady, being mindful and aware of when feelings of discomfort or anxiety attempt to derail your progress. We feel discomfort when we do things differently or when we implement changes in our lives. It is vital that you avoid letting discomfort cause you to quit or think that you're doing the wrong thing. In the words of Susan David, PhD, "Discomfort is the admission price to a meaningful life." Don't give up—you're stronger than you think, and you've got this.

To begin, I'll provide some new ways to think about your anxiety and the role it plays in your life, and I'll share some important mindset shifts you can make. We will also learn about anxiety from a variety of different perspectives so that you have a complete understanding of its purpose in your life. We will then review the journey I have seen clients and patients travel through as they work to get their anxiety under control—the Anxiety Recovery Process. These steps will ensure you not only know where you are beginning but where you are going and your end goal.

Once we have built a firm foundation of understanding, I will walk you through The Eunoia Approach—a comprehensive system that I have created to guide my management of women's mental health symptoms and disorders. Eunoia is a Greek word meaning beautiful thinking; a well mind, which is exactly what we're all striving for. The Eunoia Approach will provide a framework with which you can organize your efforts and understand how different parts of your life are interrelated with your mental health. This approach will comprise the majority of this book as we break down how biological, psychological, and social factors can be addressed and changed in the pursuit of a well mind. Each subsection within The Eunoia Approach will provide a number of tactical tools, strategies, and habits so you can apply what feels most effective for you in your life.

To ensure consistency with your anxiety management and mental health habits, you will need a clearly defined and regular ritual for caring for your mental health. For this, I will provide guidance for creating an effective and enjoyable self-care plan for you to integrate everything you have learned into a grounding and effective daily ritual.

Finally, we'll dig beneath the surface of your day-to-day anxiety and bring to light some of the harder-to-examine aspects you may be avoiding (whether consciously or subconsciously). We'll discuss how to use your anxiety as a homing beacon for alignment in your life and how to find the courage to truly choose yourself and your happiness in your one and only life. *It's going to get juicy.*

How to read this book

I recommend that you read the book from the beginning to end, as certain concepts and tools build upon one another as we progress through. At the completion of certain sections, I have provided opportunities for you to reflect on what you have learned. The Self-Checks spread throughout the book will ask questions designed to inspire self-reflection. Take time to respond to the questions honestly and thoughtfully in your journal or notebook.

Like most things in life, you will get out of this book the same effort that you put into it. Remember, this book is not a magic bullet and will not help you without you doing the work. Trust me, I know that getting your anxiety under control and feeling well is not easy. It can often feel like hiking uphill on a steep incline while someone is throwing boulders down at you at the slightest sign of progress. However, I know that even the weakest hikers can make it to the top with enough time, patience, and persistence. I know this fact to be true because I have been where you are.

chapter 2

THE SHAPESHIFTER: MY STORY

I want to start by telling you a little about my journey and how I came to write a book on anxiety management. I share my story not because it is unique, dramatic, or even inspiring. While there are a few surprising twists and highs along the way, most of my story is actually quite ordinary. I (thankfully) haven't experienced any devastating trauma, nor have I been the recipient of divine, spiritual guidance (unfortunately). Nope, I'm just your average woman who has lived a somewhat average life, and I hope that you can find similarities in my story that make you think, *Wow, she's just like me.*

I realize now that I have had anxiety for most of my life (read: all my life). I was a perpetually worried child, although the flavor of my fears and worries changed into various personas as I became older. As a little girl, the younger of my mother's two daughters,

I was conscientious, too responsible for my age, and terrified of almost everything. I would be up for nights on end, wracked with guilt and worry after even the most minor of indiscretions, ruminating on countless albeit fervent fears and concerns for the future that should have been far beyond my comprehension at my age. I remember many nights, after wrestling with the fears and demons in my mind for hours and finally summoning up the courage to get out of bed, walking silently in my sockless feet to my mother's door and knocking quietly, half hoping she wouldn't hear me. Each time, she would wake up and listen patiently while I tearfully confessed all my seemingly terrible sins and worries to her between choked breaths. None of them were ever as bad as I thought they were. My mother, a hardworking and mostly single parent working three jobs as a registered nurse to pay the bills, would listen intently and reassure me that no, she wasn't going to die on her way home from work. It was okay that I had found the porn magazine under the porch while playing at the neighbor kid's house, it wasn't mine. And no, those women weren't being hurt. Our house would not catch on fire while we were sleeping, and yes, the baby hamsters we had given away were warm and taken care of. A vivid imagination paired with heightened anxiety does not a calm or sleepy child make.

As I grew older, my anxiety shifted and switched forms. The most overt and silly childlike worries slid quietly below the surface and a sneakier and more damaging form emerged. I can't clearly recall when my anxiety morphed from a more general fear of everything to a paralyzing fear of social interactions and judgment, but it was definitely around the time I developed breasts. An early bloomer, I recall becoming the unwanted focus of my male classmates seemingly overnight. My body betrayed me and presented me as more of a woman than I was ready to be. The fallout was that I also became the target of considerable animosity from my female peers, and so emerged the damaging words and names that no adolescent girl wants to be labeled with, including *slut*, *tramp*, and *easy*. A precocious and intelligent student, I was frequently the first to finish a test and was reliably at the top of my school classes. This, paired with the new development of my more abundant-than-others bust, was all too much for my fellow females to tolerate. The silent whispers, sideways glares, and suddenly silent cafeteria tables as I approached did nothing for my self-confidence and fed the beast that was social anxiety.

As almost any woman who has lived through middle and high school can attest, other females can be one of the scariest groups of people on the planet. They travel in packs, ruthlessly single out their prey, and can treat someone terribly without ever speaking to them at all. My anxiety was helpful in keeping me safe at this time: It taught me how to shrink, how to dress in just the right way to avoid attention, and how to hide my head diligently in my schoolwork so I wouldn't see their sideways looks or hear the hushed trash-talking whispers. I had a few friends and even braved a few high school parties, only for my anxiety to remind me that home was safer, and my schoolwork would never bully me. This coming-of-age-as-a-woman ostracism motivated a change of schools late in the eleventh grade, a retreat to a quieter and (hopefully) less damaging environment for me to finish my high school years. I graduated with all honors, and I was rewarded for my academic diligence with a full scholarship to the university nearest to my home.

University was better. Now an "adult," I thrived on the independence of choosing my own major and class schedule, but I mostly loved that I no longer sat in the same classroom with the same people more than once per day. My anxiety transformed again, and instead of being a paralyzing adolescent form of social anxiety, it became a more socially acceptable perfectionistic, organized, and academic form of anxiety. Being in university meant that I didn't have to attend any parties that I didn't want to. It meant I could spend countless hours perfecting essays and chemistry reports until they were surefire ways to maintain my 4.0 GPA. I had a few close friends, but I mostly spent my time with my then-boyfriend-now-husband and our little rescue dog. My anxiety helped me during these post-secondary years, fueling the fire of productivity, perfectionism, and pursuit of academic excellence, which paid off when I graduated at the top of my program and was admitted to medical school on my first attempt. Things were looking up, and my anxiety and I had finally found our groove. It's like we were frenemies who finally found some common, hallowed ground with each other. As long as I listened to its guidance around writing a perfect paper and working for hours to avoid losing my edge, I would be successful in anything I tried. I became a proud and unrelenting perfectionist and even added this trait to my list of qualifications and skills on my résumé.

Life continued. I married my high school sweetheart at twenty-three years old during the two-week break in my three-year accelerated MD program at the University of Calgary. In love with my new husband and my life, it seemed that my anxiety no longer would have a role to play. I had become accustomed to doing what my anxiety told me to do, and I had been successful because of it. So successful, in fact, that I didn't even realize the role my anxiety played in my life; it had become so ingrained in my personality, habits, and lifestyle that it wasn't a hindrance, it was a help. It helped me meet all the socially expected milestones with grace and seemingly little effort:

> Get good grades: check. ✔
> Graduate with honors: check. ✔
> Full-ride scholarship: check. ✔
> Get admitted to medical school: check. ✔
> Find partner, marry early: check. ✔
> Become a doctor by twenty-five: check. ✔
> Get pregnant: check, and check. ✔ ✔

My husband predicted we would have twins long before we were married. He would joke with me about it, and my highly risk-averse medical brain would easily dismiss this idea: *much too risky*. Twin pregnancies were too high risk.

I told him I was pregnant on our fifth wedding anniversary. We were pregnant quicker than expected. Throughout those early and nauseating weeks, he would jokingly ask me how my two little buddies were doing, and I would laugh and shake my head. *Much too high risk.*

Cut scene to me, one foggy day after the birth of my beautiful twin girls. My anxiety was back. It had mutated into its most vicious and powerful version yet. Postpartum mood disorder (PMD) is a beast in any form, and mine was no exception. Within weeks, I became a shell of my former self. I was chronically exhausted with babies who would wake on opposite schedules no matter what I tried, and my anxiety encouraged me: *Carly, a more rigorous schedule and doing things in just the right way will fix the issue.*

Although I had previously spent time helping women with position and latching at a breastfeeding clinic during my residency and considered myself to have extra knowledge in this area, nursing my own babies was overwhelmingly painful, emotional, and felt futile at times. I remember feeling so worried, so trapped, so out of touch with the old version of myself that existed pre-motherhood. I was constantly tense, cried on a dime, and had an explosive temper that knew almost no bounds. To this day, my baby monitor is cracked open, a wound sustained from me throwing it at the wall or across the room in overwhelming fits of postpartum rage. I believed that controlling the twins' schedule would help me feel more control over my mind and my anger, which only made me angrier when they didn't comply with my plans. My sleep, at best, was fitful and wrought with nightmares, interrupted frequently by newborn twins who seemed to need more of me than I was able to give them. I second-guessed my competency to be their mother and even believed in moments of fleeting terror that they would be better off without me. It was a very dark time.

As any pervasive mental health disorder does, my postpartum anxiety affected more than just my mood. It affected how I showed up in my relationships, what I thought about my own worth as a person and mother, and how I took care of myself (read: I didn't). It took away the confident and assertive woman I had once been and replaced her with a passive, submissive, and self-sacrificing version of my previous self. I would avoid speaking up for myself to others out of fear of them being angry with me or abandoning me. I complied with nearly every request, even though I knew deep down that it would not be right for me. I fought silently for months.

Thankfully, I woke up one morning and a realization struck me immediately as if it had been planted in my mind overnight. I realized that my life was passing before my very eyes, and this was the only chance I was getting at it. It hit me like a ton of bricks. *Was this really the life I was going to have? Was this how my motherhood experience was actually going to look? How long was this going to go on? Was this how I wanted to be living my life and acting in my relationships? Was this all there was going to be for me?* An anxious, overwhelmed, and passive vortex of feeling resentful, depleted, and irritated all the time?

I didn't sign up for this.

I remember saying this sentence out loud to myself in that moment. I remember realizing that the life I was currently living was not what I had ever anticipated or envisioned when I dreamed of being a mother, despite having "achieved all the milestones." I realized in that moment that I would not get another chance to watch my twins grow up, watch them take their first steps or make funny faces over mushy peas. I realized that so much of my motherhood experience and my day-to-day life was discolored in my memory by relentless intrusive thoughts and a constant feeling of impending dread and incredible fatigue—a byproduct of my restless nights. This realization was a huge turning point for me, as if the universe itself had given me a firm shake and told me now was the time to WAKE UP. *Whose life was I living? Whose responsibility was it to ensure I was living a life true to me? Whose responsibility was it that I became the mother my children deserved?* It was mine. My anxiety and I had finally come face-to-face.

At that moment, I decided to step up to the plate and take responsibility for my own mind. Although I hadn't fully recognized what I was going through right then, I was experiencing a severe clinical postpartum mood disorder. I was aware that something wasn't right about this experience and that this wasn't what "motherhood was like." I started by reaching out to a physician support line instead of my own colleagues in my clinic, as I was terrified of being judged by them as weak or not able to hack it. Even as a physician who specializes in maternal mental health, I could not shake the fear of being seen as less-than-okay or that I couldn't do motherhood "all on my own." In fact, it's often this exact fear of being judged as not competent that causes women to avoid going to their doctor at all and to avoid talking to friends about how they are feeling and getting the help they need in the postpartum period.

I cried on the phone to a kind stranger as I told her about my fleeting thoughts of getting in the car and driving away, never to return. I sobbed as I shared with her that there were moments when I genuinely believed that my family would be better off without me, and that those moments were becoming more and more common.

I began seeing a therapist, and so began my personal introduction to cognitive behavioral therapy and mindfulness, strategies I would dabble with at this time but not fully commit to until much later. She introduced me to the concept of self-care and highlighted the stark absence of any of it in my own life. We discussed my relationships, especially the most stressful ones, and how I had been behaving as a passive "people-pleaser," which then left me feeling resentful and bitter toward those I loved. Around that same time, I made the commitment to do almost anything that would make me feel better.

I began reading books on personal development and committed to a rigid morning routine of meditation, journaling, affirmations, and exercise. I started doing yoga nearly every single morning. I began to feel a bit better each day, but my anxiety had a different idea. So sneaky, that anxiety.

This newfound routine was exactly what my anxiety wanted to latch on to, and with a vengeance. What initially began as a healthy, supportive self-care plan transformed into a rigid, militaristic, and punitive schedule I felt compelled to follow, day in and day out. I set up a rigid 5:30 a.m. routine of meditation, journaling, reading, exercise, and affirmations. Anxiety told me that every single problem had a perfect solution and that I just had to follow a series of predefined steps for the outcome I was seeking. I applied strategies my previous life had taught me were successful, that input equals output, and that there is indeed an elusive "correct way" to fix any complicated problem. Looking back now at myself then, I realize that I was kidding myself when I thought I was getting better. The exercise, meditation, and other activities were helping, but my perfectionistic anxiety stood backstage, vigilant for any deviation in the routine so that it could be center stage again. I couldn't skip a day without devastating shame and self-hatred. I berated myself for not following the "routine" correctly, and heaven help us if the twins woke up during the defined period I had set aside each morning for self-care. My anxiety had a way of turning even a healthy change into something to control and regulate and use as a weapon against me. This cycle went on for months.

While I certainly saw improvements in my fitness level and ability to sustain my attention for longer than three seconds, my mental health wasn't improving as I had expected, much to my disappointment and shame. I began to circle back to my earlier thoughts about motherhood, the ones I had desperately wanted to be false, but they came, nevertheless. I began to wonder if *this actually was what it was like to be a mother*: chronically irritable, incessantly worried, and feeling defeated and trapped in my own life. I had begun the sad process of resigning to what I believed to be my reality. I loved my daughters and husband, I was physically healthy, and I had a good job that I was months away from returning to. Life was good, and I had no reason to complain about my mental health. This was just what it was going to be like from now on.

In *Women Who Run With the Wolves*, Clarissa Pinkola Estés, PhD, shares, "You are born to one mother, but if you are lucky, you will have more than one. And among them all you will have most of what you need." I consider myself one of these lucky ones and can bring to mind at least three of these extra mothers in my life. They are women who come into your life at just the right time and shine light into the areas you haven't seen or haven't been willing to see. With their wisdom and grace, they see your true self beneath the mask and "fine-ness" that you are hiding behind. There have been many significant turning points in my story of postpartum mental health, but this is the one I remember most clearly: my friend (I'll call her Carol) and I had returned to my house to put the girls to bed after a lovely dinner at her house with our husbands. We were soaking in the hot tub and Carol asked me, as she always had, how I was doing.

"Fine," I lied. I had been seeing a therapist and doing all the things I knew how. "I've come to realize that this is just what it's like to be a mom. People who exercise every day aren't depressed and anxious.

People who meditate and journal daily and do all the things you're supposed to do aren't depressed and anxious. This is just what it's like, I guess. I'm just having a hard time accepting it, clearly."

She paused and looked at me, knowingly. The pause was long, almost painful to me.

"What if it wasn't?" she asked. "What if it could actually be better than this?"

This question, simple and to the point, caused me to pause.

What if it could be better? Initially, I scoffed. That is what I had been thinking all along! I thought it could be better, and I was doing (in my mind) everything I could to make it better. I was frustrated. I felt like I had been doing nearly every single thing a person could do to help themselves crawl out of the dark and vast pit of mental illness.

However, there had been one important step I had been ignoring and had ruled out for myself long before. Up until that point, I had refused to consider that I may need medication to fix this problem. My do-it-myself attitude, perfectionistic sense of self-competence, and resistance to medication had forced me to nearly kill myself in trying to self-care myself better despite a busy, relentlessly ruminating and emotional mind. In my then-skewed opinion (anxiety will do that to you), I had been doing more than what most of my patients had ever done and was still feeling like shit.

But what if it could be better? What if it was possible? The possibility tickled at the back of my brain, desperate to be explored. What if I could be more present, more patient, and more joyful with my family? What if I could enjoy the time with my children more instead of just waiting until they were asleep so I could get a break? What if I could feel joy every day, laugh easily, and feel motivated again? What if I could feel energetic and inspired, excited for my life and what my future could hold? What if I could be the mom my twins really deserved?

I remember thinking that people who meditate every day religiously couldn't be anxious to the point of panic. People who spend hours working through their complicated thoughts and emotions in their journal usually find some relief after a time. People who exercise daily, do affirmations, practice cognitive behavioral therapy strategies, and go to therapy are "just not" depressed and anxious messes, or so I thought. I was trying so hard to be healthy and still was up against the wall of my neurotransmitters that refused to do what they were supposed to do.

I was right, partially. People who do all these things aren't depressed *if* their brain chemistry is working properly. People who exercise daily aren't anxious messes *if* their neurotransmitters are functioning properly. With my insistent need to be perfect, independent, and competent, and to prove to myself that I was not weak or broken, I had refused to even consider the one thing that my brain needed to finally recover from postpartum mental illness: medication.

The irony of this story is apparent to me now. Almost daily in my clinical work, I spend time with a woman who is deep in the crashing waves of anxiety or postpartum mental illness and can't see that she's swimming for her life. I share with her an analogy that one of my mentors shared with me during my training and that I use regularly now to explain to my patients the role of medication in depression and anxiety.

Take a moment to imagine that you are on a boat in the middle of the sea. This boat is your mental health, and the sea is life. We are all on our own individual boats. Some days (or seasons), the sun is shining, the water is calm, and we are enjoying life and catching rays on the deck of our boat. Life is good, and we are healthy. Other days, the waves get a bit choppy, and we find ourselves hanging on to the rails of our boat for more stability, or even going below to take cover for a while. In some seasons, however, the waves are crashing larger than our boat can handle, and we are taking on water. We desperately try to bail out the boat, but despite our best efforts, we are thrown from the safety of our vessel and into the crashing sea below.

Once in the water, we can barely keep our head above it, but not for lack of trying. We are swimming harder and harder, getting pushed underneath and working desperately to stay up, which is what depression and anxiety feel like—swimming harder and harder while trying to just keep going . . . to just keep breathing.

Now imagine there is your trusted local mental health provider on the deck of your boat, and she offers you a life ring. Would you take it?

If you were offered the chance to catch your breath, to learn to ride the waves for a bit and get a bit of relief amidst the storm of your mind, would you take it?

A logical person would. I reflect on this analogy now and feel sad for the version of myself that was in the water. She believed that taking that ring would make her feel less of a mother, make her feel less competent, and make things worse. For months, she felt that if she just swam the right way, did all the right things, and didn't rest or give herself the chance for a break, she would make everything better. Does this story sound familiar to you?

When I see women now in the thick of their mental illness, it's easy for me to identify a fellow swimmer in the waves. She is swimming harder and harder, trying to keep her head above the water, to prove to herself (and others) that she is strong enough to withstand the tsunami that is untreated mental illness. Her illness is convincing her that if she just swims the right way, goes without sleep to get further, and swims harder and harder, she will get back on her boat. That is what anxiety feels like, no matter when it strikes you.

The life ring in the analogy is medication, and despite how far we have come regarding postpartum mental health and mental illness in general, there is still so much division and stigma associated with this topic for many women. The life ring is not a fix for being in the water. The life ring does not take away the mental illness, it simply gives the swimmer a chance to catch her breath and ride the waves for a bit. Just as the life ring doesn't bring her back to the boat, it helps her be a stronger swimmer for a time so she can get back to it herself. It is medication that keeps her up and afloat so she can focus on the important work of learning how to get back on her boat, plus learn the skills to keep her there to weather the next storm, which is why mental health treatment must be multimodal—because when you're in the water and the waves are crashing so severely, you need multiple supports to get you back on the boat. Therapy, mindset work, self-care (in its MANY forms), and medication are all important tools and should be considered.

After that fateful albeit simple question, I realized that I hadn't tried everything I could to feel better and be the mother that my twins deserved. I finally decided to start medication to get my neurotransmitters sorted out.

Within what seems like days, the fog began to clear. It was

unbelievable. I caught myself mid-laugh one day and realized that I hadn't thought once that day about how crappy I felt or how exhausted I was. I felt pleasant but somewhat unfamiliar feelings: relaxation, joy, ease, peace. Over the coming weeks, I began to feel like myself again. My mind was clearer, the volume of my anxious thoughts was turned down, and with it, my mood had turned up. To this day, as I write these words, I am shocked at how quickly and dramatically my experience changed. As a physician with knowledge of the pharmacology of selective serotonin-reuptake inhibitors (SSRIs), I have been taught that these medications take four to six weeks to see full effect, but to my soul, I feel that it took mere days for me to feel facets of my personality and previous self start to return. Over the coming weeks, my busy mind slowed, and I found space between the anxious thoughts. I was able to be more present, I was more emotionally stable, and my anger had all but evaporated.

As I returned back to myself, I became ravenous for information and strategies on how to prevent myself from ever going back to that dark place I had been in just weeks prior. I began creating new habits and systems to track and monitor my mental health so I could be proactive about managing it rather than reactively responding to the low days. I began to rethink the role anxiety played in my life and learned how to manage my anxious thoughts with various cognitive behavioral strategies. I became an active agent, an intentional creator of my one life.

This sense of empowerment and agency lit a flame inside of me that I had not realized existed. I dove back into mindfulness and meditation with a new appreciation for observing my thoughts and appreciated the space that now existed between them. I gained clarity around how to negotiate with my thoughts and disengage from them rather than constantly becoming swept up in them. I read book after book on personal development now that I could focus for more than five minutes, and I filtered through what habits would work well for me. I suddenly became aware of the infinite potential I could have as a mother and woman in the world if I simply stopped being held back by my small fears and anxieties and stepped into my full self. I started to bring light to the dreams I had inside of me that had been buried for so long: I wanted to write a book. I wanted to help women get through what I had been through. I wanted to help women feel the same sense of empowerment and agency that I had. I wanted to show my children the world and bravely explore the unknown.

Although I had always considered myself a motivated and successful person, these dreams felt different in that they felt as though they were coming from directly inside of my soul—a place within myself that I had only just begun to explore the depths and vastness of. These dreams were bigger than my previous goals and successes had been. Truer, more aligned, and more soulful. They were no longer fueled by perfectionistic achievement and success but rather from a deeper place within myself, a place I could only recognize as my soul.

I also realized that to achieve all those big soul-filled dreams, I would have to do some real work on myself and in my life. I looked at my current life, and instead of feeling like nothing else would fit, I looked at what could be taken away so that I could fill that space with more goodness and purpose. In my medical practice, this looked like cutting back on general medical appointments to carve out time for seeing more women in the midst of their mental health challenges so I could help them learn the skills to get back on their boat. Outside of my medical practice, I explored ways I could work deeper with women, and this exploration brought me to life coach training and to more education around maternal mental illness, cognitive behavioral therapy, and other psychotherapy modalities. At the time of this writing, I have expanded my approach to include integrative and holistic approaches to mental health treatment and have begun applying nutritional psychiatry practices (which use food as medicine for the brain). I recently opened my virtual mental health clinic for women—Eunoia Medical—and I am on a mission to truly revolutionize mental health care for women.

However, this progress didn't happen overnight. Shortly after I recovered from my own dark night of the soul, I began working with women in both my office and online as a coach, meeting them where they were in the water and helping them learn the skills to swim back to their boats. I guided them with my own experience and knowledge to help them find their own way back to themselves, out of their anxiety, and back into being the agents and creators of their own lives. I began to teach them how to reclaim their own voices and give up their habit of passive people-pleasing. I began to teach them self-love instead of the prized self-sacrifice and martyrdom we see around us as women. I showed them that they no longer had to be the doormat in their lives and that their bodies and minds were worth taking care of without feeling guilty about it. I began to crystallize and systematize the process I myself had been through to reclaim my power, and I was leading them along the same path.

This book is this same path—the path that I have taken myself and other women have taken with my help, the path back to feeling like themselves. Your journey may not look like mine; it may be much worse or much better. You may have good days with just a few anxious thoughts, or you may be stuck in dark places for weeks, wishing you had someone to guide you back to the light. You may or may not be on medication, and it may or may not be right for you. Wherever you are, this book will help you. I share my story and what has worked for me with hope that it will help even one woman make the right choice for herself and her family: to show up, take responsibility, and to learn how to become who she really wants to be, whoever that woman is.

Perhaps you have also had a striking moment when you realized the reality of your limited time on this planet. Perhaps you have also realized that your current reality, this place in time and space that you're living in, is your ONE chance at life. Your one kick at the can, so to speak.

- If you haven't, here is a reality check:
- If you have been living in a vortex of fear and worry all the time, even though you know the worries are irrational at times, and you can't seem to shut them off no matter how hard you try . . .
- If you have been failing to take care of yourself, day in and day out, because everything is "so much more important" than your own mental health . . .
- If you have been saying yes when you know you should say no and being a martyr for everyone for far too long . . .
- If you have been sacrificing yourself for others every single day, leaving nothing for yourself and feeling bitter and resentful . . .

- If you have been burying your dreams and passions because you're too anxious and don't think you're good enough to have them or chase them . . .
- If you have been settling in your life for anything less than what you TRULY have always wanted . . .

WAKE UP.

This IS your current and only experience of being human. This, what you're living right now, whatever it looks like, IS your life. Your life is not in the future or in the past, it's happening RIGHT NOW.

And it's ticking away, one second at a time.

Is this the way you want it to be? Is this the way you imagined it would be? Or are you looking for more? Did you have a different idea in your head of what your life or being a woman or a mother would feel like? Are you okay with missing out on the invaluable moments in your life because your anxious thoughts never shut up? Do you wish you could find more time (read: get your priorities right) so that you can focus on taking care of yourself or doing what you love more often? Do you even know what you love anymore? Is this how you thought or imagined your life would go?

If not, you're in luck. Well done—you've taken the first step to changing that narrative. This book is the first step to opening your eyes to all the ways your anxiety is holding you back and then taking steps toward taking back your power. It's the first step to realizing how your own perceptions, beliefs, and thought processes are affecting your life. If you apply the steps and strategies outlined in the coming chapters, I'm confident you'll be well on your way to becoming the calm, confident, assertive, and passionate woman you envision to be.

part 1

THE BEAST THAT IS ANXIETY

So, what is anxiety? In the most basic of explanations, anxiety is how our brain reacts to a threat. It is a part of being human, and all humans have it in some form or expression. In my work, I've rarely found someone who cannot identify with the experience of being anxious or worried. Worry is a universal human experience. The degree to which it affects us, the degree to which it takes over our minds is what varies from person to person. I will repeat this concept frequently through this book. The fact that you have anxiety is not in your control; however, what we do have within our grasp is our response to the waves that overcome us and sometimes try to drown us. How we react to the worry, the role we give worry in our life, and how we manage it is what we have control over.

Instead of viewing it as a hindrance and wishing it away, hiding from it, and hoping it doesn't return, it is my hope that you will be able to understand the role it plays in your life, give it the credit it deserves, and approach it from a fresher, more positive place. It is also my hope that this section will provide you with opportunities to shift your mindset away from one of being controlled by your anxiety to feeling empowered to take back the reins. Education and awareness are the keys to personal growth.

chapter 3

ANXIETY IS A UNIVERSAL HUMAN EXPERIENCE

First of all, this section is not intended and will not serve as a full review of the neuroscience of anxiety. Full disclosure: I am not a neuroscientist. Second disclosure: Neuroscience can be *super boring*, and I suspect I'll lose you if I dig into it. Also, it's totally not my style to get all "sciencey" on you. Therefore, for the purposes of this book and our mission, I will share some basics around where anxiety lives in our brain and how our brain responds to threats, the role our anxiety plays in survival, and the structures responsible for it.

From a neuroscience perspective, there are two areas of your brain that contribute to anxiety. Anxiety is a self-preserving force that resides in the primitive fight-or-flight part of our brain, the amygdala. The amygdala is an almond-shaped mass of cells located deep in the temporal lobes of the brain and is part of the limbic system. The limbic system is responsible for many of our emotions and motivations, especially in relation to our survival. The limbic system is activated when we need to respond to a threat and triggers a cascade of downstream reactions that create our fight-or-flight response. Note also that your amygdala is not very smart and does not respond to logic. It's also important to note that your amygdala is the first area of your brain that interprets stimuli from your external world and is constantly primed for action. Stay with me here; I swear this information is important to know.

In studies of the brain, cells in the amygdala have been shown to play a role in fear conditioning, which is the development of a fear response after repeated exposures to a frightening event or situation (threat). The amygdala also connects to areas of our brain that process sensory information (what we see, smell, hear, etc.), and it receives this information first before any other locations in the brain. Finally, the amygdala plays a role in developing new brain circuits and connections in response to dangerous or stressful situations, known as adaptive learning, which was critical for the survival of our ancestors. This adaptive learning is the process by which we see a bear and panic. Our brains have learned to associate the sight of a large hairy animal with a threat to our safety and, in turn, have a well-oiled pathway in place to prepare our system to fight off or flee from the threat. This system activation is primitive, reactive, and instantaneous. Our brain perceives sensory information, our amygdala processes it as a threat, and what follows is a cascade of physiological changes to prepare our bodies to fight the danger or flee to safety. It is these physiological changes that most of us perceive as symptoms of anxiety—racing heart, rapid breathing, sweaty palms, and a sense of being on edge or panic.

Our amygdala plays two other interesting roles: 1) the processing of emotions, and 2) the organizing of memories. It's responsible for processing emotions such as fear, anger, and pleasure, and it also decides what memories are stored and where they are stored in our brains, which explains why the amygdala plays such a critical role in the development of anxiety. It is responsible for detecting a threat to our survival, instantly mobilizing an emotional and survival response to it and then consolidating that threat in our memories so we can respond quicker next time. The amygdala (and associated structures) work together like a specialized supercomputer designed to identify threats in our environment and then mobilize resources to respond to them, and it is this supercomputer that is responsible for our experience of anxiety. But it can become sensitized and cause certain individuals to experience anxiety at a higher level than others around them, a level that affects functioning (and that's what you experience).

This hypersensitization can happen for a number of different reasons, from chronic stress to trauma to even physical illness. And this hypersensitization occurs following threats to our safety, identity, or both. Many people explain that their anxiety got much worse after an accident or trauma (threat to safety), a job loss (threat to identity), a child falling ill (threat to identity), or a loss of relationship (threat to safety and/or identity). It's also possible for the anxiety supercomputer to be sensitized by chronic stress, whether from childhood trauma or an unstable upbringing in the early years of life. Chronic resource scarcity (living in poverty) or exposure to repeated violence are both reasons that someone may struggle with a sensitized threat detection system. There are obviously hundreds of reasons and causes that can be linked to the development of anxiety, and this chapter is not intended to be an exhaustive review of these. In my client work, I've found it helpful in some cases to look back with them into their personal history and unearth the events or situations in their lives that may have contributed to this hypersensitization so that we can work to reset the system and heal. Again, this book is not intended to be an exhaustive manual on healing emotional trauma, and I would encourage anyone with that history to get in touch with their friendly local psychotherapist and spend some time working with them.

When the anxiety supercomputer becomes hypersensitized, it's as though the threshold for triggering the fight-or-flight response is lowered, and it takes less to trigger an automatic anxiety reaction. In people who struggle with higher-than-average anxiety, they may notice that their anxiety is triggered by seemingly innocent changes or experiences. To the logical brain, these experiences may not be legitimate reasons to trigger an anxiety response, but in the hypersensitized anxious brain, they are.

There is another part of your brain that is also involved in anxiety generation and that is your cortex. The cortex is your evolved thinking brain that can use logic and can rationalize and plan. The cortex does not have connections to the parts of your brain that generate the anxiety response, but it does have a connection to your amygdala and can ignite the amygdala's anxiety response with thoughts. However, while the cortex can ignite the amygdala, it cannot "talk it down" (because the amygdala does not respond to logic). Have you ever thought to yourself, "I know I shouldn't worry about this, and this would never happen in a million years, but I can't help it?" You're not alone. Quite commonly, patients tell me that even though they are aware certain thoughts are completely irrational fears in their conscious brain, they can't stop their subconscious anxious brain from having them. I call this The Gap; it's the conceptual space between the anxious part of your brain and the conscious part of your brain that knows your anxious thoughts are irrational. If you're resonating with this paragraph, it is likely because you have experienced The Gap yourself. If you're experiencing The Gap, see it as a good sign because it means you're able to separate yourself from your anxious thoughts and label them as such, which is one of the most important first steps to reducing the thoughts. It's also evidence that you have become aware of the impact of the amygdala versus the cortex, and you can apply strategies relevant to the responsible pathway.

Now that we've got the basics of brain science out of the way, I want to share with you some alternate ways to think about your anxiety and the roles it plays in your life. I am a huge fan of shifting our mindset and the way we view complicated or overwhelming problems. I believe that by simply changing how we view things in our lives, by shifting our paradigm or perspective, we can grow and learn in new and expansive ways. So, let's dig in.

Your ancestors gave you anxiety

Let's examine our anxiety from an evolutionary perspective. It's important to recognize that anxiety, no matter how annoying it is to us, is actually an evolutionary adaptation. Anxiety has served an absolutely critical role in the survival of our species. In the words of Catherine Pittman, PhD, "We are descendants of the scared people."

Cut to scene: Your cavewoman ancestor is foraging for food in the forest with her clan mate. She comes upon a cave. It is dark and smells of rotting animal carcasses. Your ancestor uses her senses, her amygdala recognizes a potential threat, her anxiety is triggered, and she quickly flees to safety. Her foraging partner, who has less anxiety, wanders fearlessly into the cave of a bear and becomes a carcass herself. What trait just saved your ancestor's life? Anxiety, thank you.

While this scene is an exceptionally simplified micro-example of the process of evolution, it makes it simple to understand that anxiety, way back when and throughout history, has been a trait that has been carried on to subsequent generations due to its utility in maintaining survival. Without it, our ancestors would likely not have survived very long in a harsh environment with near-constant threats to their survival. Without anxiety about their safety, they would not have learned how to avoid predators or seek safe shelter. Anxiety (among other skills and characteristics) helped our ancestors be aware of threats in their environment and adapt their behavior to ensure the survival of themselves and their offspring.

When a trait contributes to increased chance of survival of a species, evolutionary theory supports that this trait will be carried on to future generations, and that is where you and I come in. Although we believe it at times to be pesky and detrimental in our day-to-day life now, our anxiety is actually a gift from our predecessors (oh gee, thanks). It has been a psychological trait strongly selected for us through the process of evolution. Those individuals who had anxiety regarding their safety would be more likely to survive, as they would be motivated to avoid dangerous situations, motivated to learn how to feed themselves, and motivated to acquire other adaptive behaviors. Anxiety has essentially been hardwired into our brains along with other biological drives for survival and, by way of it, is not going away easily.

The issue with this hardwiring is that this threat detection system that served our ancestors so well in primitive times is now a bit over the top in modern day. Luckily for most of us, we live in a modern world and our environments have evolved such that we do not often live with constant threats to our safety. This is good. Unfortunately, the primitive part of our brain where our anxiety lives has not evolved at the same rate. It's as though we are running a very primitive operating system in a highly evolved environment. Think DOS in an Apple environment. We need to become aware of the wiring patterns and work to rewire them in a way that allows us to be calmer and more present, more often.

Your alarm system is a bit overzealous

Most buildings have fire alarm systems to detect smoke and fire and set off those alarms to notify of an impending threat to the building's safety. Similarly, all humans have anxiety that is designed to detect threats to safety. It can be helpful to view these two systems as analogous to each other.

It's generally preferable that the fire alarm system in a building be appropriately wired to respond when there is legitimate fire or smoke threatening a building, otherwise its occupants may end up standing on the lawn in their nightgowns in the middle of the night for no reason. Similarly, most women I speak with about anxiety would like theirs (their fire alarm system) to only respond when there are actual threats to their safety rather than silly things that are not true threats.

If you're like most women I see, you likely have an alarm system that is a bit hypersensitive. It's as though the detection threshold is set a bit too low, and it rings far too early. Instead of "going off" when there is legitimate fire in your life, your alarm likely goes off at the mere possibility that there could be smoke. Sound familiar?

You may find that the fears or worried thoughts you experience are sometimes so irrational and "silly" that you cannot believe you are anxious about them. You have this reaction because your cortex has rationalized the situation as "not a threat," but your amygdala still believes it is. Nonetheless, the mere thought of a potential threat is sometimes enough in highly sensitized systems to cause the amygdala to mobilize resources to respond to it (i.e., cause you to have symptoms of anxiety or experience a panic attack).

Returning to the analogy of a fire alarm system, it's important to acknowledge that at the end of the day, the fire alarm exists for a very important reason: to prevent the building from being engulfed in flames. We'd just prefer it didn't go off when someone burns toast. Similarly, we do need our anxiety to keep us safe as well, but we would prefer it didn't trigger a panic attack because of a harmless trip to the grocery store. It's imperative for our enjoyment of our lives and peace of mind that our alarm system be "appropriately wired" so that the threat detection level is appropriate. It is by way of strategies and practices in this book that you will learn not only to determine the level of your threat detection of your alarm system but also to rewire it to a more appropriate level.

Your anxiety serves an important purpose

Among psychology and mental health junkies, cognitive behavioral therapy (CBT) is a well-known and effective therapy modality that utilizes the interaction between our thoughts, feelings, and behaviors to affect therapeutic change (i.e., make people feel better). It can be helpful to view anxiety from this perspective as well. In fact, many of the strategies I suggest in this book come from CBT models. Cognitive behavioral therapy helps explain why we behave how we do and what parts of our thoughts and emotions are motivating that behavior. By understanding this interaction between our thoughts, emotions, and behaviors, we can begin to change our experience of life and feel an improved sense of control over it.

The CBT approach to anxiety management is invaluable in that it provides us with a framework to work with our anxious thoughts. The basic premise of CBT is that our thoughts, emotions, and behaviors all influence one another. For example, an anxious thought can trigger the emotional experience of anxiety and what follows is behavior motivated by that emotion. This CBT triangle also provides us with some clear areas to direct our efforts when we want to tackle a complex problem like anxiety. We can direct our efforts toward challenging our thoughts, regulating our emotions, or changing our behaviors. Some of these strategies are easier than others.

I also find it helpful to reflect on the CBT theory of the motivational triad of human behavior and how anxiety fits into our behavior. In fact, this triad explains a lot about human behavior in general. In its most simplified form, the motivational triad theory asserts that all human behavior comes from one of three primary motivations:

to seek pleasure, to avoid pain, and to increase efficiency. I refer to "pain" in this regard as "distress" and can equate it to any type of negative emotional experience, such as sadness, anger, loneliness, etc.

When it comes to women with anxiety, I see their anxiety playing a few different roles in the motivational triad of human behavior. In many situations, your experience of anxiety is the pain that you are seeking to avoid when you behave in certain ways. That is, you behave in ways that serve to reduce your own anxiety (distress). This simple concept helps explain why you might engage in certain behaviors that might not be very healthy for you but serve to minimize your pain in the moment (i.e., emotional eating, drug or alcohol use, etc.). These buffering behaviors help you reduce your distress and pain in the moment and become reinforced because they are effective in that moment for deflecting the pain. This concept also helps us understand some of our more deeply ingrained behavioral habits such as perfectionism and people-pleasing. In fact, the interaction between anxiety and passive behavior is a particularly challenging one that I find many women struggle to break free of having.

The other way that I see the motivational triad helpful in explaining anxiety is that your anxiety serves as a distress management system. Recall that your anxiety's primary goal is to keep you safe from threats, and your anxiety views any form of distress or emotional pain as a threat. When anxiety detects distress or pain, it motivates your behavior to reduce the pain. As an example, if you anticipate a conflict when you speak up for yourself in a relationship, your anxiety will work to reduce that distress by directing you to behave in a certain way (i.e., passive behavior).

chapter 4

IT MAKES NO SENSE TO RESIST YOUR ANXIETY

I am right-hand dominant. It's my natural tendency to pick up a pen with my right hand and use right-handed scissors. I feel most comfortable doing most things with my right hand.

As it's my natural tendency, something that is just a part of "who I am," I don't really think twice about my handedness. I don't wonder if I'll still be right-handed next week or wish away the fact that I am right-hand dominant. I don't look at a pen and worry about how I'll use it—I just pick it up and write. Similarly, I also don't really assign much value to my being right-handed or feel any shame or criticism about being right-handed. It just is what it is. It is my tendency.

Are you right- or left-handed? When you go to write something, do you give it a second thought or act surprised by your tendency?

Do you think, *Damn it, I'm still right-handed?* Of course not. You accept that your hand dominance is a tendency.

Similarly, you may have to alter your behavior to accommodate your tendency to be right- or left-handed. Especially if left-handed, you may avoid sitting next to someone who is right-handed or you may seek out left-handed scissors. You likely have adjusted some of your habits to accommodate your tendency, but still, it's relatively emotionless because, hey, it's your tendency. It's unlikely that you've ever tried to force yourself to be the opposite of your tendency or wished you were just less "left-handed." If you've tried to be ambidextrous, it's likely been quite messy. With lots of practice, lots of dedication and intention, you may learn how to write with the opposite hand, but it would likely feel awkward most of the time.

Why am I talking to you about handedness in a book about anxiety? Well, just like handedness, your anxiety is a tendency. Just like you naturally pick up your pen with your dominant hand, you similarly "pick up" your life with anxiety. When changes occur in your life, your natural reaction is to react with anxiety. It is your tendency. There's nothing right or wrong about it.

Similarly, it's important to shift your mindset around your reaction to life. When new or unexpected events happen, when you have a change in schedule or an increase in demand at work, your natural reaction will be to feel anxious about it. It's expected that you will react to life with anxiety, similar to how you pick up a pen with your dominant hand. You expect it, and it doesn't surprise you. When we can expect ourselves to react a certain way, we can be more prepared to deal with it in a constructive and healthy manner.

Just how it wouldn't make much sense to feel ashamed for having a right- or left-hand dominance, the same applies for your tendency to be anxious. To do so would be futile and self-defeating. Your anxiety is simply the reaction you have to your life. As you would change your environment or life to accommodate your handedness, the same applies to the approach that is healthiest to manage your anxiety. Perhaps this change means that you learn how to adapt your own behavior, or learn thought management strategies to work with your anxious tendency, or ensure that you limit your exposure to unhealthy anxiety triggers such as substances, toxic relationships, or social media drama. You acknowledge and accept that anxiety is your tendency and that you need to work with it rather than force yourself (or otherwise numb yourself) to not be anxious.

And yes, you can learn how to have the opposite tendency, but like handedness or training yourself to be ambidextrous, it will be messy and uncomfortable and awkward at times. But with practice, intention, and consistency, it is possible to learn how to react to life (and pick up your pen) with a different or slightly adapted tendency.

Your anxiety is an overprotective helicopter parent

> "Don't go out into the street. Okay, honey?"
>
> It's summer, and my twins are two-and-a-half years old. They have adorable red, blue, and yellow tricycles and are just learning to master the pedals and steering at the same time. It's a warm sunny day, and our quiet street is surprisingly busier than usual for a summer day, as it's rodeo weekend in our little rural town.

"Faye, the street is busy with cars. Please stay on the driveway."

No answer. She continues pedaling toward the street, and my heart beats louder and faster.

"Are you listening?! Faye! Faye, STOP! You could get hit by a car!"

Still, no response.

"FAYE, STOP RIGHT NOW! YOU COULD DIE!"

She stops, thankfully. I take a deep breath.

Crisis averted, at least for today. My dramatic response was valid, indicated, and now has been reinforced. Now imagine this situation goes a different way:

"Don't go out into the street. Okay, honey?"
"Okay, Mom! I will stop." End scene.

When heard and acknowledged, the parent in this second version doesn't feel the need or urge to get louder, more intense, or dramatic.

Your anxiety is just like an overprotective helicopter parent. Although I don't consider myself a "helicopter parent" usually, it can be helpful to use this term as an analogy for your anxiety. A helicopter parent is hell-bent on protecting their child and will hover around on high alert for threats, at all times. When a helicopter parent is ignored by a child, it only increases the insistence and fear that the parent displays in an attempt to keep the child safe (as in the first aforementioned situation). Helicopter parenting is a helpful way to conceptualize anxiety because we can learn how ignoring it or trying to silence it can actually make it become louder and more insistent.

Do you see how, when ignored over and over again, the parent becomes more insistent and, I hazard to say, dramatic? Do you recall any situations in which you behaved this way? In this situation, a parent is very much like anxiety. Our anxiety is simply trying to protect us, just like a parent is trying to protect a child. Just like our proverbial, ever-present, and anxious parent, our anxiety similarly does not like to be stifled or ignored. It thinks it knows what is dangerous, and it is very insistent on making sure you know. The more you try to stifle or ignore it, the louder and more dramatic it gets, just like anxiety. Your anxiety is controlling; it wants you to do exactly what makes it comfortable.

I have often recommended that women view their anxiety as a helicopter parent and to take the approach that you would want from your kids when you're giving them guidance about their safety:

"Don't go into the street, okay? Make sure you watch for cars."

Response: "Yep, sounds good. I'll keep it in mind. Thanks."

And then carry on with your day.

When we can recognize what's happening (that our anxiety is trying to protect us), acknowledge it, and thank it for its help, it can help us calm down in the moment. This analogy is designed to help us conceptualize our anxiety in a way that helps us approach it differently, in a more adaptive and constructive way.

Remember that at its core, your anxiety wants to keep you alive and views any deviation from what's normal as a threat to your safety. It also wants to keep you from doing new things or making changes in your life. If you're afraid of driving, it wants you to remain afraid of driving. If your anxiety tells you flying is terrifying, it wants you to keep believing that it is terrifying, so you'll be safe and never fly. If your anxiety believes starting a new business or being an entrepreneur is a threat, it will freak out when you decide to take that step. It doesn't trust anything new to be safe, and it tells us at every opportunity to second-guess, doubt, and question each step. But we don't have to listen to it and believe everything it tells us. And that is the trick.

You are not your anxiety

As you can see, there is more to anxiety than just feeling worried. Viewing it in these different perspectives can help you understand more thoroughly the role your anxiety plays in your life while helping you feel more empowered to manage it. There is one more way to view your anxiety that I believe is critical to your anxiety recovery. It is imperative for you to realize that YOU, yourself, are NOT your anxiety. Your anxiety is not you. Your anxiety is simply a part of you that has gotten a bit out of control.

I often ask my patients to consider their anxiety as a separate being within their brains that has its own motivations and characteristics. I've even gone so far as to encourage them to create a separate persona in their minds, a name or character to represent their anxiety. It's critical that you are able to cognitively separate your anxiety from your own self if you are to successfully manage it. I've often referred to my own anxiety as a nattering little parrot sitting on my shoulder, annoyingly telling me things all day, but I can choose to listen to it and indulge it, or not. The reality is that your anxiety is a force that exists within your brain, but it is not who you are. By separating yourself from your anxiety, you can develop a sense of agency that allows you to make changes to quiet down your anxiety and to choose whether you engage in its patterns. If none of the previous perspective shifts have felt helpful for you, this is, quite honestly, the most important shift. If you continue to cognitively associate your anxiety as being who you are, it will be incredibly hard to distance yourself from the anxious thoughts and disagree with them.

Your anxiety is ruining your health

I know that you bought this book to take the first step toward getting your anxiety under control, and I'm so pumped about it. There are many good reasons why regaining control is important, and your physical health is one of these reasons. The truth is that despite it being an evolutionary advantage that has contributed to the survival of our species over centuries, anxiety is actually not very good for us.

Our bodies are not designed to function at a high level of vigilance at all times. Rest is crucial for the body to regenerate its cells, maintain homeostasis, and consolidate memories. When we exist in a heightened state of anxiety, with such a sensitive and vigilant threat detection system constantly surveying our environment for threats, our body's systems can burn out. In fact, research has shown that chronic anxiety has been linked to an increased risk of many other chronic illnesses, such as cardiovascular disease, respiratory disorders, and gastrointestinal issues. There is a complex and dynamic relationship between having chronic physical illness and the impact it makes on your mental health as well. Living with a chronic illness can elevate your baseline level of anxiety simply because you are living with constant concern about your health condition(s).

Many nonspecific physical symptoms such as nausea, heartburn, abdominal cramping, tightness in the chest, and shortness of breath can all be manifestations of anxiety (once all other serious conditions have been ruled out, obviously). I have known women who experience headaches, increased constipation, and intermittent rashes when their anxiety is out of control. As if you needed another reason to get it under control (or another reason to have anxiety about having anxiety), right?

Furthermore, your anxiety can wreak absolute havoc on your sleep. Many of the women with whom I work say that they struggle to fall asleep in the evening, their brains bent on solving all their problems as soon as they settle down for bed. Other women tell me that after they fall asleep, they struggle to stay asleep, experience frequent and prolonged night wakings, or wake earlier than they would like. When we consider that our anxiety is an ever-vigilant sentry that monitors our environment for threats to our safety, it follows that our little sentry doesn't just settle down at night and go to sleep. It remains at-the-ready, prepared to respond to any anticipated threats, despite it being time to rest and sleep. The elevated cortisol levels that are pumping through our bodies from chronic anxiety remain elevated at night, thus contributing to difficulty falling asleep or broken sleep. However, all is not lost. Many women I've worked with have also found that as their anxiety improves, their sleep improves and becomes more consolidated. We're going to dig into some specific strategies to improve your sleep when we review the Biological Pillar of The Eunoia Approach. Stay tuned.

chapter 5

ONLY YOU CAN DECIDE HOW TO MOVE FORWARD FROM HERE

Rule your mind or it will rule you.—Horace

Now that you've become more aware of where your anxiety comes from and have some alternative perspectives on how to view it, it's time for you to reflect on the relationship you have with your own anxiety and decide (once and for all) what you want to do about it. In the section to follow, I give you an overview of the process of anxiety recovery so you can identify where you are in that journey and see where you are going. In order to do that, however, I would be ignoring a critical element to this process if I did not encourage you to examine the approach you are taking with your anxiety, the relationship you have with it, and your mindset around it.

In my experience, I usually see two approaches to managing anxiety. One is a self-pitiful, woe-is-me approach, and the other is an objective, no-bullshit one. I refer to these as the Victim Approach and the Agency Approach. They are very different approaches, and you have the choice right now over which one you want to take. No one can make this decision for you, and we all come to this decision in our own time in our journey. Whether knowingly or unknowingly, many women believe they are trying to manage their anxiety when, in fact, they are not.

Here are a few descriptions of a Victim Approach to anxiety: Anxiety has happened to you, and it is *terrible*. Your anxiety has complete control of your life, and there isn't much you can do about it. You believe you are broken, and the fact that you have anxiety means you are unfixable or damaged. Whether knowingly or not, you have submitted to the fact that your anxiety is going to run your life and there isn't much you can really do about it. Constant worry, rumination, and panic attacks will just be "how it will always be." You may try to ignore it, wishing it away, but then are surprised, annoyed, and irritated when it comes back yet again. You may complain and vent about your anxiety like a petulant child, wondering what you did to have it "so bad" and that you "never sleep" or "just can't" do all the things you need to do to really make a difference in your anxiety management. You throw your hands up in the air, admitting defeat, and indulging the fact that your anxiety is in control and there just isn't much else you can do but live in misery. You may frequently ask for help from others and thank them for their advice, but somehow the strategies they suggest "just never seem to fit in your life." Part of you is committed to managing your anxiety, but the other half is okay with it being around because it gives you a damn good excuse to get out of things or behave in ways you normally wouldn't. You walk around continually "wondering" why your life has to be so hard. You may think: *A lot of people have anxiety, but mine is just way worse. What works for everyone else just doesn't work for me. I've tried meditating once or twice and it didn't really do anything, so it doesn't work. Therapists never understand me, and I don't like talking to people. I guess I'm just broken and destined to live with this anxiety. My life sucks. Humph.*

While this description may seem harsh, it's unfortunately a very common situation. If it sounds like you, that's okay. Honestly, don't beat yourself up. It's not my intent to shame anyone who may behave in this way because mental illness is hard, and learned helplessness is a genuine psychological phenomenon that happens to the brain. However, I draw attention to it because if this is the flavor of the thoughts in your brain regarding your anxiety, it's time to cut that crap now.

These sorts of self-defeating and victim-based beliefs are not going to serve you in your desire to legitimately get your anxiety under control. It's time to take an honest look at how you've been feeling about your anxiety and be honest with yourself if your mindset and beliefs could use a tune-up. It can be helpful to contrast the Victim Approach with the other approach I see women taking to managing their anxiety, the Agency Approach.

In the Agency Approach, you believe that you and you alone are in control of your life and that instead of anxiety taking over, you are ready to genuinely take back control. One of the hallmarks of this approach is the willingness to try. You are open to learning more about your anxiety and the possibility that there are things you don't know about it that may help you. You are willing to learn more about how your anxiety works and what your triggers are. You are ready to develop a deep understanding of how it feels in your body and mind when your anxiety is high. You are willing to be objectively curious about your own behavior and learn what helps bring you back into equilibrium when you're out of balance. You are willing to actually do those things and ditch your excuses. You are willing to get over yourself and learn how to meditate once and for all and stick with it until it becomes a habit. You stop living behind your excuses and do some damn self-care for your own good, even when it's hard and it feels like you don't want to. You learn how to observe what your mind does and watch it for patterns, knowing that each time it flares up and overcomes you, you're that much closer to being in control of it. You begin to intentionally plan your self-care times and moments in your life because they become nonnegotiable, and you increase them appropriately when you anticipate your stress and anxiety levels will be higher. You work to become a mindful observer of what happens in your mind rather than hiding from it. As the person who is responsible for managing your anxiety, you may seek out someone who knows more than you do and can teach you more about it. You have given up claiming that you don't like "talking to people," and you hire a frickin' coach or see a therapist who you connect with to help you work through it. You learn how to reparent yourself and your mind, and you plan for stressful times. You can be a motivated player in your life, no longer being fine with having your life controlled by your anxiety. You can stop letting your illness or struggle define your personality.

If you're not at this point yet in your anxiety journey, that's okay.

Remember, it's simply a willingness that's required: a willingness to learn new things and do new things, even when it's hard or seems to not fit in your life; a willingness to decide once and for all, no matter what, you'll do what is needed to get your mental health under control. If you can approach your anxiety management journey with an open-minded willingness, you'll be taking the Agency Approach, and that's the first step.

It may seem that I'm implying that having your anxiety or any mental illness is a choice, but I'm not. Mental illness is a disease, and the human race as a whole suffers from it. If you're someone who has been #blessed with anxiety that's more severe than average, that's not a choice you've made. It's not your fault. And more than anything, you are not broken. What I am telling you, though, is that *how you handle your mental illness is a choice*, as is the reality with any illness really, from anxiety to diabetes to chronic pain. In many cases, having the disease or illness is not a choice because if it were a choice, you wouldn't have it. However, if you were a diabetic and wanted to live well and thrive with and in spite of your diabetes, you would be dedicated to learning everything about it. You would probably make changes to your life so that you could minimize the risks of the disease on your body, set yourself up for success by kicking bad habits and incorporating new health-promoting ones, and you would stop being surprised when your blood sugar was high after a big meal. You would realize that being diabetic is your new reality and that you can choose to ignore it and complain about the effects, or you can accept it and take meaningful action. This is the Agency Approach. This is your choice. Which do you want to choose?

chapter 6

THE ANXIETY RECOVERY PROCESS

Now that we have our mindset in check, it's time to get a lay of the land for where we are heading through this book. Taking a trip is much easier and more enjoyable when you have an idea of where you're going and what to expect along the way. It's also important to be aware of who is driving. I often use the analogy of a car to explain the journey from feeling anxious and overwhelmed to calm and in control.

In my work with women in both my coaching and medical practices, I have noticed many similarities in their experiences. In fact, I have helped enough women now that I have distilled the anxiety management and recovery process down into three main phases. The Anxiety Recovery Process is the same journey I took as I worked to manage my own anxiety and can serve as a roadmap on your journey.

As you read through this section, try to determine where you fall on this path. Most women reading this book will likely be late in Phase 1 or early in Phase 2. See if you can identify where you are starting. Let's dig in.

Phase 1: FULLY IN THE VORTEX

The first phase of the Anxiety Recovery Process is what I call being *fully in the vortex*. The vortex, in this case, is a tornado of anxiety, and the sufferer is seated directly in the center of the storm, unable to see through the swirling funnel of their relentless, ruminating mind. In this phase, women often don't have any idea that anxiety is making an impact on their life. They haven't yet recognized the role their anxiety is playing or separated themselves from it. In this phase, your anxiety is like a tornado and you are completely engulfed in it, unable to see through it. When you're in the vortex, you can't see the vortex.

Women in this phase may consider themselves "worriers" or experience a constant need to be validated or reassured. They may experience many irrational worries and thoughts throughout the day, but they may think that's what other people experience as well. The anxiety they suffer from has become so powerful and so all-encompassing that they're unable to discern a difference between their anxious thoughts and reality. They fail to recognize that anxiety is what is actually causing them to worry about that seemingly innocent symptom that won't go away, causing them to be relentlessly indecisive, or causing them to be awake for hours with insomnia. People in this phase are either completely unaware of their anxiety and its power or they have just started to realize it.

In the first phase, anxiety is firmly in the driver's seat, and you're a mere passenger. Anxiety drives dramatically while you cover your eyes in the back seat. Your anxiety is constantly surveying the environment around you, avoiding every potential accident or perceived catastrophe with emotional twists and turns, uncharted courses, and bumpy roads.

Anxiety is driving way too many women around erratically without them even realizing it. Women in this phase are often using less-than-ideal coping skills to buffer the constant feelings of tension. Maybe they're bingeing on food, alcohol, sleep, social media, etc., to try and numb their feelings of distress. They're keyed up with the near incessant thought of something being wrong with them. They're afraid of everything, they worry about seemingly silly things and can't "not worry" about them, even when they know logically that they are ridiculous. Often women in this phase tell me that they spend each day hoping the next one is better and feel devastated when it isn't. Each morning, they wake refreshed (or not) but with a sense of impending defeat, wistfully hoping that "fingers crossed, nothing goes wrong today" that will throw off their mood. This feeling plunges them into a cycle of worry, irritability, emotional outbursts, and shame. They fear something "setting them off," leaving them in a pit of defeat and self-hatred that will be hard to climb out of for days. Despite it all, they are either completely unaware of their anxiety or are suspicious of it, but they're afraid to explore the possibility of having it. Heck, even the idea of having a diagnosis is terrifying to them. They may know that anxiety is to blame for much of their mental health struggles, but they feel powerless and lack the knowledge, tools, and support they need to step out of the vortex.

I want to tell you a story about one of my patients and how we came to discover that she had been in the vortex without realizing it. Let's call her Ashley. Ashley is a vibrant young woman who came to me many months ago, seeking yet another opinion about a rash that she had been struggling with for nearly two years at the time. She had seen countless specialists, had multiple rounds of autoimmune work-up, and had tried more elimination diets than she could remember. She was at a loss as to how to explain this rash that would cause her chest and face to flush with red patches and hives multiple times a day. Nothing had worked so far. Despite her best efforts to cut out dairy, gluten, and sugar and to use organic, vegan skincare, the rash persisted. I remember the day we met when she spoke at lightning speed and without a breath in my office for at least ten minutes straight. She recounted the dermatologists, immunologists, and rheumatologists she had seen, none of whom had given her a diagnosis. Admittedly, had she not been so thoroughly investigated so far, I may not have realized the connection, but to me, the cause of her rash was obvious.

> "Do you have anxiety?" I asked.
> "No, I don't think so. I mean, maybe? Do you think I do?" she answered. I smiled.
> "Do you worry a lot?"
> She paused, then replied, "Actually, all the time."

On further questioning, it was clear that Ashley worried about more than just her rash. She worried about everything. She constantly sought reassurance from her friends and family about her fears. She explained how she couldn't make a single decision without running it by others or being reassured repeatedly that it was the right choice. She shared how her rash flared when she was stressed, when she had an emotional reaction, or when she was "worried about something." She had become so fixated on her rash and finding the answer for it that she was preoccupied by it and living in fear of it flaring. She was living in a prison of anxiety.

When I drew the potential connection between her rash and her anxiety, Ashley was in disbelief. She had all but given up hope on finding a cause or fix for this rash and the worry about it that was taking over her life. Could her rash really be related to her anxiety? Could her excessive worry really be causing her body to react in this way?

During our first visit, I walked her through my approach to anxiety management and recommended some specific strategies for her to try over the next few weeks. These approaches were some of the same ones I share in this book. For the first few weeks, Ashley was understandably resistant to the connection between her rash and anxiety. It wasn't until she began to see a measurable decrease in her worried thoughts and anxiety symptoms that an incredible thing happened: no rash. She returned to my office in amazement, and to this day, by getting her anxiety under control with the strategies I outline in this book and some medication support, her rash has not returned.

I share Ashley's story for a few reasons. First of all, it is one of many cases of women who are so deep in the grips of anxiety that they cannot see the impact it's having on their lives. They may know that they are "worriers," but they genuinely believe that everyone worries like they do or that it's just how they are. They have yet to gain the perspective that those thoughts that keep them up at night, their tendency to second-guess and doubt every decision they make, and their fervent fears about day-to-day things are not "normal." What she didn't see at our initial meeting was not only the connection between her rash and her worry but also how much her anxiety continued to affect the rest of her life. It wasn't until we explored her thoughts and how persistent, irrational, and uncontrollable they felt that she realized how her anxiety had been in control of her life for so long. She was "in the vortex."

Second, I believe it's imperative to discuss the connection between our minds and our physical bodies. While this perspective may not be fully researched or supported in the Western medical paradigm, I firmly believe there is a beautiful and complicated connection between the mind and body. It is possible (and exceedingly common, I might add) for our bodies to manifest anxiety in physical symptoms, which is not to say that every physical symptom that hasn't yet been diagnosed is related to anxiety, but it's important to consider and acknowledge this perspective. I have seen more women than I can count whose physical symptoms either resolve completely or improve when they begin the hard work of learning about and managing their mental health. Our minds and bodies are connected, and it's high time to acknowledge that distress in one will cause distress in the other.

While I'm certain this reaction happens in men as well, my experience has been more often with women. We have become really good at repressing painful emotions or refusing to see flawed thinking patterns in our own minds because it's easier to treat a physical symptom than it is to become aware of or manage our mental health. It's easier to have a "fixable" physical illness than a chronic mental illness. It's easier to direct frustration at a medical system that cannot explain your symptoms than to consider whether there is something going on deep inside your mind that you are refusing to see or manage, something that also occurs in people with a history of trauma that has not been processed and healed. What we can't see or refuse to acknowledge in our minds will come out in our body.

I explained Ashley's rash to her this way: I believe that all thoughts and emotions are energy, and they must be released from the body in one way or another. If we cannot or refuse to acknowledge and process the energy that is building up and rattling around in our minds, our bodies sometimes have no choice but to let it out in another way. If we think of anxiety as energy, the healthiest way for us to release that energy is through exercise, meditation, journaling, and self-expression. If we are not mindfully aware of the presence of anxious or worried energy and managing it in a healthy manner, it will manifest in other ways. While I have not personally proven this belief through scientific study, I do believe it to be true. Our bodies will express physically what our minds cannot (or will not) process and express. This theory has also been extensively researched and documented in trauma and work with post-traumatic stress disorder (PTSD). Unprocessed emotions from trauma can also manifest in very real and painful symptoms in our physical bodies, whether it be chronic pain or chronic digestive issues, etc.

It's common for women in the vortex to struggle with physical symptoms such as chronic tension headaches, digestive issues, rashes and skin changes, and chronic joint pain, among others. If you are struggling with any of these symptoms and have not yet been given a clear diagnosis, consider the possibility that perhaps it's a physical manifestation of unprocessed emotional or mental energy. To be clear, I am not saying that your symptoms are in your head or that your symptoms are made up. I hear from too many women that they have been made to feel "crazy" because their symptoms have not yet been diagnosed by the traditional medical system. I can only imagine how frustrating, defeating, and powerless it must feel to be told that your symptoms are unexplainable or that there is no objective proof of them on investigations.

I genuinely believe that modern medicine as a field has yet to catch up to the depth of the connection between mind and body. It's a challenging and nebulous concept that rigorous scientific research, the foundation upon which modern Western medicine is built, cannot fully evaluate with confidence. But that doesn't mean it doesn't exist or that it's not real. It doesn't mean that just because your symptoms haven't been diagnosed in the traditional paradigm of Western medicine that they don't exist or that the provider doesn't believe you. The fact that someone doesn't speak a certain language doesn't mean the language doesn't exist, it simply means the framework for speaking and understanding does not exist (yet). If you are someone who has struggled with being diagnosed for chronic symptoms and are frustrated with how you've been made to feel in the medical system, please understand that the majority of medical providers do genuinely want to help you, they just don't have the language or understanding to do it yet. It's only through my work with women and intimately following their progress that I've seen without a doubt that some symptoms are absolutely physical manifestations of mental health distress, but not all of them. I have seen symptoms that have been undiagnosed and unrelenting for years resolve after proper attention, acknowledgment, and effort has gone into processing unresolved trauma or repressed emotions. This is not to say all undiagnosed symptoms are related to mental illness either.

There is an additional important point to be made about women who are on the verge of realizing they've been in the vortex, and it happened with Ashley as well. Reliably, just as women are becoming more aware of their anxiety and the impact it's been having on their life, their anxiety gets worse. They often experience an uncomfortable and unwelcome increase in their worry and anxious thoughts. Their sleep becomes even more disrupted than it has been. Their physical symptoms increase. It's as though the awareness of the presence of their anxiety causes anxiety about being anxious. What the heck is going on?

Recall that your anxiety is hell-bent on maintaining the status quo, and it prefers to be in control at all times. It wants to keep you safe, doing what is familiar and what has kept you alive successfully so far. The more we become aware of how our anxiety is affecting us, the more reconnaissance we do on it and the more we become "in on the plan" that our anxiety has for us, the more our anxiety will flare up as if in an attempt to keep itself alive. Anxiety likes things exactly how they are and does NOT want to be found out or be managed. It doesn't want to change. Your anxiety is quite happy being in the driver's seat. If you've been controlled by your anxiety for a long time, that is your norm and your anxiety really likes it that way. Thus, when you begin to work on your anxiety and begin to take steps toward managing and reducing it, your anxiety freaks out, which is something you have to be prepared for and accept so you can finally reclaim your control. In fact, it is a sign that you are on the right track. You are likely stepping into the Awareness Phase.

Phase 2: THE AWARENESS PHASE

The first step toward change is awareness. The second step is acceptance. —Nathaniel Branden

In order to change something in our lives, we have to first become more aware of our mind's patterns, thoughts, and behaviors. Whether it's dealing with thoughts of self-doubt, self-sabotaging behaviors such as overeating, overdrinking, or avoidance and procrastination, awareness of our brain's inner workings is the absolute first step toward managing it and making changes.

The second phase of anxiety recovery is the Awareness Phase. It's a phase of discovering and learning more about our anxiety and its intricacies. In this phase, I often describe our work as similar to that of a soldier doing reconnaissance on an enemy. If you were gearing up for a battle with something or someone, one of the first steps is reconnaissance so you can learn as much as possible about your enemy and what you're up against. This awareness defines the second phase of anxiety recovery.

The Awareness Phase begins when you start the process of learning about your anxiety. You learn the ins and outs, the triggers, what it feels like, what makes it worse, and what makes it better. This learning is done through mindfulness practices and obtaining new strategies to manage anxiety in the moment. You become familiar with the physical symptoms that herald your anxiety is flaring and start to identify and recognize your own personal version of anxious, false thoughts. You learn the ways that your anxiety uses false thoughts and physical symptoms, confusion, and mental noise as a weapon against you to keep you stuck in status quo, in "normal." You may also catch on to some of the sneakier factors that make an impact on your anxiety, like perfectionism, people-pleasing, or an obsession to productivity and achievement. Of all of the phases, most women remain in the Awareness Phase for the longest period of time.

It is in this second phase of anxiety recovery that some women have their first experience of feeling calm. I've often had women in this phase tell me that they are actually beginning to have "good days." It is such a beautiful and critical moment in the process of anxiety recovery, as they can now see the light on the other side and know that relief from anxiety is possible. The experience of "having a good day" motivates them to experience that state more often, which reinforces the good habits and strategies that have gotten them to this point. There is an overall awakening to the impact that anxiety has had on their life, and many women find themselves amazed at "how bad things really were until now."

One important thing to recognize about the Awareness Phase is that although you may see glimpses of relief and improvement, these likely will not last (yet). More often than not, women in the second phase oscillate between being back in the vortex on anxious days and then being out of it. When they are out of it, they are better able to see it for what it is, identify what is happening, and start to manage it, but they still have days when their anxiety takes back control. And it might get worse before it gets better, sorry.

In the Awareness Phase, anxiety has moved to the passenger seat but is still quite opinionated. It gives unsolicited advice, and it's sometimes hard to avoid listening to its lies. Ignoring its lies is an important part of the Anxiety Recovery Process because we continue to oscillate between calm and anxious states. This experience in itself, although unwelcome and uncomfortable most times, provides us with repeated exposure to the emotional transition that happens when we move from calm to anxious. Although we may feel that this rotation is a sign of failure in our recovery, it's not. In fact, when our anxiety returns or we get wrapped up again in an emotional vortex, it's a very necessary and helpful part of the process. I've worked with so many women to manage their anxiety, and almost inevitably, after a few weeks of seeing progress, someone will return with her head hung low, feeling ashamed or as though she is failing because she had a bad day or even a bad week with her anxiety. She often wonders if she's "not doing this right" or if the process isn't working.

You, too, will also likely feel as if you are failing at managing your anxiety. It is not true, so don't let your fears get in the way of your progress. Instead, it's important to realize that these steps backward are necessary learning experiences. Each time we step "backward" and are overcome with our emotions or have a meltdown or bad day, we are provided with a learning opportunity. The transition from calm to anxious can be subtle and sneaky. Anxiety is very stealthy and can often catch us off guard as we go about our day. How often have you experienced a moment when you suddenly feel as if you are in the middle of a panic attack? Did it feel like you were unaware of it slowly developing? Did it sneak up on you and overtake you?

The more often we are exposed to the subtle transition from calm to anxious, the more skilled we become at noticing when it is happening and intervening. If you can work to become an aware observer of that transition, if you can be alert to the moment when that first symptom starts to creep back in (that physical symptom or that particular type of anxious thought), you can lean into the transition and see what happens. This information is invaluable. When you experience the transition between calm to anxiety over and over again, as well as its counterpart, the transition from anxious to calm, you become an expert in your own emotional and mental processes. When you become an expert, you are also perfectly positioned to know exactly how to intervene and when, what to do, and the impact it will have. Trust me. Although it feels awful, transitioning and your awareness of it, it's truly some of the most helpful information we can gather on our recovery journey.

Remember this information about transitioning when you're working through this book and making progress. It is so common to have our anxiety flare back up and take over, similar to the tornado coming over us again. It is not a failure; it is part of the process. Each time our anxiety flares and comes back, we're afforded another opportunity to learn and practice our skills, which is all part of the process. It will take some time and a lot of effort, but you will get there.

Phase 3: THE AGENCY PHASE

In the final phase of recovery, you have stepped out of the vortex and are standing next to it. You have mastered your awareness and management of your anxiety and feel more in control of your emotions and your behavior. You have now stepped into the Agency Phase.

Your anxiety is now something that you are aware of as separate from you, you are aware that it can come and go, but you no longer resist it so strongly or are overtaken as often. In earlier phases, where being anxious and keyed up feels more like your status quo, in this phase, the balance shifts. You are now experiencing more and more days of calm presence and peace as your norm. When you inevitably do experience stressful events or anxiety-inducing situations, you're more prepared and able to identify what's happening and can observe your thoughts from an objective position. You're aware and mindful enough to decide whether to challenge your false thoughts and remain calm or indulge the anxious thoughts and go down the emotional rabbit hole. It doesn't have power over you anymore, and you have more control. You come to the point where you realize that you no longer have to be a victim to its lies and chaos. You're now firmly seated in the driver's seat of your own life. Your anxiety has moved from the passenger seat into the trunk, and you've turned up your favorite music. You can sing out loud to your favorite song. You know what calm feels like, you are clear on what the transition from calm to anxious feels like, and not only can you identify when it's happening, but you can change the trajectory. You know exactly how to manage it because you've had practice managing it over and over again.

One of the best parts of this phase is how much easier everything gets, especially when it comes to curating your life, your habits, and your environment to support your improved mental health. In this phase of anxiety recovery, you become highly sensitive to recognizing anything that brings you closer to or further away from your calm "equilibrium." When you're in this phase, the contrast between your good and bad days is very stark. It's as though you have become a finely tuned instrument that detects anything that will bring your mind into or out of alignment with your new normal. Just as your brain becomes comfortable in a chaotic environment, it also quickly equilibrates to this new calm state as your norm. When this happens, you become very acutely aware of what makes you feel more anxious. With conscious, intentional action, you can easily work to reduce or eliminate those habits, relationships, or situations that bring you out of alignment. You also become clearer on what brings you closer to your calm state. You may begin to notice the connection between different healthy habits (such as exercise or meditation) and your desired calm state. If you begin an exercise routine, you may notice that you feel calmer and for longer periods of time. You may also notice that exercising more often helps reduce your anxiety when it does come back. Although you were already likely aware of this connection before this phase, it now becomes clearer and easier for you to believe and maintain. As with a veil lifting, you gain clarity around what small changes in your habits and routines do to your mental state, and it becomes easier to commit to those small changes. Now healthier habits (i.e., exercise, self-care, and mindfulness techniques) replace negative buffering activities (i.e., binge-eating or drinking or online shopping) and become reinforced as you create and strengthen new reward pathways in your brain. You are gaining positive momentum, and it feels amazing.

While it's certainly possible for this connection to develop in the earlier phases of anxiety recovery, the brain is often too chaotic in those phases for the connection to be very clear. In the initial phase of anxiety recovery, it can feel exhausting and require a ton of effort to begin a new healthy habit, in part due to the cognitive work it requires to be in the anxiety vortex all the time (even unknowingly). The connection between your healthy habit and your reduced anxiety is not there yet. And because your anxiety is so chronically high, it can be difficult to discern anything that makes it feel better. It can also be difficult to discern what makes your anxiety worse. It just feels bad, all the damn time. However, the further you move through the Anxiety Recovery Process, the easier the noticing gets. When your anxiety is chronically high (in the Vortex Phase), it can be impossible to determine what triggers your anxiety at any given time. There may be a few triggers that you know will make your anxiety worse, but for the most part, it remains chronically elevated with little fluctuation from day to day. I've had women tell me, "I just feel anxious all the time, about everything."

If you were to quantify your anxiety on any given day on a scale of ten, what number would you say? If you are walking around with your anxiety at a level eight or nine on most days, it can be difficult to determine what brings your anxiety down to a seven or a six. Your brain is so chaotic, and the noise of your thoughts is so loud that it's hard to have a finely tuned awareness of what's really going on. It's like being at a rock concert and trying to hear your phone ring or have a conversation with the person standing next to you.

In contrast, as you progress into the Agency Phase, your anxiety level is perhaps more often sitting around a two or three out of ten. At this lower anxiety level, it becomes very obvious when your anxiety is higher, creeping up even to a four or five, because the experience of anxiety is so noxious to you now. You're familiar with what it feels like to have anxiety at a level eight or nine, but it's apparent to you now as you're more sensitive to it. This lower level of anxiety in the Agency Phase clears your mind and allows for a heightened awareness of your anxiety and what triggers it. It's as though the volume of your thoughts (the rock concert) has been turned down.

It's not uncommon at this time for women to identify many more anxiety triggers than they'd previously been aware of in this phase. With longer periods of calm in their lives, they are now able to detect very subtle changes in their anxiety level, identify the trigger, and take action to mitigate it. In my own case, I had no idea that a few glasses of red wine would cause my anxiety to flare for days after drinking them. It wasn't until I had experienced an extended period of calm and gained an awareness of my own anxiety that I could monitor and identify wine as the causal trigger in my anxiety flares. As the volume in my mind had been so beautifully turned down, it was so clear to me what had turned it up. It allowed me to alter my habits and be more intentional about my alcohol intake. Now, my ability to detect changes in my anxiety level and identify triggers of that change is so heightened and fine-tuned that I continue to refine my knowledge of my anxiety and become more and more empowered to manage it.

Self-Check:
1. If your anxiety were with you in the car of your life, where would it be sitting right now? Who's doing the driving?
2. What are some checkpoint thoughts or emotions you can watch for that will help you identify when you move from one phase to the next?

chapter 7

ANXIETY'S LAST STAND

Your worry will pretend to be necessary. But I promise you, it's not. When you reach the stage of your anxiety recovery where the balance struck between feeling calm and feeling worried is tipping toward calm most of the time, an interesting thing often occurs. I have worked with many women who make amazing progress in their anxiety journey only to find themselves experiencing a gripping albeit false realization that perhaps they have made a grave mistake. Without the protective force of their anxiety to keep them on guard for all threats, they suddenly find themselves worried about the fact that they are not worried. It's like having a void in your life that you think needs to be filled, when really, this state is ideal—you experience spaciousness, you are connected with your mind and soul, and you're not living in a heightened state of chaos and worry all the time.

It's a bizarre moment in your life when you realize that you're not worried or anxious anymore, or at least that your anxiety is no longer in complete control of your life. It's an interesting mix between feeling empowered, freed, unburdened, and limitless combined with a nagging sensation that *perhaps you needed your anxiety after all.* You wonder whether all that worry was actually important.

Chronic anxiety sufferers often carry beliefs (conscious or subconscious) about their tendency to worry. They often think that although troublesome, their anxiety actually prevents bad things from happening. Essentially, their worry is pretending to be necessary. Due to this deep belief, when their anxiety begins to lessen, they often experience an intense resurgence of it. It's as though the anxiety has realized it has received an eviction notice and is now doing everything in its power to retain its residency and control in your mind. As a result, I've seen women whose worry becomes fixated around the fact that they're not worried anymore. *What if all my anxiety has kept me safe so far? Will something bad happen to me now?* These thoughts are merely manifestations of what I call your Anxiety's Last Stand, its last attempt to remain in control and push you back to where you have been safe and comfortable.

It can be very unsettling to realize there's been such an abrupt change in our mind's usual state. Our brains prefer what they know. They quickly become acclimated and comfortable in whatever environment we are in. The easiest way to understand this phenomenon is to consider the fetus in the womb. The in-utero experience is chaotic. A high level of noise is the norm: the rushing blood of the mother's body, her heartbeat, her voice, and the sounds from the environment. The fetus is almost never still as the mother moves about her day. The in-utero environment is not a calm state. The developing brain, rapidly creating neuroconnections to prepare for life outside of the womb, quickly acclimates and becomes comfortable with the high level of chaos and activity.

The baby is born. Shortly after birth, the environment changes dramatically. There are now periods of intense silence and stillness. We swaddle them to mimic the tight space of the womb and typically lay them down in darkness to sleep. Instead of falling to sleep as all new parents wish, the infant is jarred by the sudden change in environment. They instead fall asleep in moving vehicles, loud shopping centers, and against their mothers' bodies where they are warm and listening to her heart beat. Their minds are accustomed to and comfortable in familiar environments—in this case, a chaotic, high-movement, and loud situation. As many women reading this book may attest to, it can take some time for an infant to be able to adapt to a quieter, darker, and stiller environment to sleep.

This scenario is similar to how our brain adapts to experiencing high levels of anxiety and worry. Our brains become used to living in a state of heightened vigilance and cognitive noise. The excessive rumination, panic attacks, and feelings of being on edge in a chronic anxiety sufferer is analogous to the chaotic environment in utero. This heightened state has become our norm. In fact, the deviation from this occurred way back in the earlier phases of anxiety recovery when we first realized that we had an issue with anxiety, but it becomes very apparent in this later phase. Therefore, as we transition to a calmer state in the third stage of our anxiety recovery, it's very common to experience a surge of anxiety as we nearly complete that transition. While unsettling and uncomfortable, try to avoid being caught off guard. Instead, see this surge as a good sign: *You've almost reached the goal.*

So, how do we manage our Anxiety's Last Stand? Personally, I see it as an excellent checkpoint in the Anxiety Recovery Process. It's time for celebration.

That being said, being anxious about something is uncomfortable and distressing, so I hardly expect you to simply celebrate the fact that you're anxious. First of all, the most important thing to do in this moment is to anticipate that it will occur. Reading this chapter has now let you in on your anxiety's plan, and you'll be better prepared.

When you can anticipate that your anxiety will rear its ugly head to make its last attempt to remain in control, you will be less caught off guard and shaken. You will be less likely to indulge the thoughts as reality. When you do experience the surge of anxious thoughts around your anxiety going away (the irony is apparent), the important thing is to recognize what is happening. It's imperative to lean on the skills you will learn in this book to identify the thoughts, disprove them, and let them go. Even these fears and worried thoughts regarding your anxiety's importance are just that: false thoughts. They are no different from any other anxious thought that you have ever had. No matter what anxious thoughts we have, it's not the anxious thoughts that are the problem, *it's the fact that we believe and indulge the thoughts.* If you are having thoughts of your anxiety being necessary and important, but you choose to objectively identify, challenge, and label them as false, you don't change course or backpedal. In contrast, if you believe the thoughts and change your behavior, you will backslide and revert to old ways of allowing your anxiety to direct and control your life.

It's also important to realize that while we are working to manage your anxiety, we are mainly focused on reducing the anxiety that is causing the most trouble: the overzealous part. We don't want to completely remove the fire alarm system from the building, we merely want to turn down its sensitivity. The appropriate fight-or-flight response will still remain, but ideally, it will not be triggered by conversations with your boss or being stuck in traffic. So, when your anxiety is panicking and telling you all the reasons why it is critically important to your survival, keep in mind that it will still be there when you need to escape a rabid dog or whatever such terrifying future example your brain is creating.

chapter 8

IT'S NORMAL TO FEEL OVERWHELMED

I want to take this opportunity to check in with you about the goal you have for getting your anxiety under better control. This goal is one of the most important ones you can have for yourself and your family, but I also know it can feel quite overwhelming to start. When I first began my journey of recovering from my severe postpartum anxiety disorder, I remember seeing people further along in a similar journey, or reading books that felt so far from my current reality, that I would feel defeated and even worse about my mood disorder. It can be so hard to overcome something that has such a powerful grip on your mindset, and it exerts so much influence over your day-to-day life. In this modern time of social media and mental health awareness, you also don't have to look far to find a story of someone else overcoming mental health challenges and surpassing their own expectations for themselves. It can sometimes feel like the goals that we have for ourselves are so far out of reach from where we are at this time.

This feeling of your goal being out of reach doesn't just apply to the goals you have for your mental health. Whatever goal you have for yourself, whether it's to manage your weight, start a business, or pay off debt, there's always someone who is further along in that journey than you. Thankfully, these are the ones you look to for inspiration and how to get where you want to be—where they are. Maybe I'm that for you. Who knows. But sometimes seeing those people far ahead of us can feel very defeating and overwhelming, and it can be unclear how to even get started moving in their direction.

Before we go on, I want to share three strategies I take to reduce the overwhelm that comes with reaching for personal goals or self-improvement. I remember feeling this way when my kids were very young, when my anxiety disorder had a white-knuckle death grip on me, and when I felt like I was always so exhausted, so anxious, and so defeated. The first few months of motherhood were overwhelming, and I remember feeling like I was trapped in my life. I would look at other moms who seemed so put-together and calm. *How did they do it all? How did they manage everything AND enjoy it?* I would see them exercising, planning meals, and doing many things every day that would help them stay organized and calm. I felt like I didn't even know where to start. So, how did I reduce the overwhelm and move forward?

I realized that I was only seeing parts of their reality. Anytime we see someone who seems to be in a place that we want to be, whether it be with our family lives, our financial lives, or our personal lives, we forget that we are only seeing parts of their reality. There is usually a LOT behind the scenes that we don't see, or there is a lot of their process that we haven't been able to see. In this day and age, we see SO much of the stories of others on the Instagram highlight reel that it can be easy to think we're seeing the entire picture when, in reality, we're only seeing the good or the imperfect parts that are curated in just the right way. We see women doing impossibly impractical things in perfect clothes with perfect hair. We see families on holiday outings that appear perfect and scream-free when, in actuality, we're only seeing a snapshot. When we only see the good parts of someone's story, it can be easy to think that we're the only ones struggling. Not true. The same applies to our goals. No one, and I mean NO ONE, gets to a goal without struggle, sacrifice, tears, and stress. So, if you're feeling those things, you're not alone. *It is all part of the process.*

I also realized that I could take a series of very small steps forward, and although it would feel slow and painful and like I wasn't making much progress, I would get there eventually. While it may seem that some people become overnight successes with different things, most people (read: all people) actually achieve their goals not in one giant leap but rather in innumerable tiny and slow steps. With such a gap between where we are and where we want to be, it can be tempting to think that it's one BIG step to get there. But the reality is, there are actually hundreds of tiny micro-steps when we are working toward a goal. If you've ever had a goal of losing ten pounds or writing a book, it was unlikely that reaching it happened overnight. Even as I write this chapter, I am writing only one page of hundreds. I am taking just one small step today, writing a certain number of words that when all combined after weeks of the same behavior, will create something amazing. You need to have the same mindset when you are working to manage your anxiety. Today, you may have started reading this book as your first tiny step. Tomorrow, you may put into practice some of the strategies or mindset shifts I recommend. Perhaps the next small step will then be choosing to carve out ten minutes each day for yourself and your mental health. Once those small steps feel comfortable, perhaps you will experiment with meditation or journaling on a regular basis. Every step, no matter how small, when taken intentionally and in the direction of your goal, will move you closer toward feeling the way you want to feel. The challenge is to not become impatient or feel defeated when the multiple small steps don't seem to be creating the dramatic overnight results we all crave. The key is discipline, consistency, and trust that what you are doing will bring you to your goal.

Finally, I trusted in and allowed for the magic of compounding habits. Have you ever noticed how one positive habit tends to ripple out into our other behaviors? Consider the last time you started an exercise routine, for example. You likely started small, maybe just walking in the mornings or going to a yoga class twice a week. This shift starts the process, and within a few days, you have seen some success in that small habit. Fast-forward a week or two into your new routine, and now that extra serving at supper or the bag of chips that you usually binge on in the evening doesn't seem so appealing anymore. You think, *Why would I work so hard for my health just to waste all that effort eating this?* Before you know it, you're eating healthier and making better diet choices. You start drinking more water and your skin becomes clearer, radiant even. You begin to see results in your weight and fitness, which then compounds further, and you find yourself feeling more motivated to exercise and stay committed to your progress. Other negative habits start to stick out like sore thumbs—smoking doesn't seem to make much sense anymore and is holding you back. Drinking alcohol makes you feel sick, and you love feeling healthy now. It slowly slips out of your habits, and you're drinking less frequently than ever before. Within a short while, by making just one small habit in a healthy direction, you have become a different person, which is the magic of compounding positive habits. They build on each other. They gain momentum.

I have seen this exact process occur in women who begin to get their anxiety under better control. The habit of observing your thoughts on a regular basis throughout the day leads to an increased awareness of your triggers. When you are more aware of your triggers, you begin to increase your self-care in response to your anticipated increased anxiety. You begin to feel better, and your awareness of your own emotional state increases such that you become acutely aware of everything in your life that causes you to feel out of alignment or anxious. You begin to feel calmer because you are able to manage the noise in your mind. You can begin to curate your life in a way that supports your mental well-being and can more clearly identify what is most important to you. You can hear the inner knowing that was previously drowned out by anxious and chaotic thoughts. You then become aware of the relationships that make you feel uncomfortable, and you begin to explore your boundaries and learn how to more assertively speak up for yourself. These all compound, and before you know it, you're a more confident and calmer version of your former self, living a life that you only had previously dreamed of but never thought would be yours. Trust me, I've both experienced this transformation in myself and observed it in the women with whom I've worked.

So, when you start to feel overwhelmed about whatever goal you're looking at, be it managing your anxiety, your weight, or your finances, remember that struggle is part of the process. Success happens in baby steps. Allow for the magic of momentum to guide your every next step. You'll get there. You'll be amazed how far you can go.

Self-Check:
1. In your goal of improved anxiety management, what is one tiny micro-step that you can take today to just get moving forward?
2. If your goal is better anxiety management, what can you commit to this week every single day to move closer to that goal?
3. Who can you look to for inspiration and support on this journey?
4. Reflect on a time when you have experienced the magic of compounding habits.
5. What is one mantra or reminder you can create for yourself to help you stay motivated when things are feeling hard?

part 2

LET'S GET DOWN TO BUSINESS

"To genuinely manage your mental health and get your anxiety under control, we need to leave no stone unturned."

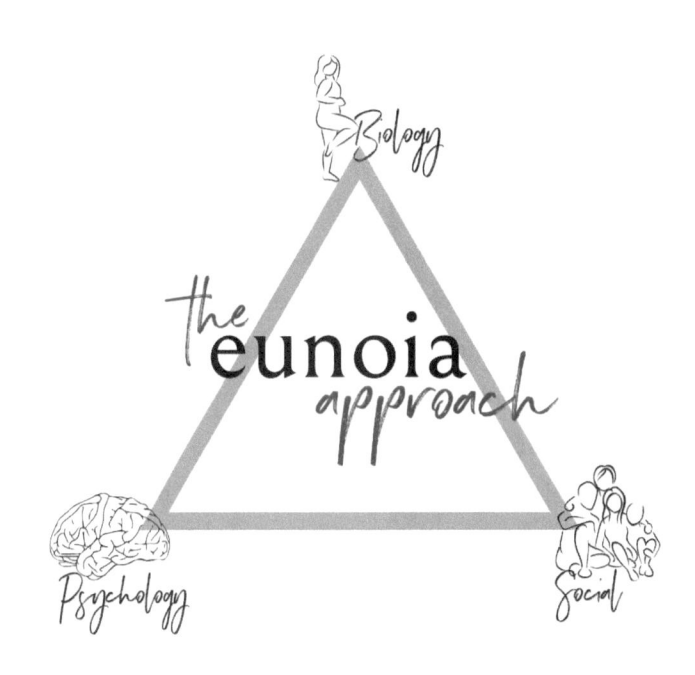

the **eunoia** approach

Biology

Psychology

Social

How are you holding up so far, friend? My hope is that you are starting to see the flickers of light pouring into the darkness that consumes you more days than not. As you learn to manage your anxiety better, we will dig into the practical aspects of what needs to be done. Allow me to introduce to you The Eunoia Approach—a framework that organizes our efforts in the pursuit of a well mind and less anxiety. When I work with women in my virtual clinic, Eunoia Medical, I approach their mental health in this very comprehensive way. Mental health is multidimensional and a fragmented approach that only covers some aspects of a woman's life and mind will not do, which is why I created The Eunoia Approach.

First, we need to examine your biology—aka how you currently care for your body and mind. We need to look at how you nourish your body, sleep, and at whatever chemicals may be circulating in your system and messing with your neurochemistry. After we tackle your biology and implement mind-friendly strategies, we will take a closer look at the psychology of your brain. I'm referring here to the thought patterns and cognitive distortions (also known as false thoughts) present, how they affect your behavior, and what needs to shift to have healthier, more adaptive thoughts. We will also examine pathological mindsets such as perfectionism and people-pleasing. As women, we are inherently social creatures. As such, we need to examine your social life and the ways you show up in your relationships—personal and professional. We need to take an honest look at the relationships you are tolerating, whether you have healthy boundaries, or if you're chronically passive and self-sacrificing. Finally, we need to create a system for you to partake in a daily self-care ritual—a designated time of day for you to reflect, connect to yourself, and make adjustments in your life as needed based on your deep connection to yourself and how you're doing. This self-care ritual is meant to help you connect with your mind, body, and soul. It is also meant to be an expression of your own belief in your worthiness.

I typically present the Eunoia framework as a triangle, with the biology aspect as the top point followed by the psychological and social aspects forming the foundation. This design is intentional because similar to an iceberg where we can only see the tip above water, making changes in our biology is only part of how we manage mental health and anxiety. The two lower corners of the triangle—psychology and social, which involve emotions, thoughts, relationships, and other social situations—literally and figuratively are the deeper, more submerged parts of our lives that are not only harder to change but are also critical and form the basis of the whole approach. To genuinely manage your mental health and get your anxiety under control, we need to leave no stone unturned in any of these areas. I get that this process may seem overwhelming, and I encourage you to just take it step by step. The miracle of compounding habits will work for you as well if you just keep at it. Trust in your mind and body's ability to make progress with each small step.

chapter 9

THE EUNOIA APPROACH

The Eunoia Approach Pillar #1: YOUR BIOLOGY

Our minds and bodies are connected. Many of us inherently know and believe this fact, yet for many of the women with whom I work, paying attention to their body and its overall health and well-being is sometimes the last thing they think about when they're trying to manage their anxiety. It is also uncommon that women are asked about their physical bodies and their physical health when they visit their health care provider for help with their anxiety. The reality is, however, that if we want to have mental wellness, we need body wellness as well because our brain and body are connected. We only have one mind, one body, one life, remember? So, we need to ensure they are cared for and nourished in all the ways they need to operate at their best. Conversely, physical health problems can drastically affect our mental health and anxiety levels. Chronic illnesses and disabilities are powerful factors to be considered in the pursuit of better mental health, which is why it's invaluable in our pursuit of better anxiety control to explore the impact that our biology has on our mental health.

When I speak about body wellness and physical health, I'm referring to how we fuel our bodies, how well our bodies rest, how much rest we get, and how we care for our muscles, joints, and gut. I'm also referring to any chemicals or artificial substances we may use in our daily lives, from medications for our mood to caffeine, alcohol, cannabis, and even nutritional supplements. I'm referring to how often we move our bodies and whether we are keeping our organs healthy with the right nutrients and hydration. If we have access, are we eating wholesome, nutrient-dense food, or are we constantly living life in the drive-thru lane, stocking up on lattes and the latest fast-food trend? It's important to note that this book provides an overview of healthy changes that can support your mental health and is not meant to be a comprehensive review of nutritional psychiatry, a review of the evidence on diet and mood, or even half of what I typically teach about sleep. Rather, this section is intended to be a starting point, a way to introduce you to the connection between your mind and body, and it will hopefully inspire you to implement some mood-enhancing habits into how you care for your body.

Your Diet

There is an incredibly complex, dynamic, and nuanced relationship between food and mood. From *what* we eat to *how* we eat to *when* we eat, if we are emotional eaters or emotional fasters, whether meals are social events or not, our mood and anxiety are often influenced by our diet, food choices, and relationship to food. Our conditioning around food from childhood and our learned relationship with food influences our enjoyment of meals, whether we see food as a reward or as something that needs to be controlled. What we fuel our bodies with is also important because our brains are organs that have unique nutritional requirements.

There are a few basic principles I recommend for all my patients when I'm working to help them manage their anxiety and optimize their mental health. As you read through these next sections, consider how you may be able to better fuel your body.

Eat regularly

How many times have you felt angry, irritable, overwhelmed, or emotional because you were hungry? How often do you find yourself reaching for something less than nutritious to address your "h-anger?" If you have ever experienced the absolutely dramatic and illogical chaos that is a hungry toddler, you can likely attest to the connection between hunger and mood swings. To make matters worse, crappy, high-calorie, sugar-and-fructose-laden, sodium-rich, nutrient-deficient foods abound in our daily lives. While you may be someone who is conscientious about eating a lot of fresh, unprocessed foods in your diet like I am, I know that even I have fallen victim to leaning on something easy, quick, and unhealthful to stave off hunger (and the resulting mood swing). Picture the Snickers chocolate bar advertisement where everyone is hangry until they've doused the hunger fires with the sugar-rich bar. Unfortunately, the crappy food that seems like a good idea when we're hungry usually makes us feel even crappier after we eat it. The reality is that due to our jam-packed schedules and busy lifestyles, we tend to be very reactive in our approach to hunger, which results in us experiencing dramatic lows in our blood sugar (and enhances impatience and irritability) throughout the day. These large biological energy swings can wreak havoc on an already stressed and anxious brain. If your brain is already working overtime to process and react to your daily life when you have anxiety, the last thing it needs is a gap in its available resources or the emotional changes that accompany low blood sugar and a grumbling stomach.

Maintaining a consistent blood sugar and ensuring we have adequate and readily available sources to fuel our bodies and brain is one of the simplest strategies I recommend to my patients with mental health concerns and anxiety. It may look like throwing a bag of almonds in your purse or keeping a high-quality snack in the drawer of your desk. The key to this strategy is being intentional about how you're going to fuel yourself throughout the day. I am not referring to planning each and every meal in your day (unless that works for you), but rather having a stash of readily available, preferably micro- and macro-nutrient-dense foods so you can maintain your blood sugar. I recommend eating a small snack every two to three hours to help ward off emotional hunger swings. Nuts are my favorite snack, as they have a reasonably decent shelf life, are portable, and pack a solid protein and fat punch to sustain blood sugar. Plus, they are chock-full of nutrients and vitamins that are beneficial for brain health. If you can't eat nuts, a homemade energy bar or whole-wheat muffin can also satisfy when hunger strikes.

What you eat matters

I have recently become interested in the field of nutritional psychiatry—a field of brain and clinical science that uses food choices to enhance mood and improve mental health. In his course on Nutritional Psychiatry for Mental Health Practitioners, Dr. Drew Ramsey, a nutritional psychiatrist and one of the foremost clinicians in this new field, reviews some of the more compelling research behind certain nutrients and their benefits or risks to mental health. While I am by no means a full-fledged nutritional psychiatrist, I will review some of the more important foods for brain health that have been identified in the recent research literature, as well as some easy ways to incorporate them into your diet. If you are interested in learning more about nutritional approaches to mental health, I highly recommend Dr. Ramsey's books, which are listed in the Resources section at the back of this book.

One of the easiest ways to eat for your brain health is to ensure you're eating a diet rich in a variety of fresh foods and low in packaged, processed foods. If you do nothing else in terms of managing your diet for your mental health, increasing your intake of fresh, unprocessed foods is likely the most beneficial. As mentioned earlier, although some convenience foods are marketed as being "healthy," on the whole, highly processed foods are calorie-rich, nutrient-deficient, and are, frankly, terrible for us. There are also often many preservatives, synthesized chemicals, and "unpronounceable" ingredients (read: toxic and unnatural) that may make an impact on our mental health in ways that we may not even realize. These "empty calorie" foods do not support our bodies or brains to function well (although this doesn't mean we can never eat them at all).

I know many women I work with have a "guilty pleasure snack" that they eat when they're feeling down or anxious or when binge-watching Netflix in the evening. There should never be shame around food, so instead of telling you that you can't eat it, or you have to go cold turkey and just cut it out, one strategy may be to just cut down how often you do consume it or reduce your portion size. In his course, Dr. Ramsey recommends his patients make simple swaps: replacing processed snacks with higher nutrient-dense ones, such as eating dark chocolate-covered almonds instead of milk chocolate-covered peanuts and baked kale chips instead of potato chips. These small swaps in your typical diet can do more for your mental health than you may realize.

When it comes to making dietary changes for your mental health, I am all about making things very simple and doing what you are able to do. For example, I encourage my patients to try to eat as many colors of foods as there are in the rainbow on as many days as possible, as many of the most nutrient-rich plants and foods are also the most colorful. This simple premise can help you be more mindful of what you are putting on your plate and can also create a fun challenge for you with your family to see who can fill their plates with the most colors. Try it the next time you sit down with your family and review how many colors you're eating at each meal. When was the last time you tried a deep purple Concord grape? How about dark green kale? Or the bright rich pink of a fresh filet of wild-caught salmon?

Another helpful and simple strategy I love is to focus on increasing certain food groups in a patient's diet, if it is possible for them. While it may seem obscure to focus on increasing magnesium or folate in your diet (where the heck do we get magnesium anyway?), we can be mindful of increasing the frequency of seafood, greens, nuts, and beans in our diet. Seafood, specifically bivalves (like mussels and oysters), small fish such as anchovies, and wild-caught salmon are loaded full of brain-powering nutrients and minerals, including B12 and omega-3 fatty acids, which have both been found to improve symptoms of depression, mood, and memory. Greens, with an emphasis on a variety of different types, provide a mix of folate, magnesium, and vitamins critical for the production of mood-enhancing hormones in our brains. Beans and nuts provide high-quality protein and fiber, which supports a steady blood sugar, feeds the bacteria in our gut, and provides us with brain and heart-healthy fats.

If you're feeling overwhelmed already, take a breath. I am not proposing you go toss out everything from your pantry and refrigerator today and do a total overhaul. Instead, I suggest exploring one particular nutrient or mineral that has been shown to benefit mental health and start by simply adding a few sources of that nutrient into your diet weekly. While supplements are helpful and can be beneficial in replacing what's lacking in our diets, it is much better to get our brain food from actual food rather than a pill bottle, if possible. Many commercial supplements are either hard to absorb or very expensive, so focusing on high-quality fresh and unprocessed food that provides natural sources of these nutrients is preferred. If you're looking for a comprehensive review of how to change your diet to support your brain and mental health, Dr. Ramsey's books are an excellent place to start.

Your sleep

It's no secret that our sleep affects our mood. In fact, like food and water, sleep is vital to our survival. I've never met anyone who can function optimally without quality sleep. Similar to the relationship between food and mental health, our sleep and mood also make an impact on each other. If your anxiety is out of control or unmanaged, your sleep is likely suffering. You probably struggle to fall asleep at night due to overthinking or rumination, you may wake frequently in the night, you may have prolonged periods awake at night of restlessness, or you wake earlier than you would like. If you're really unlucky, you may have all of those things and your sleep is just really crappy. I find sleep difficulties and anxiety so often in the same patient that I actually consider broken sleep a sign of unmanaged anxiety. I've seen the pattern time and time again. When your anxiety is getting worse, your sleep begins to become more fitful. When this happens, you often begin to become anxious about sleep itself and become borderline obsessive about getting enough of it, which only further worsens your sleep, as anxiety about it is the antithesis of sleep. It's a vicious cycle.

I know for certain that I feel much worse from a mental health perspective when I've slept poorly the night before, and I'm sure you're nodding your head in agreement right now. The truth is that when we are tired, our brains are even better at creating catastrophes out of all the bad things in our lives than they are when we're well rested. Every emotion, every thought, every incident, every stressor is heightened when we are stuck in this vicious cycle. The good thing is that when your anxiety gets better, your sleep also improves. The converse is also true: If you work to improve your sleep, you will be calmer during the day and be better able to react calmly to whatever life throws at you.

What can we do to improve our sleep? There are a few simple things I recommend to patients. Again, this section will review some basics, but for a more comprehensive review, I'd encourage you to check out some resources at the back of the book.

Let's break down some common sleep myths before we move on to strategies to improve your sleep.

First, there is no "right" amount of sleep. There is not some elusive "normal" amount of sleep or defined number of hours you need to get that is "correct." While popular opinion and media may state that seven to eight hours of sleep each night is the goal, the true hours of sleep that we biologically need varies from person to person, and throughout our lives. The issue with believing that there is a specific number of hours of sleep we "need" each night is that it creates an incredible amount of anxiety and stress about sleep and can create obsessive thought patterns about it. For this reason, I recommend my patients avoid smart watches and other technology that tracks their sleep, as they can create an unhealthy fixation on sleep, which then inadvertently causes worsening insomnia. I have met many people who feel perfectly rested and satisfied after four to six hours of deep sleep, and others who definitely need a higher number of hours, perhaps ten to twelve, to feel rested. The number of hours that is right is individual to you and is based on whether you feel rested after waking or not. Finding the ideal amount of sleep you need will take time and self-awareness. To start, each time you wake up feeling rested, reflect on how many hours you slept, what you did before bed, and what time you woke up. By tracking this basic data, you will begin to understand what "a full night's sleep" means to you.

Another very common misconception about sleep is that we should fall asleep almost immediately after laying our heads on the pillow and then not wake at all through the night. That almost never happens. It's actually completely normal and healthy to take up to thirty minutes to fall asleep. It's also normal to wake up one to three times a night, provided you take less than thirty minutes to fall back to sleep. Sometimes simply learning the facts about something you're struggling with can help put into perspective your own experience and provide support.

The next myth I want to dispel is this one: Not sleeping will kill you. Not true. It may sound silly, and you're probably thinking while rolling your eyes, *Geez, Carly, I know that.* The truth is, however, that on the days that you don't sleep well, your brain makes it out to be quite literally the worst thing that has ever happened to you in your life. Humans have a tendency to fixate and catastrophize on not sleeping because it does feel terrible to not sleep well. It's as though a bad night of sleep (or even a few nights of bad sleep) might literally kill them. We worry and ruminate, change our schedules, and basically obsess about how we can get better sleep. What we don't realize is that this fixation on not sleeping (even if it's not intentional) further damages our ability to sleep. If you struggle with sleeping or are someone who "has always been a bad sleeper," you likely worry about it a lot. Some of the worry is likely subconscious, but you still worry. It might sound like "Oh, I hope I sleep better tonight" or "I really need to go to bed because I slept terribly last night."

To improve our sleep quality, we need to be intentional about not worrying about it, which is easier said than done. As trying to suppress our thoughts and "stop worrying" doesn't actually work, the best strategy to reduce our worried thoughts about sleep is to replace them with more reassuring ones. The next time you catch yourself having a worried thought about sleep or obsessing about how many hours you got last night, try replacing those thoughts with ones like "It's normal to have a rough night of sleep every once in a while" or "I know worrying about my sleep only makes me sleep worse" or "My body knows how to sleep, as it is biologically wired to sleep." My favorite replacement thought is "I've had a bad night's sleep before, and I've been fine the next day." When you can replace the anxious thoughts you have about sleep throughout the day, you reduce the stress and arousal you experience when you go to bed, which helps you fall asleep quicker. Well done!

Create a sleep routine

Our brains love routine and habit, which is good when it comes to sleep. Unfortunately, many people who struggle with sleep maintain erratic routines around it. They may go to bed super early to try to "give themselves more time" to fall asleep or stay up excessively late watching TV to try to tire themselves out. (Or in some cases, to catch that bit of alone time they desperately need to do something mindless.) If they have a rough night of sleep, they often let themselves sleep late in the day (if they can) to catch themselves up. Unfortunately, none of these strategies are helpful (even if they seem like it at the time).

Instead, if you're struggling with your sleep, it is imperative to go to bed at the same time each night and wake up at the same time each morning, even on the weekends (at least initially). The more consistently you can maintain your sleep and wake schedules, the better your sleep will be because routine helps your brain learn to anticipate when it is time for rest, similar to how a bedtime routine helps a baby to settle before bed. Predictability is your brain's best friend, in this case. I have often recommended creating your own bedtime routine as well—a series of habits that you do every night before bed to help signal to your brain that it is time to sleep. Your routine may include drinking a certain kind of herbal tea (chamomile is especially sleep-promoting), using a special lavender body lotion, and reading quietly for thirty minutes prior to tucking yourself in. Whatever you choose, your activities should be relaxing rather than stimulating and be consistent from night to night to build a strong habit.

Furthermore, only go to bed when you're actually feeling sleepy rather than going to bed early with hope that you'll fall asleep after lying in bed for a few hours. The reality of lying in bed hoping to fall asleep is that it only creates more stress about sleep. What follows then is a stressful association with your bed and then bedtime becomes a trigger for anxiety. When your bed is a source of stress, you release excess cortisol, which results in less sleep. The best way to minimize your bed turning into a source of stress or sleep anxiety is to use your bed only for sleep (and sex), which means no watching TV, reading, or working in bed. Referred to as stimulus control therapy, these sleep rules help strengthen your brain's association with your bed and sleeping.

Avoid napping

Ah, napping. Who doesn't love a good nap? I certainly know many of my anxiety patients love napping, usually because it helps them shut off their anxious brains for a while. The trouble with napping during the day is that it fragments our sleep and causes more difficulty sleeping at night. Recall that we all have a biologically defined number of hours we need to get each day. For example, perhaps you have determined that you feel pretty good with seven hours of sleep. If you fragment your sleep by taking a two-hour midday nap, your body is unlikely to sleep through the night for a full seven hours. Additionally, nighttime sleep is typically the most restorative, as we are more able to cycle between phases of REM and non-REM sleep, so the priority is to keep the majority of sleep in the nighttime hours (and when it's darkest). The goal is to increase the pressure your body feels when it needs to sleep so that it can consolidate its sleep during the nighttime hours. Therefore, if you're working to improve your sleep, consider dropping your daytime nap. You'll thank me later when you're sleeping soundly through the night.

Darkness and light

Our bodies have a natural cortisol cycle that helps regulate our sleep and wake cycles referred to as our circadian rhythm. Based largely on exposure to light, our circadian rhythm depends on us going to bed when it's dark (or keeping our room very dark) to stimulate melatonin production (a naturally produced sleep hormone). Melatonin is released in response to darkness and this production is disrupted by light. If we maintain erratic sleep and wake cycles, spend large chunks of daylight sleeping, or spend a lot of time in environments with artificial light, we can dysregulate our body's circadian rhythm and make our sleep worse. For optimal sleep, aim to sleep in total and complete darkness. Black-out curtains or blinds can be helpful. Turn your digital clock away from your bed as well.

Finally, with our increasing dependence on technology and screens, it is very important to be mindful of how your screen use affects your sleep. I've often said that your phone is like a tiny sun in your hand, signaling to your brain that it's time to wake up. I recommend putting phones and devices that emit artificial light away sixty to ninety minutes before bedtime to avoid the suppression of melatonin production. If you must work in the evening on a screen, wearing glasses that block artificial light in the blue spectrum can help prevent interrupting melatonin production.

Your physical body

Aside from ensuring you are fueling your body properly and giving it adequate rest, it's also important that we maintain our physical bodies to keep our anxiety under control. Much like how you bring your car into the auto shop for regular maintenance to ensure it continues running smoothly, the same goes for our bodies.

In my role as a family physician, I often see patients who are flabbergasted at the realization that their bodies are beginning to break down over time. Although they have not been exercising, monitoring the health of their organs, or paying much attention at all to their body, they're surprised when the machine that they haven't maintained begins to break down. In truth, our bodies are very complex machines—a full system—with motors, hinges, plumbing, and one big important pump. We are full of muscles and tendons that will become stiff, sore, and injury-prone if we don't regularly move, strengthen, and stretch them. Put simply, our bodies are designed to move, and move often. I'll cut to the chase. If you're not moving your body in a way that's accessible to you regularly and keeping your body strong and flexible, you're leaving out a critical aspect of your anxiety management strategy. (Note: Exercise or movement looks different for everybody and every body. If you're not able to regularly move your body due to a disability or illness, try watching a hilarious movie and laughing your tush off or having sex to replicate some of the same benefits of exercise. Sounds good, right?)

For many of my patients, the possibility of something being wrong with their physical bodies is a powerful trigger for their anxiety. It makes sense when you recall your anxiety is designed to keep you alive, so it only makes sense that it will be at least a bit dramatic about any possible risk to your physical health. To combat this feeling (known as health anxiety), we need to not only be aware of our anxious thoughts and seek to replace them, but we also need to take good care of the bodies we inhabit so they are at least somewhat less likely to become ill and break down. If you are disabled or chronically ill, it also means taking good care to manage symptoms, giving yourself time to rest, taking medications as prescribed, and collaborating with high-quality health professionals who listen and support your health and wellness.

Chemicals and substances

There are a number of different substances and chemicals that can influence our moods. I often talk to my patients about returning to a biochemical baseline when I work with them. That is, we will systematically and slowly work to reduce and eliminate any unnecessary or mood-altering substances from their life so we can establish their neuro and biochemistry baselines, something that can be very enlightening. This process may involve cutting out coffee or energy drinks and sometimes means tapering off certain medications (under the supervision of a medical professional only). Patients who cut out caffeine are sometimes surprised to find how much better their anxiety becomes, while others have noticed a connection between their consumption of alcohol or cannabis and their mood.

Caffeine
Caffeine is ubiquitous in our busy lives. A daily ritual, from our morning coffees to mid-morning soda or energy shot, that green tea latte in the afternoon, and even chocolate in the evening, caffeine can be a sneaky and potent aggravator of anxiety. I recommend all patients do a thorough audit of all the sources of caffeine in their day and reduce or eliminate them completely for at least a few weeks to assess the impact it has on their mood and anxiety. At the very least,

I recommend cutting down to one cup of coffee or tea maximum in the morning and consuming no other caffeine-containing products after 1:00 p.m.

Alcohol

Alcohol is often viewed as an anxiety-relieving substance. It's also very socially acceptable and part of many of our celebrations and rituals. Not surprisingly, many anxiety sufferers self-medicate or overindulge with alcohol in an attempt to "treat" themselves and numb their constant anxious feelings. What many women do not realize, however, is the delayed activating effect that ethanol (alcohol) has in and on our bodies. Have you ever had two or three glasses of wine in the evening, only to find yourself lying awake at 2:00 in the morning? Have you ever felt unpredictably more anxious or emotional the day following a few gin and tonics? If so, you are experiencing the deleterious effects of alcohol on mood. While it may serve to reduce feelings of anxiety initially, many of my patients become very aware of the more negative effects on their mood and anxiety as they progress through the Anxiety Recovery Process. If you don't feel like completely abstaining from alcohol, that's okay. What I would encourage you to do instead is simply become more mindful of how you feel before, during, and after you consume alcohol. The goal is to become aware of how alcohol consumption affects your mood and then find a level of consumption that feels healthy and right for you.

Medications

I saw your eye roll. You almost had a mini freak-out and shut this book because you have your own preconceived notions about antianxiety or antidepressant medications. Not so fast, friend. I want to take a moment to speak about what is likely the most controversial strategy in anxiety management and mental health treatment—the use of medication. Mood medications are chemicals that alter your neurochemistry to make an impact on your experience of your mood. Now, I am fully aware that the word "medication" can either strike fear into your heart, making you certain you're reading the wrong book, or it can make you feel curiously hopeful. While I tend to believe that medication is actually one of the less important strategies in anxiety management, I want to discuss it early so that 1) we can get it out of the way and focus on more important things, and 2) we can be on the same page about what medication *can* and *cannot* do in your anxiety management journey.

To be clear, my approaches to anxiety management and mental health are not anti-medication. I am trained as a medical doctor and prescribing medication is kind of what I do a lot of the time. That said, I also do not believe that medications are necessary for every single case or that they will work for every single person. Are they game changers for some people? Absolutely. Are they required for every person with a mood disorder? Definitely not.

So, let's clear up some common misconceptions about medications and mood disorders (like anxiety and depression). For one, I am certain that if you solely depend on a particular medication to treat your anxiety, you will likely not get your anxiety under control in the long term (or at least feel as good as you want to). Medications are not an island. Even further, I believe that if you solely rely on medication as the only treatment for your anxiety, you might as well stop reading the rest of this book because you likely won't fully commit to following all of the strategies I recommend. Your mood medication will handle it all, am I right? (*That's sarcasm, by the way.*)

Conversely, I also know that if you dismiss medication entirely because you simply refuse to consider it could help or for a number of other reasons, it can make anxiety management challenging. I have prescribed more than enough antianxiety drugs to know that success with medication therapy requires a very careful evaluation of the patient—the symptoms of her disorder, her beliefs, and her goals. Medication therapy is not for every woman. Yet for some, it can be an invaluable tool in their journey to wellness and mental health. It all comes down to each individual's symptoms, body chemistry, diagnoses, medical history, values, and goals. Being a little skeptical of using medications to treat mental illness is more than okay. It's natural to feel that way. All I ask is that you stay open to the possibility that it may work for you.

There are a few things that I believe are important for everyone to know regarding the treatment of anxiety with medication. By medication, I'm referring to a pill or drug that you take with the intention to treat the symptoms of anxiety. A medication does not necessarily need to be a prescription for the following to apply (i.e., over-the-counter anxiety relief supplements such as magnesium and cannabis are also included).

Medication will not treat your anxiety by itself. #Sorrynotsorry, but pills don't build skills. There. I said it.

Medication is not for everyone, meaning everyone does not need to be medicated, and not everyone will do well or get better with medication. In fact, I would say medication is needed in perhaps only 30 to 40 percent of my patients.

There is a myriad of medications and chemicals we can use to treat anxiety or augment our other strategies to manage anxiety. In some cases, it can take a bit of trial and error to find the right one (something that's incredibly anxiety inducing for most people). This process takes time, a healthy amount of trust between patient and provider, and a strict rule on not visiting Dr. Google or Dr. WebMD, you feel me?

Just because you tried one medication in the past and "didn't like how it made you feel" doesn't mean there is no other medication that can help you. You need to keep an open mind if you're genuinely trying to feel better.

No, you won't get dependent on your anxiety medication (unless you're popping Ativan like candy when you're anxious—a strategy and medication that I never use or recommend). Also, unpopular opinion here: Your personality will not change as some people think. In fact, many of my patients feel more like themselves once stabilized on the right medication for their mood. You may be calmer and become less reactive, but isn't that the point?

No, you don't need to be on medication forever if you start it. I started on Sertraline at nine months postpartum and remained on it for about nine months. I've since been off of it for three years and counting and have been able to depend on the other strategies in this book to manage my anxiety since then.

I obviously cannot, and would not, make sweeping statements about the type of medication, dose, or frequency that would be effective, safe, or therapeutic for every woman reading this book. Medication therapy of anxiety requires a close, honest, and trusting relationship between a patient and their prescriber. It requires a willingness to see through a medication trial without totally freaking out and never returning to the doctor's office. It requires a level of trust and rapport with your physician that you are comfortable enough to share your honest feelings about how a medication is making you feel and what you do and don't like.

Most of all, it is most important to note that medication therapy requires you to actually do the deep work within the other parts of The Eunoia Approach to see results. Medication alone is not a cure-all for anxiety. I so often see people in my office who come to seek a medication as a "quick fix" for their mental health disorders, and this strategy does not work. All mental illnesses, anxiety included, are multifactorial—they are influenced by a million other things. A medication cannot replace your shitty job or help you leave a toxic relationship. A medication will not heal your trauma or help you become more assertive. A medication will not help you reconcile a loss or become more self-confident. These things require more work on your part, and that is what the majority of this book is about.

The medication yo-yo

Now that we are on the topic of medication, I want to review something I refer to as the "yo-yo medication pattern." I have seen this pattern so often in my practice that I even have a canned speech of sorts I share with women when they present in this situation. The pattern goes something like this:

1. Start a new anxiety medication. Feel brief relief that you're *doing something*.

2. Experience a medication honeymoon effect: a welcome, albeit brief respite from the loud, anxious thoughts, relief from panic attacks, and a little mood boost (*thank you, serotonin*).
3. Continue doing all the crap in your life that contributed to your anxiety in the first place (i.e., no exercise, no self-care, no boundaries, no examination of anxious thoughts and perfectionism, no examination of past trauma or flawed beliefs, no cutting off toxic relationships, etc.).
4. Feel resurgence of your anxiety symptoms after about three to nine months. Wonder if your medication isn't working and if you need to change it. Book doctor's appointment.
5. Increase your medication or switch to a new medication over a period of weeks and repeat the cycle (sometimes four, five, or even six times).

To paraphrase Albert Einstein, do you really expect things to change if you do the same thing over and over again? This pattern is essentially what takes place with the yo-yo medication phenomenon. Both patients and providers can fall victim to this trap because of the variety of medications available, and to a point, medication trials are required to find the correct medication that will work best for a patient. It makes sense that a different medication may work differently for someone. However, if the same symptoms continue to return after a period of successful treatment on a particular medication, I believe it is likely due to not doing all the foundational work (like not going to therapy, not committing to self-care, etc.) than the medication losing its efficacy or the patient "becoming tolerant" to it. You must be committed to the foundational parts of The Eunoia

Approach and genuinely put forth a good effort in those areas before you will see sustainable change with your medication.

Medication is not THE treatment, it is a treatment *adjunct* for anxiety, meaning it adds something to the treatment plan. While its effects vary between patients, medication typically helps to turn down the volume between anxious thoughts, creates spaciousness between them, and reduces the physical manifestations of emotions (including anger, sadness, anxiety, panic, etc.). I've often had patients tell me, "I don't get so upset about little things anymore" or "It feels like I'm just happier and less frazzled." I've also heard, "I am enjoying my kids more" or "I can concentrate more." Notice that I didn't say patients tell me, "It helped me quit my shitty job" or "It helped me create boundaries with my family." I didn't say, "It helped me take time for myself every day to check in" or "It taught me to stop putting everyone before myself" or "It helped me exercise regularly." Nah, that stuff is all on you. That is the hard work.

Self-Check:
Now that you have learned about the impact of your biology on your anxiety, take the time to reflect on your own life and habits.
1. Where in your life can you improve your biological habits to manage your anxiety better?
2. What are one or two small changes you can look at making over the next two weeks? Starting small is important.

3. What is the most important thing you want to focus on with respect to your biology? What is one action you will take to improve that today?

The Eunoia Approach Pillar #2: PSYCHOLOGY

Now that we've gained an understanding of how our biology affects our anxiety and mental health, we will dive into one of the meatiest sections of The Eunoia Approach: Psychology.

Our mind is incredibly powerful. Given that we only ever have access to our own inner workings and our thinking patterns, it can be easy to assume that everyone else thinks like we do or that how we think is "normal." However, that's not the case. We each have our own unique cognitive patterns and systems of beliefs that inform how we interact with our environment, how we interpret social cues, and how we frame things in our lives and process external stimuli. We often have long-held, unexamined beliefs that are unhelpful or damaging to our mental health. Unless we shed light on these common albeit false beliefs and thought patterns and work to accept them without judgment and shame and then transform them into healthier, more adaptive ones, we will struggle to feel well and happy.

In this section, you will find a diverse collection of therapy strategies and mindset shifts to help you be more aware of your brain's patterns, reframe your thinking, and help you gain control over your anxiety. Although each strategy or section is separate and distinct, combining them and mastering these shifts will help propel you into greater power over your anxiety. If you find yourself not resonating with a particular section or strategy, that is fine. Skip over it and come back to it when you're feeling fresh or looking for more support.

chapter 10

YOUR EXPERIENCE AND YOUR SUFFERING

My patient had experienced months of harsh workplace bullying that ultimately resulted in her forced resignation. She was devastated. She couldn't think straight in the immediate days that followed, and tears flowed nearly every time she opened her eyes. She was understandably worried about her future, whether she would find a new job, whether her coworkers would believe her or her abusive boss, and whether she would be able to pay her bills next month now that she didn't have a steady income.

I sat with her in the office and held space for her to feel all the emotions that continued to surface. I held space for her to feel safe in her uncertainty, to feel sad and ashamed about the way she had been treated, and to be devastated about the sequence of events that had unfolded. The emotions were raw.

"I just don't understand why I'm feeling this way. Is there something wrong with me?" she asked. "I had a head injury when I was five years old. I didn't black out, but I did have a concussion. Do you think that is why I'm so upset?"

It's an interesting phenomenon I notice among many people I work with in that we have a tendency to believe that our emotions are false overreactions to our life experiences. It's as though we trust physical injury and symptoms more than any emotional responses. I've had many women ask me the same question my patient did that day. In their extreme distress, they are so uncomfortable with feeling their emotions that they are certain something in their brains or bodies has gone terribly wrong for them to be having such a powerful and painful emotional response.

"I can't possibly feel this much; it hurts too bad. If there is something wrong with me that makes me feel this way, we can fix it."

This logic makes sense from an outside perspective. The reality is that humans, on the whole, have a very low tolerance for distress (emotional pain). One of the primary motivators of human behavior is to avoid distress or pain. Our natural inclination is to find a way to remedy the situation, and fast, which translates into a frantic search for the "reason" why our emotions are so powerful and so painful. In the case of most women, they tend to look inward for the flaw instead of looking outward at the situation in their life that has triggered the emotional reaction in them. Translation: If I feel this bad, it must be because I am broken or something is wrong with me.

In many anxiety sufferers, it's also common for them to immediately judge their anxious response or emotional reaction to an event in their life as completely inaccurate or overzealous. They have lived with anxiety long enough that they've come to believe that their own natural reaction is an overreaction because they have anxiety. They struggle to see if perhaps there is some legitimacy to how they are feeling. I often ask my clients to quantify how much they feel their reaction is legitimate versus overzealous in a particular situation. I will ask them if they feel that any other person might feel the same way in a similar situation, or what proportion of their anxious response is extreme. This reflection is helpful because we're not working to completely eliminate anxiety, we simply want to manage the part of our reaction that affects our functioning and mental health. Try it the next time you have an anxious reaction to something.

Most people hearing my patient's story would completely understand why she felt so devastated and emotional in response to what happened. Months of bullying and harassment followed by a dramatic and painful coerced resignation that led to uncertainty about employment and financial instability is a pretty legitimate reason to feel so distraught. In that moment, however, and in the weeks that followed for my patient, she continued to wonder if there was something else within her that caused her emotional experience to be so dramatic and painful. She failed to understand that when terribly painful things happen to us, it is normal to feel terrible pain.

Some of the more common everyday emotions can also cause a lot of distress. I highlight this fact because even our less powerful emotions can be accompanied by shame and guilt and a need to discredit the emotional experience as if feeling anything at all is incorrect or wrong. When we feel an emotion in response to another emotion, it is referred to as a secondary emotion. For many people with whom I work, it seems like displaying or feeling any emotion at all is sometimes viewed as something to be ashamed of, annoyed by, or resented. When women tell me about their emotional experience, it's rare that they describe it in self-compassionate ways; rather, they use a tone that signifies the inconvenience, the irritation, or the shame that is entrenched in their emotional experience.

> *I'm so angry with my son, and I'm a terrible mother because of it.*
> *I'm really frustrated with myself that I can't get over this.*
> *I feel afraid of trying this new medication; I'm such a chicken.*
> *Why am I still sad about this? I should probably just get over it, right?*

It's human and normal to feel the whole spectrum of emotions, including anxiety, sadness, and anger. Reacting to a job loss with grief, sadness, anger, and frustration is normal. Being frustrated about your progress is normal. Feeling afraid of making changes is normal. Yet many of us desperately try to shut down these emotions, shame ourselves for having them, or search desperately for a cause of "why does it feel so bad?"

And I usually say this to them: You feel this way because you are human and are going through a terrible event/situation. You're experiencing human emotions. Yes, it hurts badly. Yes, it's very uncomfortable. I totally understand. We're designed to react to painful experiences with emotions, and when we do, it's human nature to want to remove the emotion completely. Instead, we need to shift our mindset toward developing a tolerance of the emotions we feel rather than eliminating them entirely. The point is not to erase emotions (or even erase anxiety) because without emotions, we would also not feel love, happiness, or pride. The goal is to regulate and sit with emotions that are uncomfortable for us. One of our goals in improving our ability to tolerate our emotions is learning how to identify them and then develop skills to help regulate our emotions so that they affect us less and cause less trouble for us.

When we resist our mind's natural reaction to life and try to force away our emotions, it doesn't work, plain and simple. However, we tend to be very skilled at making emotional experiences more painful for ourselves by fixating on them and trying to find a fixable root cause. We spend hours and days wondering if we are somehow inherently sick or damaged because we feel the way we feel. We invalidate our own experience and make ourselves feel even worse. We work hard to make our emotional experience mean something about us, and typically, those meanings are something about us being unworthy, weak, or "bad." We succumb to the belief that we are broken or not living or functioning properly. We try to find the defect in ourselves that explains why our feelings are so powerful and so painful. We believe that we must be malfunctioning, that our bodies are not doing what they are "supposed to do."

This belief that we are broken or responding incorrectly to life's painful events is fundamentally flawed. In her book *Untamed*, Glennon Doyle writes that most of us have created in our minds the idea that there is a perfect woman who reacts to life in just the right way, without anger, fear, worry, or sadness. She processes her world "correctly"—with poise, grace, and ease. She doesn't get overwhelmed, doesn't snap at her kids, and certainly doesn't freak out and throw an embarrassing tantrum when something doesn't go her way. Doyle says that we all compare ourselves to this false "ghost" and find ourselves lacking when we experience the painful and mundane emotions of our humanness. In reality, though, this woman doesn't exist, and painful experiences and emotions are the norm of being human rather than the exception. Experiencing painful emotions doesn't mean we are wrong or broken. We are not damaged or malfunctioning because we fear for our children's safety or because we experience grief and sadness at the loss of a loved one or anger toward a backstabbing friend. Being human is a painful experience, and as Doyle says, "If it hurts, you're doing life right."

Our brains are amazing supercomputers, hardwired to find solutions and answers to our questions. If we believe that our painful reaction to life's hardships is due to a flaw in our operating system or a malfunction of our human system, our brain will work hard to find the flaw, even if it doesn't exist. Our brains are extremely creative at finding any reason, no matter how false it may be, to find our flaws, to find anything that explains why we feel what we feel. So, if the experience of emotional reactions themselves are not the problem, then what is?

The reality is that 99 percent of emotional experiences are not only healthy and normal but are fully justified reactions to life events. It is the way we react to the emotions that causes us additional distress. In Eckhart Tolle's book *A New Earth: Awakening to Your Life's Purpose*, he asks, "Can you see that your unhappiness about being unhappy is just another layer of being unhappy?" He is referring to the concept of finding space around your emotion, seeing it objectively, and practicing radical acceptance for whatever you're feeling in the moment. I often ask my patients these questions as well: What if it didn't matter that you were sad? What if you weren't upset about feeling anxious? Could you just be anxious and be in that moment? When we become aware of our tendency to have negative reactions to our emotions, we release the need to explain why we experience such powerful emotions. We remove the need to look deep inside ourselves for the "flaw" that is causing our powerful emotional experience, allowing ourselves to feel what we need to feel in that moment without judgment or shame. We remove the need to eliminate our emotional experience and can work to develop acceptance and tolerance for our humanness.

In my sessions with clients, I often refer to this concept as their experience and their suffering. The truth is that in many cases, our everyday experiences often are painful enough. When we experience a loss, fail to reach a goal, or have panic attacks, those experiences are painful. We often feel a lot of emotion in response to these situations. However, we often make our experiences worse by layering additional suffering on top of our pain in the form of judgment of our emotion and "meaning-making" about our experiences. You need to approach yourself and your experiences with self-compassion and without judgment. Work to be mindful of how often you may be making your experience of anxiety worse by adding additional suffering on top of it through your judgments.

Self-Check:
1. Reflect on how you react to the emotions that you experience. Do you notice and accept them, or do you immediately judge and work to remove them?
2. Do you tend to feel that there is something wrong with you because of your emotional experiences? What has your brain come up with as the answer?

3. Is it possible to allow your emotions and your anxiety to just be what they are without layering on any additional suffering?
4. Consider one of the more recent experiences of anxiety you have had. How much of that reaction was legitimate versus overzealous? How does this change how you feel (your secondary emotion) in relation to your anxiety?

Let's get your mindset in check right away

Mindset is the critical ingredient to nearly everything we do. I have learned over my thirty-something years of life that it doesn't matter what strategies you employ to do a certain thing or accomplish a certain goal if you have a crappy mindset about your endeavor. For example, if you have a goal to be debt-free, it doesn't matter if you have the most foolproof budgeting strategy ever if your mindset is crap. If you feel like a budget is a negative thing, or if you believe you will always have chains of debt holding you down, you will never achieve your goal. Mindset is everything, and this fact applies to anxiety management as well.

There is one particularly prevalent mindset obstacle I have identified in women who are trying to get their anxiety under control. That is, they believe that if they do all the right things and follow my plan to the letter, their anxiety will completely go away and never come back. They will be "cured" or "fixed," and they will live happily ever after.

If this is your mindset, I hate to break it to you, but it's false. As I stated earlier, anxiety is an intrinsic characteristic within all humans evolutionarily selected—a powerful behavioral motivator that has likely become deeply embedded in your conditioning. It doesn't matter how many books you read, kilometers you run, joints you smoke, or medications you take, your anxiety will never be gone forever. While this fact may be disappointing to many of you reading this book, trust me it's a good thing.

Many women I work with ask, "What can I do to make this go away?" They are desperately searching for a "reason" why their anxiety is so bad. They often think that if they can just find the cause and fix the issue, their anxiety will be a thing of the past. Again, recall earlier when I spoke about the fact that your brain will work to find the "flaw" that is causing your anxiety and will be very creative about it too. Commonly, women will wonder whether an underlying biochemical or physical reason is to blame (like thyroid disease, for example). Seeking a simple physiological fix for your anxiety is an understandable approach because anxiety is not comfortable to experience, and it feels better to find a medical or physical reason for the issue than to face the truth sometimes. I completely get it. While it may occasionally be the case with some women, it isn't for most. That being said, it is important to rule out any medical illnesses or conditions that could be contributing to your anxiety with your health care provider.

The desire to find the "clear solution" to your anxiety usually stems from the belief that a quick fix is possible. The trouble with "quick fixes" is that they often don't produce meaningful long-term improvement in symptoms. To experience lifelong benefits with your anxiety, you need to do the harder things that many of us are not motivated to do. Like almost anything in life, the harder path is almost always the one that yields the most profound results, which is why it is a good thing that your anxiety will never completely go away because in you realizing that it's going to be sticking around for a while, you will be more motivated to do the hard things. By choosing to do the "hard things" outlined in this book, you are more likely to be in control of your anxiety for the rest of your life rather than just for this moment.

If your anxiety was going to pack up and leave, would you be as motivated to learn the strategies in this book and apply them? If you could just take a pill that would make your anxiety go away easily, would you take the time to read this book and apply what you're learning? Would you spend hours journaling your deepest fears and working through false beliefs if you knew that one day your anxiety would never bother you again? Probably not.

Spoiler alert: The reality is that anxiety and most mental illnesses are chronic illnesses. Though they vary in the intensity of symptoms and severity of impact on functioning, the illness itself remains. However, as with all chronic illnesses, we have a choice in how we approach managing that illness. We do not need to be defined by them. We do not need to allow our illnesses to take away our personal power or change how we show up in our lives. You are more likely to experience greater success if you play the long game with this one instead of seeking short-term results.

One of the most important mindset shifts you can make is shifting away from hating your anxiety and wishing it away to moving toward a radical acceptance of it. With radical acceptance comes radical commitment toward learning how to live with it and work with it rather than against it. Your anxiety is your tendency, it's a natural part of you, so resisting what's inherently natural makes little to no sense. To be clear, accepting your anxiety does not mean that you approve of it or that you like that it's around. It simply means that you're willing to accept that it is here to stay and that you are learning to live with it in the most effective and healthy way you can. Using the analogy of a chronic disease like diabetes, you could choose to wish it away, or you could accept what is happening and learn how to thrive with your disease. Furthermore, when you can accept your anxiety as a part of you, you can also stop being surprised by it when it returns. Time and time again, women will come to me panicked that they are becoming anxious about something that is happening in their lives. They are often either completely unaware of why they are experiencing more anxiety, or they can't seem to figure out why this event should cause so much anxiety. Perhaps they are returning to work after maternity leave, packing up their house to move across the country, or caring for a sick family member. More often than not, women are surprised when their anxiety is flaring in these situations.

Recall that your anxiety is your tendency, and it's the way you "pick up" life. So, it follows that whenever there is a change in your life (even if it's not logically a threat to you), your anxiety is likely to flare up. Remember, anxiety prefers the status quo and what has kept you alive so far. Again, if you were a diabetic, would you forget that you were? Would you just eat something and then be shocked when your blood sugar was high? Probably not.

Learning to accept that your anxiety is not going (completely) away and then learning to expect that it will be present in your life are some of the most fundamental mindset shifts when it comes to managing your anxiety. I often refer to this concept as "Expect and Accept." When you expect your anxiety to increase or get worse when life happens, you are less thrown off when it does. You can be more proactive by implementing additional self-care to support yourself through it. Too many women live in a fantasy world, hoping their anxiety will never come back and are repeatedly shocked and dismayed when it does. If you continue to be surprised by your anxiety, you have not yet accepted that it is part of you.

The next time you find yourself becoming more anxious and your gut reaction is to panic about becoming anxious again, I encourage you to shift your thoughts. Instead of thinking, *Oh here we go again*, try *I respond to life with anxiety, but I can handle it.* Instead of spiraling into panic, remind yourself, *I have survived anxiety before, and I will do it again.*

Expect and accept. Expect and accept. And so it is.

Acceptance of your anxiety and every other emotion you experience is the first step toward changing your experience. When you arrive at the doors of self-acceptance where you accept every single emotion for what it is—that experiencing fear, pain, and other emotions are not blemishes on your human experience but rather ARE your human experience—you can eliminate many of the obstacles to your healing. We need to stop making our emotions and our anxiety mean something about us as a person. We need to stop resisting our experience because what we resist persists. We can then learn how to regulate and master our emotions so they no longer cause us any distress.

Self-Check:
1. How would you approach your anxiety differently if you believed it was never going away?
2. Consider a recent emotional response to your anxiety. Would the "expect and accept" mindset have changed that for you?

chapter 11

YOU ARE NOT YOUR THOUGHTS

To become experts in learning how our minds work and be more attuned to how our anxiety shows up in our lives, we have to first become aware of our thoughts. We have to become objective observers of them, which is why it's important that your self-care routine includes some sort of mindfulness activity.

For some of us, becoming aware of our thoughts may be a completely brand new and foreign concept, since many of us have lived our lives fully immersed in them, mindlessly identifying with our thoughts and assuming we are one with them. The truth is, however, that you are not your thoughts, and your thoughts are not who you are. You are a being who experiences thoughts, and to be honest, about 95 percent of them are nonsense.

If this concept is entirely new to you, you're in for a surprise. Perhaps you haven't been aware of it all this time. And that's okay. But hear me when I say that you are not the voice in your head that you have identified with your whole life. Some call it *ego*, but I call it *anxiety*. And *you* are not your anxiety (or your ego, depending on what you believe). The true "you" is the observer of this voice. Have you ever gone about your day and realized there is a full-blown movie production taking place in your mind—a voice that directs, judges, and assesses everything? That same voice may be the one urging you to avoid certain things, or it may be whispering things like "You're not good enough." It's a vital life skill to be able to observe, identify, and separate yourself from that voice and the thoughts it creates. When you can choose to observe, distance yourself, and assess thoughts from an objective place, you are less likely to be swept up into emotional vortexes.

So, step one: Practice distancing yourself from the voice in your head that is constantly chattering away, running a commentary on your life all day, every day. When you can distance yourself from it, you will also gain more control over how emotional you feel throughout the day. Our thoughts directly affect our emotions, and so the more we can be aware of and direct our thoughts, the less often we will feel all the yucky emotions of anxiety. We can learn this valuable skill by practicing meditation and mindfulness. There is a vast amount of powerful research supporting the practice of meditation and mindfulness for improving mental health and managing anxiety. It is something I recommend to every single woman I work with who is trying to get her anxiety under control.

Why is meditation important?

I get it, meditation can seem intimidating, especially if you're trying it for the first time. Anxious or not, when we live life on autopilot, letting that voice in our head run the show, it can feel incredibly uncomfortable to quiet our mind and observe our thoughts. Furthermore, many people, when they hear the word "meditation," picture silent yogis sitting cross-legged on the floor while doing bizarre hand gestures and saying mantras. It can seem a bit weird and new agey. *Stay with me here.*

Thankfully, with meditation becoming more mainstream, we are seeing a surge of more modern interpretations of it. There are various apps and technology all around us to help us learn and embrace the habit in a practical, less intimidating way. It's important to realize that the intention of practicing meditation does not need to be spiritual or religious. Many women do associate meditation with spiritual health, but if this description doesn't fit with you, that's totally okay. Personally, I use my meditation practice as an opportunity for me to connect with my mind and my spiritual self. There are so many ways to meditate. For the purposes of this book, a simple definition will suffice: Meditation is the practice of observing your mind objectively and watching what it does without judgment.

You may have already attempted meditation once or twice, then gave up. Perhaps you said to yourself, "My mind is too busy" or "I can't keep my mind quiet." Many of the women I work with who have attempted it feel the same way. They get frustrated after one or two sessions, believing that their mind is supposed to be "quiet" while meditating. My response to them almost always is "That is exactly why you should be meditating." There are three important reasons why I believe meditation is very important for women with anxiety.

1. Meditation helps us learn how to observe our thoughts.

The most critical skill we need in order to work with our anxious thoughts is to be able to observe and be aware of them. We need to learn how to catch when we are having a thought, objectively evaluate that thought without indulging it, then decide whether it's a thought worth believing. No other place in our life asks us to do this process other than our meditation practice. The more often we meditate, the more distance we gain from ourselves and our thoughts. It's this distance that allows us to evaluate our thoughts objectively rather than identify with them. I've often said that your degree of mental health will be directly proportional to your ability to remember that your thoughts are not you and that your thoughts are not facts.

2. Meditation is a form of attention training.

An anxious mind is a busy mind—it struggles to maintain focus and to concentrate for long periods of time, often resulting in an inability to complete tasks due to intrusive worried thoughts. Many women with anxiety (and especially my patients with attention deficit disorder) struggle with concentration and maintaining focus. In part, it's likely because we've never been taught how to focus and how to be intentional with our focus of attention. I don't remember ever taking a class on paying attention, yet it is such a vital skill to our day-to-day productivity and ultimately, our success. Meditation provides us with this opportunity.

3. Meditation teaches us how to not indulge our thoughts.
This skill is absolutely vital to managing anxiety effectively. With its powerful emotional hold on us, anxiety has a tendency to grab us with terrifying thoughts, and before we know it, we're whisked off on an emotional roller coaster. When we practice meditation, the goal is to observe thoughts *objectively* rather than *emotionally indulge them*; that is, when a thought arises during meditation, we can practice watching it come and letting it go. When we can observe objectively and avoid getting caught up in our thoughts during meditation, we can use this same skill when we have anxious thoughts throughout our day. This skill is one that requires considerable time, practice, and self-compassion, so stick with it.

Remaining present with mindfulness (and how it differs from meditation)

While I consider meditation to be a practice that you engage in for a brief period of time (preferably daily if you struggle with anxiety), mindfulness is both similar and different. I consider mindfulness as meditation on a macro scale. Mindfulness is basically a practice of being an intentional, objective observer of your cognitive and emotional experience throughout the course of your entire day and frequently redirecting your focus and attention to your current moment. Applying this skill throughout your day outside of your formal meditation session is what I consider to be mindfulness. I feel that the best way to illustrate this concept is with an example.

Right now, you are reading this book.

Likely, your mind is fully engaged in reading the words on the page and your brain is working to process the text. As this book is (hopefully) engaging, entertaining, and relevant to you, it commands all of your attention. It's unlikely that you're reading this book and thinking about a disagreement you had with your coworker or what you're going to make for dinner this evening. You are, effectively, "present" in the task at hand. You are mindfully engaging in the task at hand. You are being mindful.

Note also that because you are present in your current-moment experience and not lost in some thoughts or stories about your life, you are also emotionally neutral in this moment. It is unlikely you're feeling sadness, anger, anxiety or really anything right in this very moment reading the words from this page. There is no emotional experience happening in your mind or body because your mind is actively engaged in the present moment.

Now let's continue with our thought experiment.

Imagine you are doing something less engaging now such as washing the dishes or folding laundry, for example. These tasks do not require your full and present attention, essentially making them mindless tasks. It's natural for your mind to drift off into other thoughts about your day or stories about your past or future. Perhaps you're thinking of your plans for the rest of the day or reflecting on the argument you had with your spouse. Often, when our minds bring up these thoughts, they also bring with them emotional baggage. While thinking about an argument with your spouse, you may experience the emotions of anger, resentment, or shame. By getting swept up in the story of that argument, you are now actually experiencing the emotions of that past moment in your current moment. You feel the pain of the argument from days past, but yet, you are here, just folding laundry. You are in a completely neutral moment but are feeling the pain of a past moment. You have unknowingly created an emotional experience in your current-moment experience by engaging and indulging thoughts around an emotional story. A gentle reminder that the occurrence of the thoughts and stories coming up is not within your control, and many emotional stories come up without our active participation. However, it is within these mental stories that our painful emotions (such as anxiety, sadness, or anger) exist. By being aware of when our minds are lost in stories, we can avoid experiencing the emotional activation of past or future concerns.

Now, to be clear, I am not encouraging you to not feel emotions. Emotions are meant to be felt, and they are valid and justified. They play an important role in motivating our behavior and helping us communicate with others and ourselves. The point of this discussion is to help you recognize the connection between your thoughts and your emotions so that you realize just how much power you have in choosing your own emotional adventure. Too often we get wrapped up in stories and don't realize it. Have you ever been stuck in your head for days on end only to one day realize that everything you've been ruminating about has not even come to pass, but in your mind, it's the worst thing that has ever happened to you? It's the realization of how much control we have over our emotional experience that is paramount to developing a sense of agency and control over it. By catching yourself throughout the day in these stories and redirecting your mind to your present task, you are practicing mindfulness and strengthening your ability to regulate your emotional experience.

The trick is being able to identify when you are swept up in an emotional story in your mind so you can bring yourself back to the present moment as often as possible. In a nutshell, this is practicing mindfulness. Let's dive into a simple way to do it now.

Grounding yourself in your present-moment experience with your senses

Engaging your senses is one of the simplest and most effective ways to reorient your mind in your present-moment experience (and out of an emotional story). A very simple way to do it is with an exercise commonly referred to as The Five Senses Exercise. It is a powerful practice that can be used when you catch yourself in a story, and it can be repeated as many times throughout your day as you need. Catching when you are in a story can take a lot of practice, and often the first clue we are swept up is the physical sensations that occur when we experience emotion. It is important to simply identify the sensations, see if you can label the emotion you are feeling, and be aware that it is due to the story you are creating in your brain. Once you have identified you are in a story, you can use mindfulness exercises to reorient yourself into your present-moment experience. With practice and patience, you will gradually catch yourself earlier and earlier in your emotional story and redirect your mind to your present-moment experience. By doing so, you reclaim your power and free yourself from the clutches of the emotional experience in that story.

The Five Senses Exercise

The next time you catch yourself lost in a story, take a moment to pause and engage your senses.

> Ask yourself:
> *What are five things I can see right now?*
> *What are four things I can hear right now?*
> *What are three things I can feel right now?*
> *What are two things I can smell right now?*
> *What is one thing I can taste right now?*

By engaging all your physical senses intentionally, you prevent your brain from getting swept up in the story. Thankfully, your brain cannot actually do two things at once. Therefore, it cannot engage the senses *and* take in your environment *and* think about the emotional story at the same time.

Furthermore, by actively grounding into all of your physical senses and truly taking in all of the sensory experiences that exist around you in the current moment, you are bringing yourself back into your present moment. Here, in the present moment, there is no distress, no fear, no sadness. By snapping yourself out of stories in your mind and back into your present moment, you maintain control of your emotional experience throughout your day. And that is where and when the magic happens.

chapter 12

YOU ARE THE SUBJECT OF A SCIENCE EXPERIMENT—GET CURIOUS

It's often not enough to simply observe our thoughts or be more mindful more often. We also need to check how we react to the thoughts and emotions we experience. The principles of mindfulness encourage us to be nonjudgmental in our experience, which on the whole is challenging for most women. Although we may not outwardly consider ourselves "judgmental," it is a natural reaction for almost all of us. When we react with judgment, we label our experiences (including our thoughts, emotions, and behavior) as either good or bad. In most of my clients, the default judgment is *bad*, which leads to shame. Many women hold themselves hostage for thoughts they had as if they meant to have them. One of my patients referred to it as "holding yourself hostage for thought crimes," and I have used that phrase ever since. A strategy I often recommend to my patients to help them remain objective (and avoid judgment) in the midst of emotional chatter from their anxiety is to be curious about what it's doing. When I find my anxiety going haywire and freaking out about something, instead of getting sucked into the vortex and believing everything it says or immediately judging and shaming myself for being "an anxious mess," I work to become a detached, nonjudgmental observer of what is happening and ask questions:

Isn't that interesting?
I wonder what's happening here?
What has set off my anxiety this time?
Is this something I know is a trigger or is this a new trigger?
Is there something I'm not paying attention to that I should be?

When I was in university, my undergraduate science classes included far too many laboratory sessions and reports for my liking. Although it was occasionally exciting to watch some sort of basic university science experiment unfold, laboratory science and research did not (and will never) light my fire. The irony of this fact and my current day job has not escaped me. Although I don't recall much of those chemistry or biology lab reports, I do remember the objective, detached position with which I observed the experiments (at the time it was likely boredom, but stay with me here). When one chemical failed to produce the result that it was hypothesized to do, I didn't feel angry with it or make it feel ashamed. I just watched, observed, and thought, "Well, that's interesting."

This objective curiosity, detached from emotional judgment, is the same approach I encourage you to take with your anxiety and your behavior. When you find yourself doing something, such as using a numbing activity or having worsening thoughts, lean in and ask questions, similar to the aforementioned ones. For example, when I find myself in the pantry eating chocolate chips by the handful, instead of shaming myself and treating myself badly, I get curious instead and ask myself what's prompted this behavior in my inner experience. Rather than allowing and indulging in thoughts like, "Oh, here I go again" or "I have no self-control, I'm weak," I simply think, *Hmm, isn't that interesting* and usually, *What's going on here?*

What if you observed yourself as a research subject? What would it look like if you could approach your own behavior with curiosity rather than shame or judgment? It's likely that you would look for more data. You might look at what is happening in your life at the time or how you feel when you engage in that behavior. When you can observe, become aware, accept, and take action about what's happening in your life, what's happening in your mind and how you respond to it, what improves your mood, controls the thoughts, and makes you feel better, you are unstoppable.

> **Self-Check:**
> We've covered a few of the mindset shifts you will have to make to get your anxiety under control. Take time now to reflect on a few of these questions:
> 1. What would it look like if I radically accepted my emotional experience exactly as it happened?

2. How often am I adding suffering on top of my experience? How often am I judging myself for feeling or thinking something?
3. What approach am I taking with my anxiety? Am I wishing it away, or can I tolerate it being in my life if I can learn how to manage it?
4. How willing am I to learn new skills and adopt new habits (such as meditation and mindfulness)?
5. How can I approach my thoughts, emotions, and behavior with more curiosity and less judgment?

chapter 13

YOUR ANXIETY IS SEPARATE FROM YOU

"My mad is back. I HATE my mad."

It was what seemed like the millionth tantrum that day, and my daughter was overcome with her powerful emotions once again. I swear I could see steam coming from her tiny, adorable ears. Her little face was twisted in rage, the skin on her nose was scrunched up, and her eyes were shooting daggers through me as I bent down to talk to her. She was certain someone had moved her *How to Train Your Dragon* toy, and she was infuriated.

"I can see you're really angry right now."

She growled, a confirmation that her little mind couldn't put into words. "My mad is back, and it's really bothering me!" she screamed, not realizing how insightful she was with her response.

My mad is back.

Without realizing it, my daughter naturally saw her anger as something separate from herself that would come and go, something that bothered her when it came but would then leave. We had recently watched *Inside Out*, a movie based on the premise that within each of our heads is a little team of personified emotions that direct our behavior and create our responses to the world. In the movie, the emotions take turns responding to what is happening throughout the course of the day, taking over control of the brain depending on the events that are unfolding. Whether she was remembering that movie or not at the time, my daughter distinctly felt as though her anger was separate from her in that moment, and it helped her process her powerful emotions.

Personification, or the practice of assigning an identity to an emotion—as a separate and discrete identity—outside of ourselves is a powerful tool I often recommend to my clients. For mine, I chose an irritating, know-it-all parrot that perches on my shoulder and peppers me with negative thoughts:

> *Don't do that! You'll fail at it.*
> *Why did you say that? She probably thinks you're so rude.*
> *Don't even think about saying that, they'll get mad at you.*
> *What if you try that thing and it goes awful? What will everyone think?*

Sometimes I'd really like to tell that parrot to shove it. It natters on all day, gets much louder when I'm tired, stressed, or hungry, and tells me all sorts of crap that I don't need to hear. I often encourage my patients and clients to consider their own anxiety as a being outside of them, whether it's a big scary monster or a small sniveling snake. It doesn't matter which persona you give your anxiety, it's the practice of doing it that counts.

Conceptually separating yourself from your anxiety within your brain and thinking about it as an entity or identity who has its own motivations, habits, fears, and triggers makes it easier to become aware of it, understand it, and manage it effectively. Your anxiety as its own being has its own motivations, the most prominent one being its urgent need to keep you safe and alive at all times. Consider it a vigilant sentry, constantly monitoring your environment, its sole purpose to detect and respond to perceived threats.

You may even go so far as to give your anxiety a name, to really hammer home the concept of it being a separate force or being than yourself. By imagining your emotions as separate from you and even giving them names, you are able to conceptualize them in a different way.

If you know the enemy and know yourself, you need not fear the results of a hundred battles. —Sun Tzu

I love this quote by Sun Tzu because it encourages us to adopt a growth mindset toward our anxiety. I often use the analogy of mental warfare when I work with women with anxiety. If you were planning to go to battle with a particular enemy, it's likely you would research beforehand. You would learn what sorts of defenses they had, the types of weapons they used, and their most common strategies for winning. What you would NOT do is stick your head in the sand like an ostrich and pretend that the battle would go away on its own and resign yourself to the fates.

I want you to use this same metaphor as you learn more about your own mental enemy; view your work as a sort of reconnaissance mission. Discover and understand what behaviors surface when your anxiety is high, what it feels like when it builds up, what makes it better, and what makes it worse. No more hiding, pretending it doesn't exist, or avoiding it. Embrace it, own it, and confront it. Each time your anxiety flares, I want you to see it as an opportunity to learn more about your enemy and what you can do differently next time.

> *Self-Check:*
> Take time now to imagine your anxiety as separate from you. Reflect on the following questions and write your answers in a journal or notebook.
> 1. If your anxiety were separate from you (which it is), what form does it take?
> 2. Does your anxiety have a name? (It can be therapeutic and powerful to even consider drawing what your anxiety looks like and make a list of the characteristics of your anxiety's "personality.")
> 3. What causes your anxiety to panic?

4. What sort of changes in your life are perceived as threats by your anxiety?
5. When your anxiety is upset and flaring, how does it behave? What does it cause you to feel and experience?
6. What settles your anxiety? What makes it feel better or calmer? Is there a surefire way to cause your anxiety to relax or frankly, to shut up?
7. If your anxiety had motivations or goals, what would they be?
8. What is your anxiety afraid of? What does it want?

chapter 14

YOUR ANXIETY IS MORE PREDICTABLE THAN YOU REALIZE

One of the common disempowering mindsets I encounter when I work with women to manage their anxiety is a belief that their anxiety is unpredictable. To an outsider or to someone who is lost deep in the vortex of anxiety, it may seem this way. But if you take the time to look deeper, you will likely find that your anxiety is more predictable than you think. From the triggers that set it off, the physiological sensations you experience when your anxiety is high, and the thoughts that your brain creates when you're anxious, we all have our very own predictable "brand" of anxiety.

Now, if you are new to managing your anxiety, you may not yet be familiar with your own "brand." It's likely that you are aware of the physical sensations, however: the tight chest, sweaty palms, maybe a pit in your stomach, or nausea. You are also likely aware of some of the triggers that will, without a doubt, activate your anxiety. This awareness is exceptionally helpful intelligence in our battle against anxiety. What many of my patients do not often notice, however, are the very typical thoughts that they have in their brain that indicate their anxiety is at play in a given situation. Just as there are characteristic physical sensations that signal when our anxiety is starting to flare up, the same applies to our thoughts. I tend to refer to these thoughts as "red flag thoughts."

A red flag thought is how your cortex can ignite your amygdala to create an anxiety response. Recall from earlier that the cortex does not have direct connections to the fight-or-flight response, but it influences this response indirectly through the amygdala. When your cortex creates a red flag thought that is scary or threatening, your amygdala perceives a threat and triggers the fight-or-flight response, which is why you can be doing something completely benign with no real threat to your safety but still experience crippling anxiety and panic. It's all the work of your cortex creating potent red flag thoughts.

Almost all of the women I've worked with have come to realize that there are specific red flag thoughts that are unique to them and their anxiety, although it can take some time to learn what they are. For myself, I recognize that when thoughts of being overwhelmed such as "*this is too much work*" or "*I'll never be able to do all of this*" pop up in my brain, these are surefire signs my anxiety is taking the reins. I know that in the middle of my day if I begin having those thoughts, my anxiety is trying to slide into the driver's seat again. Similarly, increased tension in my neck and shoulders and waking more frequently at night are also key signs that my anxiety is increased.

The benefits of being aware of your own red flag thoughts are huge. Once you can identify "your brand" of anxious thoughts, they can be targeted with thought management strategies. It's this cortex-based work that is done through cognitive behavioral therapy as well. Working to disrupt, interrupt, replace, and dismiss these anxious red flag thoughts will allow you to prevent the amygdala from being ignited by changing what the cortex thinks.

Knowing your specific brand of anxiety helps you catch yourself earlier in an anxiety spiral rather than finding yourself stuck in a panic attack and wondering what happened. By being vigilant of these thoughts and sensations that are unique and typical to your brand, you will learn how to detect your anxiety at play as early as possible and implement thought management or calming strategies sooner.

Self-Check:

Let's dig into what your brand of anxiety feels and looks like. Answer the following questions in your journal to explore how your anxiety presents.

1. What are some of the more common anxious thoughts that you have?
2. Do your anxious thoughts have a particular style? (i.e., Thought of self-doubt such as *I can't do this* or people-pleasing thoughts such as *She'll be mad at me* or *What if they judge me?*)

3. How does it feel in your body when you become anxious?
4. Where do you feel the sensations of anxiety in your body? Do you feel tightness in your chest, a lump in your throat, or a sick stomach?

chapter 15

ALMOST ALL OF YOUR ANXIOUS THOUGHTS ARE COGNITIVE DISTORTIONS

As you continue to identify and catch your anxious thoughts, it can be helpful to have a general understanding about them. Many women share a lot of the same kind of thoughts that make them anxious. These kinds of thoughts are often referred to as cognitive distortions. Cognitive distortions are simply ways that our brains tell us things that aren't true. In fact, I would say that a high proportion of what our brains tell us is not true. Cognitive distortions are flawed patterns of thinking that keep us trapped in negative mental loops and reinforce our anxious tendencies and behaviors.

Let's review some of the most common cognitive distortions that I've identified in my patients. Perhaps you'll recognize some of these in yourself, something that is powerful and very enlightening. Cognitive distortions are anxiety's superpower. Without taking intentional time to identify which of your most common anxious thoughts are indeed cognitive distortions, you may have a tendency to believe everything you think, which just won't do. While you are reading through the following list, ask yourself how you might find evidence to disprove the distortions you have. I've provided some questions underneath each distortion to help you get started.

- *Black-and-white thinking: "If I can't do it right, I won't do it at all."*
    - Black-and-white thinking, also known as polarizing or psychological splitting, is the tendency to think in all-or-nothing terms, in extremes. For example, you may believe you can be either an excellent mother or a terrible one. There is a failure to recognize that there may be shades of gray, i.e., you can be a good mother having a rough day. Perfectionism is also a type of black-and-white thinking, in believing that you must be 100 percent perfect and free of flaws in order to be good enough. It often looks like not being able to start something new unless you can be 100 percent sure you will succeed at it, otherwise you won't even try.
    - Disprove it:
        - Is it possible my brain is not showing me the whole picture here?
        - Have I ever done something "not perfect," and it's been totally fine?

- Is there more gray in this situation than my brain is allowing me to see?
- *Personalization:* "*I know they did that because of me.*"
  - The tendency to believe that everything is related to you or that you are responsible for everything. This cognitive distortion tends to cause you to take everything that others do personally or believe things are somehow caused by you. The reality is, though, that most people are not behaving in ways related to you at all. The majority of people are not really thinking about anyone other than themselves.
  - This cognitive distortion is commonly seen in abuse victims as well. When someone falsely believes that their abuse or trauma was their fault, it is an example of personalization.
  - Disprove it:
    - What are other explanations for why this person behaved in this way?
    - Is there a chance that this situation has nothing to do with me?
- *Filtering:* "*There's nothing good.*"
  - This distortion occurs when you see only the negative aspects of a situation and cognitively filter out the positive ones. I find filtering comes up a lot when we are in a low-mood or low-energy state, when we are feeling more depressed. When we are feeling down, it can seem like the entire world is bad and nothing is going right. Not true. I often refer to this state as wearing a "mood helmet"

or an "Eeyore mood." Your brain selectively filters out the positive parts of your experience to reinforce your low mood. Being aware of this tendency is important, and learning how to shift your filter to see more positive things is critical. Gratitude practices are especially helpful in this situation, as they force the brain to look for things outside of its filter.
- Disprove it:
  - Can I find a silver lining in this situation?
  - What positive aspects of this situation exist that my brain isn't showing me?
  - How can I help shift my mood helmet? (Think gratitude practices!)
- *Mind-Reading:* "I just know that they're going to get angry with me."
  - Mind-reading refers to our beliefs that we can infer or know the inner workings of someone else's mind, something that can be especially common in people we feel we know very well. However, the truth is that we do not and cannot ever know what someone else is thinking or will think, no matter how well we know them. Even now as you're reading these words, you may be digging in your heels in resistance saying, "But I really do know how so-and-so thinks." Even still, this belief is just a cognitive distortion.
  - Disprove it:
    - Has there ever been a situation when I was certain this person would behave in a certain way and then they surprised me?

- Has this person ever behaved differently than I had expected them to?
- What evidence do I have that this person is thinking these thoughts? (Keep in mind that evidence is what we can observe with our eyes, not what we think we know.)

- *Catastrophizing*: "I have a headache; what if it's a brain tumor?"
  - Catastrophizing is anxiety's right-hand man. Catastrophizing occurs when your brain takes one tiny detail and blows it up into a catastrophe—way out of proportion. Catastrophizing often happens in my patients who suffer from anxiety related to their own health. A tiny physical symptom such as a common headache can spiral into a brain tumor and certain death. An increased awareness of your heart beating faster causes an instant "What if I'm dying?" thought to jump into your mind. Trust me; in this situation, Dr. Google is not your friend.
  - Disprove it:
    - Is there a chance my anxiety is blowing this situation way out of proportion?
    - What other explanations exist for this symptom/situation?

- *Should-ing*: "I should exercise more. I shouldn't be so lazy."
  - I think I could write an entire additional book on the power of the word "should" and its influence over women with anxiety. How often have you felt bad about yourself because you felt like you "should" be doing something different? This cognitive distortion exists like a set of rules

and ideal standards that can serve to create a ton of guilt inside of us if we don't take the time to examine it. When we direct our "should" statements toward other people, we tend to feel very angry and resentful toward them if they fail to comply with the "rules." The next time you find yourself feeling guilty about something, consider whether you're "should-ing" on yourself. Are you creating self-imposed rules that don't really exist?
  - Disprove it:
    - Who set up this expectation for me? Where did it come from?
    - Is there a chance I've created a rule or expectation here that is not reality?
- *Emotional reasoning: "I feel it, therefore it must be true."*
  - This cognitive distortion occurs when an individual believes something to be true because of their emotional experience. If someone feels bad about themselves emotionally, then it follows that they are bad people. If someone feels stupid for making a mistake, they believe that they truly are stupid. This distortion is also why we tend to believe we have actually done something wrong when we feel inappropriate guilt (when we take time for ourselves, for example). In this cognitive distortion, emotion is completely in control, and logic and reasoning have left the room.
  - Emotional reasoning related to anxiety underscores a lot of the challenges I cover in this book. When you're feeling anxious about something, discerning if your anxious

thoughts are true is critical to avoid the cognitive distortion of emotional reasoning. Simply because you have anxiety about something doesn't mean it's actually bad or dangerous. It's simply a flawed thinking pattern.
  - Disprove it:
    - Has my anxiety ever been wrong? (i.e., Has it ever been convinced something terrible would happen, yet it was all completely fine?)
    - Is it possible that even though this emotion is occurring that it may not actually fit the facts of the situation? Could my emotion be false?
- *Magnification: "I'm the worst mother in the world."*
  - Magnification refers to your brain perceiving a small event, situation, or experience and blowing it out of proportion. It also refers to making negative qualities about oneself seem massive, while minimizing the positive qualities you might have.
  - Disprove it:
    - If I were to look back on this situation in five years, would it matter?
    - If this were happening to someone else, would it seem this huge?
    - Is there a chance my brain is magnifying this falsely?

While there are many other cognitive distortions that exist, these are the most common ones I see in my patients. Helping to identify which of your anxious thoughts are cognitive distortions can help you feel more empowered in managing your anxiety. It can also be easier to let them go and reorient yourself into the present moment.

Identifying cognitive distortions can also be done through psychotherapy, as often times these distortions are deeply embedded in your brain and have become to be a source of truth for you. Once you have identified the specific cognitive distortions that your brain uses (your "brand" of red flag thoughts), it's important to challenge and find evidence that disproves the distortion. You can access Thought Challenge Worksheets to challenge your own cognitive distortions at CarlyCrewe.com/anxietybook.

chapter 16

YOU CAN'T JUST "STOP THINKING" SOMETHING

What you resist, persists. —Carl Jung

Now that you have become familiar with your own brand of anxious thoughts, have learned about the most common cognitive distortions, and have developed some mindfulness skills to catch yourself when you're getting wrapped up in emotional stories, you can begin to use other cognitive strategies to work with the anxious thoughts you have. Finding evidence to disprove the thoughts you have is one strategy, but many anxious women find that trying to reason with their anxious thoughts can feel futile when their anxiety is very high. They will often say things like, "Even though my rational brain knows that this anxious thought is ridiculous, I still can't seem to stop thinking it." In this particular situation, I often recommend the powerful cognitive behavioral skills of thought identification and replacement. These cortex-based strategies are excellent for in-the-moment anxiety and are simple to employ.

Before we do that, however, let's explore the concept of thought suppression. The majority of my patients and clients use thought suppression as one of their main anxiety management strategies (without realizing it, usually). That is, they simply try to "not think anxious thoughts." While this strategy seems like a good idea at first glance, I will demonstrate why it is not:

> Imagine right now that I told you to not think about a pig in a yellow bikini.
> Don't do it, no pigs in yellow bikinis . . .
> *So, what are you thinking about?*
> PIGS IN YELLOW BIKINIS.

This psychological phenomenon is what social psychologists refer to as ironic process theory, or ironic rebound. The basic premise of ironic process theory is that thoughts that we try to intentionally suppress and not think about will often rebound in increasing frequency and intensity despite our best efforts. The theory itself dates back to approximately 1987 from research by Dr. Daniel Wegner, PhD, from Harvard University, after he asked research participants to verbalize everything they were thinking about for five minutes after being told specifically to not think about a white bear. Interestingly, Wegner found that while a portion of our brain tries to follow our rule and avoid the thought entirely, another part of our brain acts as a sentry and, in effect, "checks in" to make sure the thought has not come back, ironically bringing it back to our awareness. The participants asked to not think about a white bear verbalized thoughts of a white bear more often than those participants who were not directly told to suppress white bear thoughts.

So, if we can't successfully repress our thoughts and "stop thinking anxious thoughts," what can we do when the anxious thoughts come knocking? This situation is when the practice of thought identification, also called "labeling," comes into play.

Have you ever heard the phrase, "name it to tame it?" This common catchphrase is used to help people develop the ability to name their emotion in the moment so that they can manage it more effectively. While "name it to tame it" typically refers to emotions, we can apply this same strategy to anxious thoughts. Being able to identify and label anxious thoughts in the moment is critical if we want to be able to work with those thoughts and feel less anxiety. Therefore, with our mindfulness and meditation practices, we learn how to identify anxious thoughts and label them as such: "This is an anxious thought." Doing so helps us objectively evaluate them and discern whether we want to indulge them. Recognizing a false thought or anxious thought is the first step. You can then draw upon your newfound knowledge of cognitive distortions to perhaps categorize the type of anxious thought you are having. The final step is to then replace it with a calmer, more accurate, or more reassuring thought.

While thought suppression does not work, thought replacement does. This concept was also proven to some extent by Wegner's research such that he found when asked to focus on a red car as they tried to not think about the white bear, the participants had fewer incidences of white bear thoughts. By focusing the mind on an alternate thought instead of suppressing the anxious thought, we can avoid the anxious thought rebounding more often. Given that our amygdala responds to whatever thoughts the cortex sends it, by encouraging our cortex to think of adaptive and reassuring thoughts, we reduce our amygdala activation, lessen the fight-or-flight response, and reduce the sensations of anxiety. Win-win.

Take time now to reflect on your own anxious thoughts and write down some more adaptive and accurate replacement thoughts. I've provided some examples.

> Anxious thought: "I'll never get all of this done; I'm so overwhelmed! I'm freaking out!"
> Replacement thought: "I can only do one thing at a time. I trust my future self to handle the rest."

> Anxious thought: "If I don't get better sleep tonight, I'll have the worst day tomorrow."
> Replacement thought: "I have had a rough night's sleep in the past and have been okay."

> Anxious thought: "If I say/do this, I just know that so-and-so will get mad at me."
> Replacement thought: "I can't read minds, and I'm not responsible for the emotions of others."

Self-Check:

Identifying replacement thoughts.

1. Spend time reflecting on your most common anxious thoughts and compare them to the cognitive distortions in the previous chapter.
2. Create a chart with your anxious thoughts in one column and replacement thoughts in the other column.
3. Write down replacement thoughts that you can use when your anxious red flag thoughts pop up. Keep the list handy (on your phone or in your purse) to reflect on when you find yourself spiraling.

chapter 17

AVOIDING WHAT TRIGGERS YOUR ANXIETY WILL ONLY MAKE YOU MORE ANXIOUS

How often have you gone down an anxious thought spiral after hearing some unexpected news or taking on someone else's emotions or [insert a situation you've experienced here]? Many of us can easily list at least a few things that reliably make us anxious, and these things are referred to as our triggers. In some cases, these triggers are very specific and isolated (i.e., flying in an airplane), while others are less clear and may require us to do a bit more investigating and exploring.

There are, however, a few very common triggers that I notice for women across the board when it comes to their anxiety that may or may not apply to you. As you read through them, reflect on your own experience and see if these may be triggers for you as well. Remember, triggers are not always obvious.

- *Change:* Change is a huge trigger for most women with whom I work, and it doesn't always have to be a big change to trigger anxiety. In fact, even subtle positive changes can often trigger anxiety that seems out of context or silly in relation to the degree of change. Moving, job changes, upcoming holidays, or even traffic on your usual way to work are all prime situations for triggering anxiety.
- *Illness:* When you're sick, you better believe that your anxiety is going to come knocking. I often say that anxiety is an asshole that tends to kick us when we're down. It's an unfortunate truth, but it can be helpful in that we can anticipate it, prepare for it, and manage it when it does happen. It may also look like creating a bad-day plan for managing your higher-than-average anxiety when you're dealing with a migraine, pain flare, or other illness. These are not the days to add more things to your to-do list or jam pack your schedule, okay?
- *Alcohol:* Many women find their anxiety is considerably worse the day after they drink alcohol, which is due to the delayed activating effect of ethanol. While we often turn to alcohol in the evening as a buffering activity or to wind down from a busy day, it can also be detrimental to our anxiety management in a big way.
- *Memories from previous trauma:* If you have experienced a traumatic event or been witness to one, things that remind you of that trauma can absolutely cause an elevation of your

anxiety and trigger your fight-or-flight response. In some cases, it can be actually post-traumatic stress disorder, which requires dedicated trauma-informed therapy and treatment.
- *Conflict:* Many women with whom I work have a significant fear of conflict and can find their anxiety triggered at even the slightest possibility of an argument or disagreement. In fact, avoiding conflict is how many women develop chronic passive behavior and people-pleasing tendencies. They seek to reduce the anxiety they feel about conflict and therefore default to passive behavior to avoid it.

Take time now to reflect on your own anxiety triggers. Many women find that as they progress further into their anxiety management journey and become finely attuned to the intricacies of their anxiety, they are able to identify even more anxiety triggers. Remember, your triggers will also compound. A busy week at work, having a head cold, and dealing with a rebellious teen could all be enough to send your anxiety higher and your mood lower. It's important to consider the compounding effect that multiple triggers can have on us and make compassionate allowances for when our anxiety reacts.

Self-Check:
1. Are there any situations, times, or experiences that you know trigger your anxiety?
2. Have you ever noticed your anxiety was high, but you couldn't identify a trigger?

> 3. What about each trigger causes your anxiety?
> 4. On a scale from one to ten, how much do you think that trigger actually controls you?

Some women interpret my asking them to identify their triggers as things they need to then avoid as a means to reduce their anxiety when, in actuality, it's the complete opposite. Avoiding what makes you anxious will only serve to reinforce your anxiety, no matter what the trigger. When we avoid what makes us anxious, we inadvertently tell our amygdala that the thing it is so afraid of and has determined to be a threat to our safety is, in fact, a threat to our safety. Recall that our amygdala's job is to keep us alive; it becomes activated when it believes something is a threat. If we indulge our amygdala and avoid that trigger, the amygdala's response is even more deeply reinforced. Instead, we need to put our amygdala into situations it finds threatening and have it experience something new: safety. It is particularly helpful to have the amygdala experience positive emotions (such as joy or calmness) when in the presence of a trigger so that it learns to associate that trigger with positive rather than negative emotions. This basic explanation is of the concept of exposure therapy, which is a common strategy employed by therapists to help reduce feelings of panic and anxiety related to a specific trigger (and also in phobias). Here is a simplified example of this concept: If you were bitten by a dog as a child and your amygdala generates anxiety around dogs (but you would prefer it didn't), spending time with a playful dog and enjoying yourself is a simple way to help your amygdala learn that dogs are not dangerous and to reduce the anxiety response. (A full review of exposure therapy is beyond the scope of this book.)

So, once you have created your trigger list, use it not as a list of things to avoid but rather as a list of situations you can now use to put your newfound skills to the test, thus reducing the activation of your amygdala. This suggestion does not mean that you will not still experience the physical sensations of anxiety while doing these things. In fact, experiencing physical sensations of anxiety (palpitations, sweating, etc.) while exposing yourself to triggers is exactly what we need to occur. These physical sensations mean we have our amygdala's attention! When we have its attention, it can learn a new and more appropriate response to this particular trigger.

I encourage my patients to develop an awareness of their triggers so that they can practice strengthening their anxiety management skills in light of them. Doing so helps you further understand it, learn how to anticipate it, and manage it proactively rather than reactively, which is key. Understanding what triggers your anxiety can also help you increase your self-care in response to an upcoming known trigger, allowing you to approach it from the position of being prepared rather than just *hoping* it goes well. It's the difference between "I know that my anxiety will be elevated and so I'm going to do things to support myself through this trigger" and "This is going to be terrible and I'm just hoping to get through it." It's all about your mindset and your approach to anxiety. It is about viewing your triggers as opportunities for learning how to better understand and manage our anxiety. We must not avoid what triggers our anxiety but realize that our triggers identify where we need to focus our efforts to support ourselves even more.

chapter 18

SURVIVAL OF THE BUSIEST: YOU CAN'T BUSY YOURSELF BETTER

When I think about my mind, I tend to think about my border collie. Border collies are typically a very high-energy breed of dog that have a ridiculous drive to work and "do things." Intelligent and task-oriented, they are often used as farming or working dogs, as they are known for their incessant need to have a job. A border collie without a job can cause a lot of trouble, something I know because I have a border collie at my feet as I write this chapter. Although older now and starting to go a little gray, he had many characteristics in his younger years that define his breed, including his constant need to be busy and his tendency to be a bit destructive without something meaningful to do. When he was left to fend for himself in the apartment, he inevitably became bored, and we would come home to find chewed pillows or overturned garbage cans. Pure trouble.

Your brain is just like a border collie. When busy, it's engaged in the task at hand. When bored or not "doing something," it looks for something to do and will cause trouble if not monitored. This explanation is exactly why so many women I work with tell me that they are "fine" during the day, but it's in the quiet evening hours when they are done their tasks that their anxiety rears its head. The most common times for border collie brains to become busy is right at night when you're settling down to sleep. Has your brain ever decided that 11:30 p.m. is the perfect time to solve all of the current problems in your life?

It would seem then that the cure for controlling the border collie brain would be to make yourself constantly busy throughout the day, but this is not the case. Excessive "busyness" is actually a very common habit I find in women who struggle with anxiety. They will fill their days and schedules with unending tasks and errands, not realizing that they are doing it to avoid being present in their own minds. It's much easier to busy your brain with to-dos than it is to deal with anxious thoughts all the time. The trouble is that by making our already-chaotic brains busier, we make our anxiety worse, and in turn, we feel even more scattered and overwhelmed. We believe if we just fill our days up to the brim with tasks and appointments, we won't be anxious. Wrong. To truly manage our anxiety, we need more calm and spaciousness to objectively allow, observe, and manage our anxious thoughts mindfully. Stop drowning your anxiety in never-ending tasks and give it the space it needs to dissipate and breathe. I get it; it's scary and uncomfortable, but we need to have white space in our days and on our calendars to provide time for the cognitive work that will strengthen our anxiety management skills in the long term.

The tendency to be busy all the time is simply a habit that we've developed as a buffering strategy. Overworking and overscheduling are two common buffering activities I have recognized in both clients and patients in the past. Women are often surprised to realize that they've been relying on these two behaviors to buffer their emotions for much of their lives. I believe these activities often go unchecked because of the productivity-obsessed culture we live in, where productivity and working hard are valued. However, without awareness, overscheduling and overworking are incredibly damaging and contribute to the overwhelming rates of burnout in our society. They are dangerous buffering activities because they become reinforced on so many levels. We tend to minimize the trouble our border collie brains can cause and the discomfort we feel from our emotions by constantly finding jobs for our minds to do. Again, this is not to say that working hard and being productive is bad or dangerous, but it can be when it's engaged in mindlessly—and with the intention of—avoiding what is going on in your mind (your anxiety).

Let's be honest; it also feels really good to get things done. Productivity feels good. Some of my best days are when I feel I have accomplished a lot. When you are used to feeling down or anxious all the time, feeling the high of productivity and accomplishment can be like a drug. Before long, the drive to be productive and to work hard, to create more, to be more, and to do more becomes strongly reinforced, and burnout almost inevitably follows. I know that being unproductive can be one of the more anxiety-producing triggers I have, and so to mitigate this discomfort, I will often throw myself into work and productivity as a way to take that discomfort away. The trouble is that before long, I find myself burned out from working so hard and wonder how I got to this place (again). Busyness is one of my behavior loops.

Have you ever gotten to a place in your life where you feel stuck in a certain pattern of behavior? Have you sometimes wondered why you behave in a certain way, even though you know you shouldn't? Have you ever felt powerless to change your own behavior?

Here are some examples that I've seen in my clients:

- You find yourself picking meaningless fights in a relationship just as it starts to get serious because you fear the pain of an anticipated breakup.
- You half-commit to projects at work so that when the project inevitably fails, you can blame something other than your own performance.
- You find yourself binge-eating again after a stressful day even though you know it's not what you want to do.
- You overwork and constantly strive for perfection to the point of burnout, and you have done so over and over again.
- You say yes to something you know you don't want to do and then feel resentment, anger, and shame about your inability to say no.

These are behavioral loops or habit loops (and in these examples, are self-sabotaging ones). They are automatic patterns of behavior that become reinforced over time. Recall that the motivational triad of human behavior theory asserts that humans are driven to act based on three primary motivations: to avoid pain, to seek pleasure, and to increase efficiency. Behavioral or habit loops are one way that the brain increases its efficiency while simultaneously seeking pleasure or avoiding pain (depending on the loop). With our lives being so complicated and our schedules so jam-packed, our brains need to run a few of our behaviors on autopilot to reduce the demand on our cognitive resources. Think of it as multiple apps or programs auto-starting every time you switch on your laptop. These behaviors could be simple daily habits such as brushing our teeth or the routine that we follow before going to bed, or they can be more complex patterns of behavior that serve to create our emotional reality such as chronic people-pleasing or passive-aggressive behavior.

The basic framework of a behavioral loop is simple. Each loop begins with a cue, the thing in your environment (either internal or external) that triggers the behavior. In more basic habits, the cue may be very obvious: seeing your toothbrush triggers you to pick it up and brush your teeth. In the behavioral loops that we are discussing here, the cue may be more nuanced or subconscious. What follows from the cue is typically a behavior that seeks to achieve a reward—which may be something positive (i.e., feeling joy, getting a sugar rush, etc.) or it may be the removal of something negative (i.e., anxiety). If this behavioral loop is repeated more than once (cue—behavior—reward), it becomes a deeply reinforced behavior. Our brain has now switched it to autopilot so that it no longer demands cognitive resources to perform it.

Development of a Behavior Loop

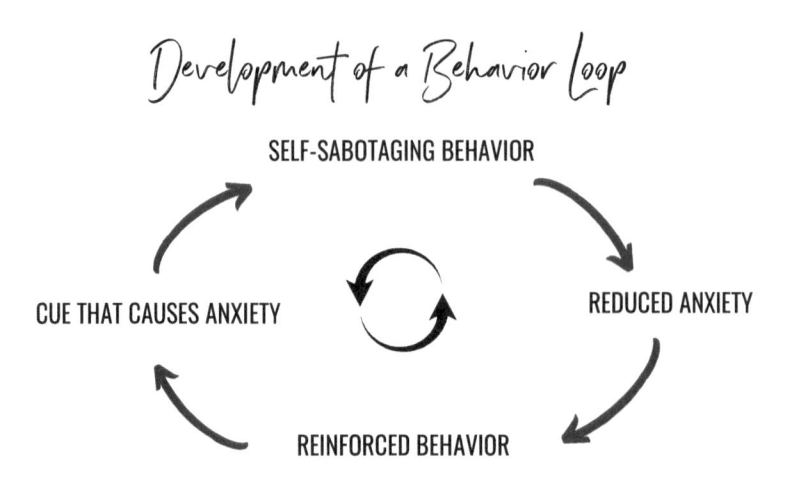

```
            SELF-SABOTAGING BEHAVIOR
                    ↑         ↘
                              
   CUE THAT CAUSES ANXIETY   ↻   REDUCED ANXIETY
                              
                    ↖         ↙
              REINFORCED BEHAVIOR
```

Smoking, avoiding exercise, overeating, and chewing your nails are all habits that are amenable to change with conscious awareness and considerable effort. For the purposes of this chapter and this book, I focus mostly on emotional behavioral loops. These loops are often more subconscious, and there may be no actual external behavior that is observed. The behavior in these loops may be patterns of how we communicate after being triggered or even thoughts that come up in our own heads. Cues in our emotional behavioral loops are often also influenced by flawed perception or cognitive distortions. For example, if you carry a cognitive distortion of you being a terrible mother, you may falsely interpret any small side glance at the food you're buying in the grocery store as a trigger and then plunge yourself into an anxiety spiral of self-shaming and self-deprecating thoughts, which is why it is so imperative to develop a mindful awareness of what is going on in your own head as often as possible. It's critical to realize that these behavioral loops and almost all subconscious patterns of behavior are deeply conditioned and automatic.

As always, how we approach and think about our behavior loops is important. Self-judgment and shame will serve no purpose here. Many times it can be frustrating to find yourself repeating a self-sabotaging behavior again and again. Truthfully, there is no set number of times that you will have to go through your own repeating pattern before you will realize it and finally redirect yourself midcourse. In an attempt to shift my mindset around these loops, I choose to see each time I repeat my predictable and damaging perfectionism and overworking cycle as an opportunity to learn more about my mind's inner workings to hopefully identify the signs of the cycle easier and to practice ways of jumping off the roller coaster to find a new path. We are all humans on a journey of becoming and developing, and sometimes we have to be whacked over the head with something a few times before we catch on. It doesn't mean you're broken or stupid, it just means you're still learning. Have self-compassion and appreciate that each time you're back on a particular behavioral pattern, you are one step closer to identifying it, being aware of it, and changing your pattern.

In many cases, anxiety may be the cue for a behavioral loop, while the awareness of a repeating behavioral loop can also cause great anxiety. Consider now one of your own behavioral loops, preferably one that you would like to reduce or stop. Perhaps the nightly glass of red wine to soothe your nerves or saying yes when you really want to say no. What triggers that behavior? Let's break it down a bit and take a moment to explore some of your own behavioral loops.

> **Self-Check:**
> Reflect on these questions:
> 1. What behavior loops do I tend to repeat? Consider one of the most common or most painful loops you have.
> 2. What is the cue or trigger that causes this loop to start? (For example, when you yell at your kids or when your mother-in-law comments on your cooking.)
> 3. What emotion is triggered when that cue occurs?
> 4. What behavior do you engage in? How is this behavior serving you? (Does it reduce distress or anxiety? Does it minimize pain?)
> 5. What is the end result of this loop?

Because you're reading this book, I'd hazard to say that anxiety is a trigger for many of your behavioral loops. Anxiety is the cue/trigger for many of the behaviors we engage in that we don't like, such as overeating, oversleeping, overdrinking, etc. We do these behaviors because we are seeking to reduce our anxiety in the moment. Anxiety can also be the trigger for people-pleasing behavior or perfectionism. When we feel anxious about something, we behave predictably to reduce our anxiety (reduce discomfort or pain), and if that behavior is rewarded by reduced anxiety, it becomes reinforced, which is how habit loops are formed.

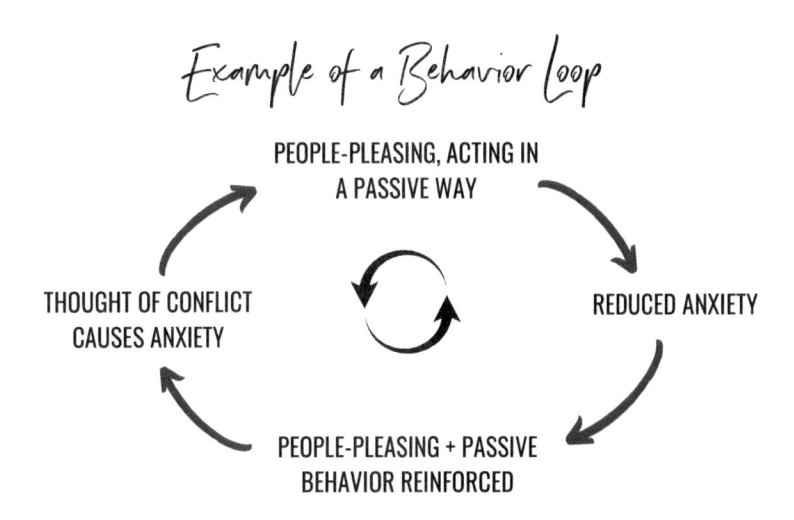

Example of a Behavior Loop

```
        PEOPLE-PLEASING, ACTING IN
             A PASSIVE WAY

THOUGHT OF CONFLICT              REDUCED ANXIETY
  CAUSES ANXIETY

         PEOPLE-PLEASING + PASSIVE
           BEHAVIOR REINFORCED
```

We can learn about our habit loops by observing the results of a certain behavior loop. If you are ever wondering why you behave in a certain way (why you find yourself overeating or grabbing that glass of wine in the evening again), take an objective step back and examine what happened after you engaged in the behavior. If you felt reduced anxiety as a result, that is the reward for the habit loop. Identifying the reward in the situation can be incredibly helpful because if you can achieve that reward in a different way, you may be able to stop the behavior.

Behavioral loops often cause incredible anxiety and distress once we're aware of them. After burning out multiple times due to overworking (a behavior I often engage in to reduce my own feelings of anxiety), I now feel anxiety when I sense that I am back on that same behavioral loop until I work to consciously disrupt the loop. The anxiety felt about an impending repeated behavior stems from feeling powerless to stop the behavioral loop. Many women feel as though they are not personally in control of their automatic behavior as if they are watching a train crash without knowing how to stop it or prevent the inevitable pain that will happen. They worry themselves sick "knowing" what is going to happen but feel powerless over how to behave differently or create a new outcome for themselves. It's important to remember that we all have the choice in how we approach the knowledge of our own behavioral loops. As mentioned previously, we can choose to be a victim to our brain's default programming, or we can become active agents and learn how to reprogram ourselves.

I know it can be hard to look closely at what we repeatedly do because it tends to bring up feelings of shame or even self-loathing. I've heard more than one of my clients say, "Oh why did I do that again? I'm so stupid. I know better." And yes, in part this statement is correct because your conscious brain, the part of you that is aware of the behavioral loop, does know better. However, the parts of your brain seeking to increase your efficiency and reduce your distress don't know any better. Working with intention to become consciously aware of our behavioral loops and examine them closely increases our ability to "know better" and catch ourselves before we enter the loop. But shame and guilt have no place here. I know many women avoid looking closely at how their own behavior is causing them pain, but it is crucial to developing a sense of agency and control over their own minds.

By taking the time to examine what causes the behavioral loop to repeat itself, you gain more insight on how to change the pattern. You become more attuned to the very subtle signs that your pattern is starting or evolving. You gain awareness of the thoughts or events that trigger the loop and can be vigilant for the behavior that follows.

By the nature of this work, it can be challenging to do alone, as we can often only see things from our own perspective. For this reason and so many more, it can be incredibly helpful to work with a coach or therapist who can help you identify what beliefs may be playing a role in your situation.

chapter 19

COGNOGENS: FALSE BELIEFS

In physiological disease, the cause or organism that contributes to infection or system breakdown is referred to as a pathogen. The word pathogen comes from the Greek words *pathos* meaning suffering and *gen* to give birth to. In modern medical sense, pathogen refers to the organism that is capable of producing disease in the body and may be a virus, bacteria, parasite, or other microorganism.

In mental health, it can be helpful to use this concept of a pathogen as well, but instead of the organism causing disease being a virus or bacteria, it is a belief that causes patterns of flawed thoughts and behaviors. An extension of the term "pathogen," a belief that contributes to distress or becoming "stuck" in a cognitive pattern or habit can be referred to as a "cognogen," as defined by Dr. Greg Dubord, Founder of CBT Canada. These cognogens are also referred to by personal development gurus and mindset junkies as "limiting beliefs."

Whereas cognitive distortions are false thoughts, cognogens are false beliefs. Our deep beliefs inform our day-to-day thoughts, and false beliefs are behind many of the mental health struggles that I see in my clients and patients. Cognogens are often subconscious, deeply programmed beliefs that stem from conditioning or past experiences. As our emotions, thoughts, and behaviors all make an impact on and interact with one another, examining the thoughts and beliefs that underlie our behaviors (and behavioral loops) is incredibly important to alter our behavior and emotional experience. There are innumerable different false beliefs and cognogens that can coexist, and one person can have many.

I'll admit, when I began my own foray into the world of personal development, anyone who spoke about "limiting beliefs" sounded painfully nebulous and impractical. As a very tactical and action-focused person, I could not conceptualize the utility of digging into "beliefs" when trying to move forward in a personal or professional arena. This section may seem nebulous to you also, depending on where you are in your own anxiety or personal development journey. If that's the case, that's alright. Just read through and plan to come back later when it resonates a bit more.

Thankfully, I have since come around to the idea of belief work and have experienced the power of belief work myself. I have also come to understand the connection between the deep beliefs I carry in my subconscious brain and how they influence my thoughts from day to day. Digging deeply into the subconscious beliefs of my clients and patients has also been incredibly effective. I am constantly amazed at the power of belief work and its ability to create dynamic and dramatic shifts in someone's perception of their situation or reach new levels of understanding.

One way I often explain the concept of cognogens to my patients is to use the analogy of a computer. Your brain is just like a big computer. When we are a child, our brain's job is to basically create or install programs that help us operate successfully in the world. These computer "programs" are the beliefs that we pick up about how the world works. They guide our behavior in relationships, in our personal achievements, and in how we view ourselves. For example, one of these programs may be "I must please others to be worthy" or "I receive love when I accomplish things." These same computer programs continue into our adult lives and depending on the program, may wreak havoc on our happiness and mental health. Identifying your own cognogens or "faulty programming" is important because often these programs that were successful in helping us learn how to interact with the world as a child (or in our earlier life) are not effective any longer. We effectively need to upgrade our software.

Most of the time, we are carrying around these faulty computer programs without realizing we have them. They live in our subconscious mind, below the surface of our day-to-day thoughts and awareness. They direct our behavior and structure our reality without us being aware of it. Beliefs about lack—not being good enough, smart enough, or worthy—are very common among the women with whom I work. We often carry such beliefs about parenting, what it means to be a good mother or a bad mother, and about money, that making money requires sacrifice and hard work or that we're not deserving of wealth. A very common money belief is that there's never enough of it, often referred to as a scarcity mindset. Other beliefs I have identified in my clients are things like "I can't sleep without a sleeping pill" or "I can't cope with pain without alcohol." When we have these subconscious beliefs directing our behavior, we can behave in ways that are self-destructive. We self-sabotage anything that comes our way.

As I stated earlier, I tend to have a behavioral loop of overworking until I burn out. Despite my best attempts to avoid this pattern by intentionally taking very good care of my mental health, trying to check in with my energy level, and prioritizing rest, I have repeated this pattern innumerable times. Each time I find myself in the pit of burnout, feeling apathetic about everything and exhausted, I realize I've done it again. It wasn't until I examined the beliefs and subconscious programming I had around my self-worth, perfectionism, and the value of productivity that I began to gain more traction in changing my behavior pattern.

Common false beliefs or cognogens:

> *I can't move forward until I have everything right or perfect.*
> *There is a correct solution to every problem and I just have to find it at any cost.*
> *I never have enough time.*
> *There is not enough for everyone.*
> *I can't cope without _____.*
> *I'm broken.*
> *I must work/sacrifice a lot to be successful.*
> *I can't say what I really feel because people will get mad at me.*

Everyone else is more important than me.
I'm a burden to everyone.
I'm unlovable unless _____.

Can you see how each of these beliefs may motivate someone to behave in a certain way? The behaviors that follow these cognogenic beliefs are among some of the more common behavioral patterns that I have identified in my patients and clients and help them work through.

To start, reflect on your own behavior to help identify some of the more common cognogens that may be playing a role in your life. Don't fret if it's hard to identify these patterns right now. It can take a considerable amount of mindful awareness and observation of your own patterns of thoughts and behaviors before these patterns become apparent.

> **Self-Check:**
> 1. Reflect on the aforementioned list. Do any of these cognogens feel familiar to you? Are there other false beliefs that you carry?
> 2. Examine one of your problematic behavior loops or tendencies. Is it possible that the behavior loop is influenced by a false belief?
> 3. What beliefs do you carry that may not be true?

The trick to self-limiting beliefs or cognogens is that they can be difficult to identify without the help of someone outside looking in. Due to the nature of them being beliefs, they can sometimes be so subconscious in our mental processing that we lack the ability to view them objectively. We don't "see them" as the barriers they are, which is why working with a therapist or coach can be very helpful, as they can take an objective view of your life and your mindset blocks—it can be easy for them to identify where the blocks are and what beliefs are holding you back. Sometimes merely identifying that the belief exists and bringing it to the believer's attention can be enough to dispel the belief and the behaviors associated with it. The identification in itself can be somewhat of a "lightbulb moment" for many people. I have witnessed it in my own work with clients. It's as though you've been carrying a large rock in your backpack without realizing it and wondering why your journey has been so hard. By unpacking the backpack of subconscious beliefs that you're carrying, laying it all out in front of you, and deciding which beliefs you want to continue carrying, you can change the trajectory of your course with only what makes your journey easier. Let that shit go, as hard as it may be. You will feel lighter, calmer, and brighter as a result.

Once you have identified your own specific cognogens or limiting beliefs, the process of replacing them is simple (albeit not easy). As I stated, cognogens are often deeply embedded in our subconscious mind and continue to loop like broken records in our brain, even without our conscious awareness. They have been around for a long time, and as such, our brain relies heavily on thinking about these beliefs as a blueprint of how to respond to life. Furthermore, these beliefs are supported by circuits in our brain that have been activated and used many times in the past. In the brain, the most often used circuits are the ones that become the strongest and are the most persistent in our thoughts and behaviors. If you have been carrying around a limiting belief or cognogen for a long time without realizing it, it's likely the circuit supporting that belief is strong and deep. To change the circuitry and cultivate new beliefs, it requires us to identify when we're stuck in the limiting circuit and intentionally choose to focus our brain on a new belief and create a new circuit. The new circuit that supports your more adaptive belief will be considerably weaker than the one for your old, worn-out limiting belief. Therefore, it will take a lot of intentionality and time to repeatedly replace the old belief with a new, upgraded one.

Self-Check:

Let's upgrade your beliefs.
1. Take some time to reflect on the list of cognogens or limiting beliefs you created earlier in this section.
2. Brainstorm some alternative beliefs to replace them. These beliefs should be not so unbelievable that your conscious brain struggles to believe them.
3. Each time you find yourself behaving in a way or thinking thoughts related to your old, outdated cognogens, intentionally pause and replace your false belief with one that is more adaptive.

Identifying your own limiting beliefs (or cognogens) is an advanced strategy when it comes to managing your anxiety because it goes beyond identifying anxious thoughts and replacing them. In fact, this strategy asks us to go beneath the thoughts to the beliefs that create the thoughts and honestly evaluate whether those beliefs are supportive to us.

chapter 20

PERFECTIONISM: WHEN GOOD ENOUGH IS NEVER GOOD ENOUGH

It's frankly shocking to me how many women struggle with perfectionism without realizing it. In my work in Eunoia Medical, I would say perfectionism is one of the most misunderstood and sneakiest cognogens that women deal with when it comes to their mental health.

I, for one, consider myself a recovering perfectionist. What does that mean, you say? I have come to realize how my own perfectionistic cognogen has created a cage around my mental health in the past. I am almost always actively working to identify and replace it with a more adaptive belief system. You, too, may identify as a perfectionist or a recovering one. Or perhaps you are thinking to yourself, *I'm not a perfectionist, my house is so messy!* I would caution you, though, as perfectionism is likely making an impact on you as well.

The most common understanding of perfectionism is the need to be or appear perfect or without flaw. However, that is not the most common manifestation of perfectionism I see. I often explain perfectionism to my clients as the program their brain-computer learned that input = output, or that there is a perfect way to do everything. Women who struggle with perfectionism often believe that there is a "right" solution for every problem and will work tirelessly to find it (to their own detriment at times). Perfectionism may present as needing to have all the details of a situation worked out and perfected prior to being able to move forward or to take action. It also can feel like not being "happy" or content unless everything is exactly how you have imagined it and then feeling despair or frustration when you cannot make it so. Can you identify with this feeling? Have you ever felt that unless you had everything figured out, exactly how it would "be," that you can't move forward with any action? Or what about feeling that if you cannot be successful at something, you would prefer to not even try?

Admittedly, in my younger years, before I realized the damaging effects of being a perfectionist, I used to write "perfectionist" on my résumé when I was applying for jobs. I wore it like a badge of honor. The idea that being someone who doesn't sacrifice, who pushes to be the best and to do tasks "perfectly," seemed ideal to me at the time. I would be "the perfect employee," and it's easy to see why it would be the case: An employee who identifies as a perfectionist needs less management, as she will manage herself ruthlessly; her expectations of herself are so unrealistically high that she'll never do anything less than her absolute best, as anything less is not tolerated. What I realize now from my more experienced position is how flawed this thinking is. As someone who reviews résumés and hires staff, I now see someone who identifies as a perfectionist (as if it is a good thing) as code for someone who has no boundaries around her work–life balance and who will strive to be perfect, even to her own detriment.

I have yet to find a woman who calls herself a "perfectionist" who doesn't also struggle with anxiety. Examining the relationship between these two cognitive habits can help us understand how getting one or both of these tendencies under control can serve to reduce both of them. If you constantly strive for perfection or require things to be exactly a certain way, you experience anxiety about not being perfect or being found out as imperfect. That anxiety is very uncomfortable and therefore, we modify our behavior to reduce that discomfort (it's a behavior loop). If being imperfect causes you to have anxiety, and striving toward being perfect helps reduce your anxiety, you'll work even harder to be perfect. In this way, perfectionism and anxiety become very much a chicken-or-egg relationship. It can be hard to determine which began first or which is the bigger issue.

However, we cannot discuss perfectionism without drawing attention to the world in which girls and women are raised. I believe we live in a society that idolizes perfection, productivity, and excellence. Despite our best efforts on a personal level to reject the concept of being "perfect," popular media continues to prize and perpetuate it. We're simultaneously told to reject concepts of perfectionism while being shown the countless places we are falling short. On the one hand, society and marketing media tell us to embrace our imperfections and reject concepts of perfection; we should show up authentically. Yet on the other hand, we're bombarded by advertising, magazines, TV and film, and social media that encourage us to lose weight, look younger, become more attractive and more efficient in every way so we can be more productive. You know, picture-perfect perfection. It's as though we're told, "You don't have to be perfect and perfectionism isn't real, but you should still aim for that."

We often pick up perfectionistic programming from childhood conditioning that demonstrates that perfection equates to being loved and "enough." It comes from a belief that something flawed is not lovable or acceptable. In my clients who are successful and high achieving, perfectionism often follows from them putting in effort in their younger years and being rewarded with achievement and success in a reliable fashion, something that was certainly my experience. Study hard, get good grades. Get good grades, get into prestigious programs. Study in that program, get a career. Perfectionism teaches us that if we just do everything the right way and put in enough "input," we will be reliably rewarded with the "output" we're seeking. It's all very predictable and "perfect."

It all works well until it doesn't. I notice that perfectionism most often becomes apparent in women's lives after they have children. In fact, I can think of at least a dozen women whose anxiety became considerably worse after the birth of their children, and I suspect it is due to the perfectionistic programming they picked up without realizing it. In their pre-child life, life was quite simply input = output. You put in the right amount of work and do things in just the right way, and you will get the result you are seeking. Frankly, there's nothing like parenting to challenge that system. In no way is motherhood an input = output situation. Any mother can attest to the fact that it doesn't matter how many different things you try to get your infant to sleep longer or your toddler to eat better, you can never predictably predict the output of a parenting situation based on your input. It just doesn't match up.

So, what happens when the program that we have been running our lives on is no longer working? Anxiety strikes. When your brain is used to the world behaving in a certain way (due to the programming it has picked up over years of experience), and it doesn't actually work out that way, anxiety rears its ugly head. It's as if the carpet has been pulled out from under your brain, and it no longer knows how to operate in the world reliably, which explains (in part) why so many women struggle with anxiety after having children. It's challenging their subconscious programming about how the world works, then anxiety comes in to save the day.

The issue with perfectionism is that by its nature, it is unachievable. While we may be able to maintain close-to-perfection in some domains of our lives, ultimately, there are going to be situations when what we input doesn't equal output, or that we won't be able to meet our own unrealistic expectations. For many women, perfectionism creates a cage from which they can never escape, and they're often not even aware of it. Having subconscious programming of perfectionism sets us up for failure before we even begin, as the end goal can never be achieved (or at least maintained).

I remember the time that perfectionism almost killed me. Upon learning of the benefits of a morning routine, the importance of consistency and habit formation, I quickly committed myself to perfect adherence to a 5:30 a.m. wake-up time for my morning routine. Anything with a clearly defined benchmark is dangerous for a perfectionist, and I've since learned to avoid anything that has even the mere perception of "perfection" being "correct." Perfectionism loves opportunities to grip onto goals and create strict expectations.

In my case, my perfectionism loved the idea of a daily rigid routine that I could adhere to without fail. My perfectionism believed (and consequently so did I) that if I just did the right series of steps in just *the* right way, I would "cure" my mental illness (note the input = output programming). Thanks to my perfectionism, I also quickly settled into the belief that I could not possibly skip one single day. This mental connection happened automatically, likely the minute I realized the benefit of a daily morning routine. If you have ever read *The Miracle Morning* by Hal Elrod, you may have felt the same way: If all these amazing things happen when I commit to a morning routine, I will commit 100 percent. My perfectionism loved it.

For weeks, I dragged my tired behind out of bed at 5:30 a.m. and committed to a rigid routine of meditation, affirmations, reading, exercise, and journaling. The majority of mornings it wasn't a problem, and I continue to experience amazing results from a regular morning routine to this day (just in a healthier way). The issue in those earlier days, however, was that my need to have perfect adherence to my morning routine morphed what should have been a fantastic and health-promoting habit into a sort of personal development prison. Whether it was after a night shift, being up all night with the kids, or being ill with stomach flu, I blindly refused to miss a day, as my perfectionistic cognogen instilled in me that 100 percent perfect adherence was the only acceptable behavior.

In hindsight, I can see how rigid and perfectionistic that was. We live in a society that places immense value on discipline and perfectionism and doesn't often acknowledge the human nature of our humanness. When I inevitably had to skip a day (being human, and all), the shame and guilt I would feel around my "inconsistency" or "laziness" was incredibly painful, almost incapacitating. I would berate and punish myself all day, saying all sorts of terrible things to myself about my inability to maintain a habit or about how unmotivated I was. I would nearly undo all of the progress I made in my mental health with my morning routine by skipping one day, and it would plunge me into a pit of self-loathing and self-punishment. I would reactively force myself to commit to an extra practice the next day to make up for lost time, and I would feel intense shame every time I saw the empty box on my self-care tracker where that morning routine "X" would have been. This is a behavioral loop.

It took months for me to realize that I had created my own painful cage. By gripping onto an unrealistic ideal of 100 percent strict daily adherence to my morning routine, I had set myself up for inevitable failure. My cognogens that 1) *perfect adherence to my morning routine was required*, and 2) *that perfect adherence was even possible* set me up for a roller coaster of shame and self-punishment. I began to lose sight of the benefits of my morning routine. It became a source of stress and anxiety, and it exhausted me. Despite it all, I forced myself to get up every single day without fail to avoid feeling the shame and guilt of "failing to be perfect." My perfectionism didn't allow for tired days, sick days, or for days I had been up all night with work or kids. My perfectionistic cognogen didn't care or allow me to have human days. I was stuck between a rock and a hard place in my mind: I couldn't realistically adhere 100 percent to my routine, and I also couldn't not adhere 100 percent because it was so painful to fail.

I recall the day I realized that the prison I was living in was of my own creation. I realized that not once did someone come to me and demand I wake up every single day without fail at 5:30 a.m. No one ruled me with an iron fist (other than myself). No one told me that I was a failure because I didn't get up one day or because I was too tired to do the routine that day. It was me. It was my mind that created this cage. It was my mind that called me a failure and made me feel terrible shame and guilt. It was the voice in my own head that had set the high bar of expectation. It was my own false beliefs about being perfect that were setting me up for inevitable feelings of failure, and the resulting pain that followed was my own fault. I realized that by creating the expectation for myself of being perfect, what I had created was a painful pattern of inevitable failure followed by crushing shame and guilt. I was being my own worst enemy. *Talk about having a lightbulb moment.* I was the creator of my own experience, and I was making it so much more painful than it had to be. My perfectionism had taken something healthy, fun, and enjoyable and turned it into a rigid, inflexible roller coaster. I couldn't humanly meet the "goal" of perfect adherence (because spoiler alert: no one can) without unhealthy forcing, and I felt incredible distress when I "failed."

Since this realization, I have become more aware of when and where perfectionism plays a role in my life. For this reason, I'm now cautious about using budgeting apps that ask me to consistently track my spending habits as well because I know that given the opportunity, my adherence will be strict and disciplined. Too disciplined, to be honest. I latch onto this sort of habit with a perfectionistic death grip and have repeated this pattern enough times in my life now to realize that it is the work of my perfectionism cognogen.

Perfectionism can also manifest as relentless striving and overworking in order to avoid the feeling of failure. Even as I write this chapter on perfectionism, I struggle to fully commit to writing this chapter and this book. My perfectionistic cognogens are still hanging around, making their presence known. I'm still not 100 percent sure of exactly how everything will be laid out in the book or whether it will all make sense. If I indulge my perfectionistic (anxious) thoughts about my writing skills not being good enough, my book not being organized enough, or the title not being "perfect," I will completely give up on writing it at all. The anticipation and drive to avoid feeling failure will cause me to adjust my behavior to avoid those feelings (stop writing the book), and no one will read this book. And I won't be able to have the impact I desire to have and change the lives of the women who desperately need to know that they're not their anxiety. Having the awareness of our cognogens, what triggers them, and knowing how to manage and push through the fear-based thoughts is the key to everything you want to do but are afraid of facing.

Self-Check:

It's important to become aware of when and how perfectionism is making an impact on your life. Take some time to journal or reflect on the following questions to explore your own relationship with perfectionism.

1. Where in my life do I feel the need to be or appear perfect?

2. Where in my life do I feel as if I can't move forward until I have all of the answers or when everything is exactly how I want it to be?
3. Do I believe that there is a right way to do everything? Do I believe that input = output?
4. Where in my life do I hold myself to unrealistic expectations of perfect adherence, and how is it affecting my ability to show up in the world?
5. What thoughts do I have that can alert me that my perfectionism is making an impact on me?

chapter 21

HABIT CREATION FOR THE RECOVERING PERFECTIONIST

You're likely wondering, *Carly, do you just avoid morning routines and tracking your finances now?* Of course not. I firmly believe these and other habits are important in our lives and consider habit formation an important part of my own success.

I still do these things, but instead of a rigid perfectionistic expectation of myself, I have worked hard to identify what is "good enough" in each of these and other situations. I've allowed myself to live by new standards of what constitutes success in nearly every area of my life. I've realized that if I had the ability to define what constitutes failure in a situation, I also have the power to define what constitutes success. By being intentional about the expectations I set for myself in my own behavior and habits, I choose to set myself up for success rather than failure.

The trouble with perfectionism is that it's a hard pattern to identify and even harder to shake. The fact that achievement and perfection are idealized in our society makes it challenging to see why it's a dangerous belief. For many years, I wore my perfectionism as a badge of honor, as if it were a good quality, one that would not allow for sacrifice in any area of my work or life. I failed to see how damaging that belief pattern was not only in my life but also on my mental health. It wasn't until I went through multiple experiences similar to what I've outlined here that I began to realize how damaging perfectionism could be and was for me. I learned to be vigilant for the thoughts that signaled my perfectionism was spiking again and trying to take the reins, directing my behavior. I began to create a system through which I set behavioral expectations for myself or set myself up to create new habits. I also became skilled at identifying perfectionism in others and learned to help them see how perfectionism was running their lives as well.

Now, when I set out to create a habit in my life, whether it's a regular running routine or setting limits on how much time I spend on social media or how many sweets I eat, I use a concept called Constraint and Flexibility to guide me. This framework for creating goals or habits is very helpful for perfectionists (or recovering perfectionists).

To illustrate this concept, think of a highway. If you're in your car on a long straight highway, imagine your success in your habit or goal at the end of the road. The guardrails on either side of the road are the constraints, but while you're on the highway, you can drive pretty well anywhere you want as long as you're in the direction of your goal. The constraints are the upper and lower limits of a behavior or habit that are acceptable for you. Your ability to drive between them, to weave between the limits of your behavioral benchmarks, are what I refer to as flexibility. Let's use creating a morning routine as an example.

In creating a morning routine, the two extremes of the behavior would be zero—to not do it at all (or zero days), or seven—to commit to your routine 100 percent of the time (perfectionism, essentially). To begin, I want you to set a minimally acceptable number of days each week that you would like to commit to, a benchmark that you would prefer to not fall beneath. Let's use three days in this example, meaning that you consider yourself "successful" if you have completed your chosen habit at least three times a week. Great. Now, the upper limit of this behavior is the maximally possible number that you want to do your habit, in this case your morning routine. Perhaps you feel like five days a week is probably good enough. These two numbers are the constraints in your habit formation. You define success between the two constraints, i.e., you are successful if you do your morning routine between three and five times each week. You can do as little as three days per week or as many as five days per week, depending on how you feel, and still be "successful" in your habit. These are the guardrails on the highway toward your success. As long as you remain between the constraints, you allow yourself the flexibility of choosing what feels best for you, and you can still consider yourself "successful." It's a win-win.

Having constraints in your creation of habits is important because it intentionally forces you to identify and avoid perfectionistic expectations. It also builds in allowance for flexibility and your humanness, teaching you how to give yourself grace. Within the two guardrails (constraints) of three to five days, you allow yourself some flexibility on a daily basis. You have at least two to four days that allow you to be human and not commit to your morning routine, if you so choose. Furthermore, if you allow for more flexibility by not strictly defining which days of your week are your "off days," you give yourself the freedom to decide each day whether you will do your morning routine based on how you're feeling that day. If you wake up one day and are not feeling it, you can choose to make this day one of your "off days" and know that you have a few more if you need them each week.

The trouble with perfectionism is that it assumes we will feel the same way we did when we set the plan in motion, every single day, but that isn't always going to be the case. Your motivation, energy level, desire, and drive to commit to a morning routine will wax and wane throughout the weeks, which is human nature. By not defining which specific days each week you will commit to your morning routine, you allow yourself even more flexibility and freedom to ebb and flow with your schedule and your energy levels, leaving yourself some wiggle room.

Constraint and flexibility work for the habits you are trying to create as well as provide structure around habits you are trying to limit or reduce. For example, drinking alcohol is a common buffering activity many of my clients have. While their alcohol intake may not reach the levels of dependence or a diagnosis of alcoholism, it's common that they want to limit or bring their intake of alcohol to a level that they feel is healthier, or make their use more intentional.

It's common when women are trying to change a habit (be it cutting down on alcohol or starting a diet), it tends to be a very all-or-nothing situation (this is black-and-white thinking, by the way). You will either drink alcohol or you will not. You will either strictly adhere to your diet or you will not. There is no middle ground, no room for humanness, no gray area that can still equate to success overall. In the case of alcohol intake, the constraints around it may be an upper limit of no more than three drinks per week and a lower limit of zero drinks per week. This way you allow yourself the flexibility of what days you choose to drink, how many drinks you have when you do decide to drink, and whether you drink at all.

This built-in flexibility also accounts for the inevitable rebelliousness that you likely feel after constricting yourself to a particular set of "rules" for a period of time. Have you ever started a diet and had a few weeks of success only to get a rebellious streak that causes you to binge-eat on everything you've been so strictly denying yourself? I know that when I have set an expectation for myself of perfectionism in a certain habit, it's inevitable that one day I will just not feel like doing it out of pure rebellion against my own plan. Building in constraint and flexibility sets you up for more success in whatever habit or behavior you are seeking to change. It helps disrupt the shame and guilt cycle while rewiring your definition of success, perfection, "enoughness"—whatever that looks like for you.

Self-Check:

Take some time now to reflect before moving on.
1. When you have set expectations or new habits for yourself, how have you set them up in your mind? Are they rigid or flexible expectations?
2. How have your previous attempts at setting expectations for yourself gone for you? What emotions do you feel when you mess up or fail to meet your own expectation?
3. What are some ways you can build in constraint and flexibility into your habit formation?

The Eunoia Approach Pillar #3: OUR SOCIAL ECOSYSTEM

The final pillar of The Eunoia Approach deals with social interactions. As women, we are inherently social creatures, and it's very difficult for us to see ourselves as completely separate from our interactions with others. Whether it's fearing an argument or conflict, or feeling guilty about something nasty we said in the heat of the moment, our relationships are important to us, and when they're threatened, it can cause incredible anxiety.

part 3

INTERPERSONAL RELATIONSHIPS AND COMMUNICATION

Our mental health and overall happiness is often heavily influenced by the relationships in our lives, the behavior and emotions of others, and how we show up in our relationships. For many women, interpersonal relationships can be some of the most stressful and anxiety-inducing things in their lives. Whether it's fearing an argument or conflict, or feeling guilty about something nasty we said in the heat of the moment, our relationships are important to us, and when they're threatened, it can cause incredible anxiety.

In fact, many of the women with whom I work are so often influenced by the emotions of others that they feel that they live at others' whims. It's like being a "yes" person at all times, or in some cases, not knowing when to say no. It means you are at the beck of everyone else's schedule, and you allow yourself to sway whichever way others' emotions flow.

Recall from earlier chapters when I explained the importance of claiming your own personal responsibility for your mental health and your anxiety. If there's one specific area that is the most important for you to reclaim agency and full control of your own emotional responses and emotional energy, it is within your interpersonal relationships. If your relationships are a source of anxiety for you, from a manipulative friend to judgmental relative, this section will hopefully be helpful and empowering for you.

We will begin with a discussion of what I refer to as your Personal Power. This concept is critical to understanding the subsequent concepts of passivity, assertiveness, and boundaries. We'll explore chronic passivity and people-pleasing, a tendency that follows from having unhealthy boundaries or no boundaries at all. We will explore my framework for how to communicate in your relationships that can help you feel more in control of your emotions and with practice, prevent damaging relationships due to our tendency to react and respond emotionally. We'll cover some of the most common obstacles women face, the most common beliefs women carry about their emotional responsibilities, and the reciprocal relationship between anxiety and passivity.

Finally, we will explore the important concept of boundaries—what they are, the ways you can identify if you need better boundaries (nearly all of us do), and how to take practical steps to create and implement them.

By the time you are done reading this section, it's my hope that you'll be able to boldly, unapologetically say yes only to what truly fuels your mind, body, and soul and let the rest go. Seriously, let go of what or who weighs you down. You've totally got this! All it takes is a little strategy, soul, and tapping into your inner power that is dying to be unleashed.

chapter 22

LET'S TALK ABOUT YOUR PERSONAL POWER

Above all, be the heroine of your life, not the victim.
—Nora Ephron

Throughout this book, I've shared a number of pragmatic and tangible strategies, mindset shifts, and perspectives to help you get your anxiety under control. Integrating and mastering these strategies into your life will create remarkable shifts in your ability to manage your anxiety effectively. Realistically, every strategy I've shared is intended to help you reclaim your **personal power** from anxiety and step into agency as a woman.

What do I mean by your personal power? It's your deep understanding and belief in your worthiness. It also refers to your unshakable ability and confidence to be in control of your life. Not what happens *to* you but rather *your response to what transpires around and within you.* In your personal power, you are un-fuck-with-able. Within your personal power, you may have anxiety, but it is not in control of you. Sounds amazing, right?

When you are in your personal power, you are the embodied version of your Goddess self. Here, anything you desire is possible. You are not focused on doing things but on being your most elevated and evolved self. You are confident, aligned, and have high standards for yourself. When you are in your personal power, you create and maintain healthy, respectful boundaries within your relationships to protect your energy and your alignment. When you are in your personal power, you are limitless and powerful. It's magical.

Anxiety robs us of our personal power. It does so in sneaky ways, such as taking a hold of us with fear and emotion or making us behave in ways that keep us disempowered and feeling small. When we're activated with emotions and anxiety, we're compromised in our ability to be objective and to respond from a place of calm and aligned power. There is nothing like fear or threats to our safety to shake us from our core, our center, our personal power. We need to be living in our personal power at all times to create the truly aligned life we desire and deserve, which is why learning to manage your anxiety is an integral part of creating a truly aligned life. If anxiety is driving the car of your life, you are not in your personal power. It is only by learning how to tap into and embody our personal power that we can truly learn to manage our anxiety once and for all. While the strategies I share in this book are very practical and pragmatic cognitive approaches to anxiety management, it's important to emphasize that managing your anxiety is not just about your day-to-day thinking and doing. It's about how you step into the fullest expression of yourself as a woman and how you truly create the life that you desire and deserve.

One of the most common reasons why I see women struggling with anxiety is because they're stuck in a chronically passive, people-pleasing behavior pattern. They're in the habit of giving away their personal power in their relationships and in their life. They have very weak or nonexistent boundaries. Often, women actually have no idea that they're stuck in this habit, and they certainly have no idea of its connection with their anxiety. Behaving in a passive way can look like many different things. It's biting your tongue when your father makes a comment about your lax parenting. It's always responding to work emails after hours or taking on extra work because you don't know how to say no. It's agreeing to volunteer for everything asked, even when you know you don't have time. It's always being the dumping ground for your negative friend who zaps your positive energy and never asks about you (I'm pretty sure we all have this someone in our lives). What I've come to realize is that continuing to be a passive participant in our own life and not learning more assertive, confident ways to communicate is like taking a jug of lighter fluid and pouring it on an anxiety fire.

In contrast, learning to advocate for yourself in a calm, confident, and assertive way allows you to speak from and be in your personal power. Recall that when you are living in your personal power, you are living in alignment with your truth, meaning that you speak from a place of being aligned with and doing what is most true and right for you. Part of being in your personal power means you maintain high standards of behavior from yourself at all times. In your conversations with others, you expect yourself to remain respectful, in control, and confident. When you experience emotions in an interaction (which you will because you are human), being in your personal power means you have enough emotional intelligence to understand that you cannot be calm and objective when you are emotionally activated and compromised. When that happens, you are able to step away from emotional situations respectfully and ground yourself back into your personal power so the conversation can continue productively at a later time using empowered communication. When you speak from your personal power, you have a salient awareness of what you are responsible for in a relationship and what you are not responsible for.

When we behave passively in our relationships, we speak from a place within us that is scared, lacking confidence, and quite frankly, powerless. When we behave passively, we give our personal power away to others and no longer have control over our own inner state. We become dependent on the whims of others and feel the need to fix things for them, manage their emotions, and often martyr ourselves in the process. We believe we are being "nice," when in fact, we are acting out of fear of being disliked or ostracized. Women who behave passively often have a deep fear of others not liking them or becoming angry with them. They also demonstrate a painful lack of personal boundaries around their emotions, their information, and their energy. They are often drained, spread too thin, and exhausted as they constantly feel responsible for things that are not their responsibility. Instead of caring for themselves and maintaining strong, healthy personal care practices, they give all of their energy away, leaving nothing for themselves. Women who are chronically passive and people-pleasing often feel resentful toward their loved ones, feeling that while they constantly give of themselves to others, no one returns the gesture. They often find themselves doing many things they don't want to do and wasting their valuable and limited resources on things that don't fill them up. The worst part about being passive is that very few women actually identify that it's their passive behavior that is causing them so much anxiety in the first place. Sound familiar?

Keep in mind that passivity looks different for each of us. While you may not resonate with all of what I describe as passive behavior, I strongly encourage you to examine when you are giving away your personal power to others in your relationships or conversations.

Self-Check:
1. Do you know what it feels like to be in your personal power? If not, what do you think it would feel like? How would you stand, speak, and look if you were in your personal power?
2. Where in your life do you give up your personal power to others?
3. Do you consider yourself a people-pleaser? Where does this behavior come from for you?
4. In what ways do you sacrifice yourself for the benefit of others?
5. What would it feel like to give up your passive tendencies and people-pleasing? What is holding you back from doing it? What do you gain from keeping these tendencies?

chapter 23

THE CONNECTION BETWEEN ANXIETY AND PASSIVITY

So, how are anxiety and passivity linked? Recall from our earlier chapters that your anxiety is designed to keep you safe and to avoid distress. Conflict, or the perception of conflict, is very uncomfortable for the majority of people, as it signifies a threat to safety. It causes distress. In response to distress, our anxiety really has only two primitive responses: fight or flight. (Sidenote: More recent research and theory of the fight-or-flight response has identified two other responses, fawn or freeze, but for simplicity, we'll stick to just fight and flight.) When the fear of conflict strikes (causing distress) and our anxiety takes over, we have essentially two options of how to behave and respond unless we can manage our anxiety and reclaim our personal power. Although more common in males, the tendency toward *fight* triggers aggressive communication styles—using overt threats, intimidation, and physical dominance in an attempt to deal with the situation. In women, however, it's more common to have our flight mechanism triggered, which then results in passive behavioral patterns to avoid conflict.

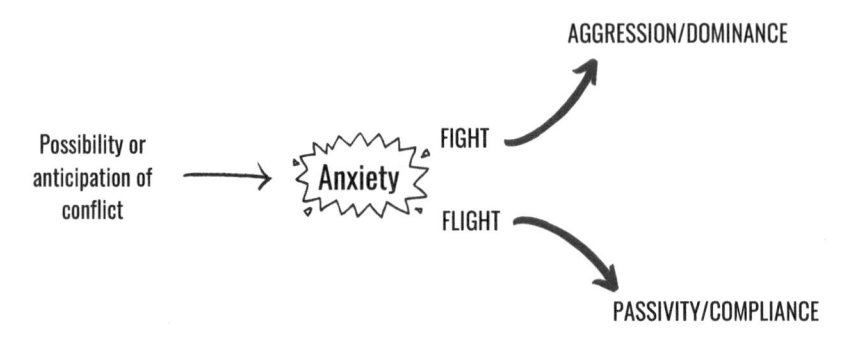

```
                                              AGGRESSION/DOMINANCE
                                           ↗
Possibility or                        FIGHT
anticipation of   →    Anxiety
conflict                              FLIGHT
                                           ↘
                                              PASSIVITY/COMPLIANCE
```

There are many reasons why women tend to default to a flight mechanism and behave passively. For one, as females, much of our sociocultural conditioning has directed us to "be nice" and to "get along." The dominant stereotypical female gender role has been a submissive, subservient, and passive archetype. Evolutionarily, our ancestors were more likely to survive when they were in social groups, so it also follows that any behavior that risks us being "kicked out" of our social group will trigger anxiety. As little girls, we're praised for being "nice" and "kind." We are given more stereotypically "female" toys and encouraged to not rock the boat, to not make waves. As we grow up, many women are labeled as bitchy or domineering if they are vocal about their opinions and needs. As a result of all this social conditioning, it makes sense that speaking up and being assertive feels very uncomfortable and unnatural. However, as with so many false beliefs that we carry, the fact that it is our conditioning does not mean it is true.

Second, passive behavior serves to reduce distress since most of us perceive conflict as distressing. When we behave passively, we lower distress by reducing the chance of conflict, which then reduces our anxiety. This behavior becomes reinforced over time, and before we know it, we're in a behavioral loop. It becomes even more deeply ingrained if we've been raised in a household where we learned to be passive from a young age when our brains were developing. Generational and cultural dialogues are so powerful, habitual, and deeply ingrained within many of us that the mere thought of being more assertive is terrifying.

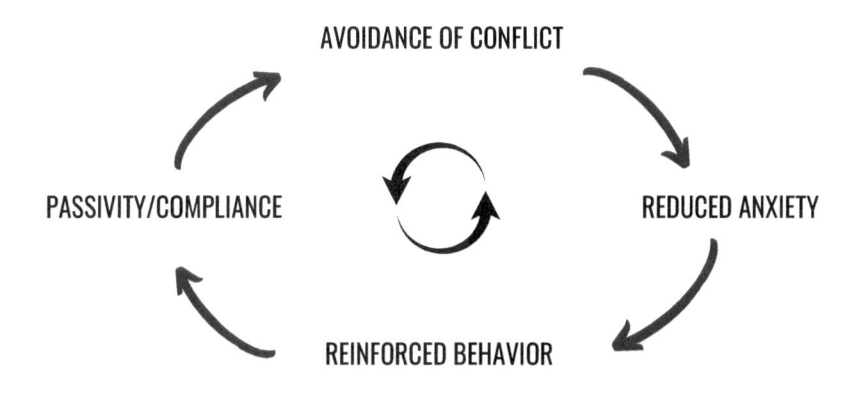

AVOIDANCE OF CONFLICT → **REDUCED ANXIETY** → **REINFORCED BEHAVIOR** → **PASSIVITY/COMPLIANCE**

But what if they get mad at me?
What if we get into an argument?
What if they think I'm selfish?
What if they stop loving me?
They'll think I'm such a bitch! They'll never talk to me again.
I'd feel so guilty; I could never say that.

These are just some of the responses I hear from women when I do coaching or seminars on assertiveness and boundaries. I can sense their stomachs flip when I ask about the relationships in their lives that need better boundaries established. The problem is that they often don't realize how this behavior is intertwined with their anxiety. They don't realize that by constantly giving away their personal power, they will continue to experience a terrible cycle of worsening anxiety until they do something about it.

When I was in the darkest night of my anxiety disorder, I remember these fears so clearly, and I know that is why I avoided speaking up for myself for so long. Like so many women, I was focused on being liked and not ruffling feathers. I had so much anxiety about upsetting or disappointing others. I remember feeling like I absolutely had to do what others asked of me because my anxiety told me it was far too scary to try the opposite. They wanted to do something; I went along with it. They asked me to do something for them; I did it. They needed me to fix their problems and make them happy; I would sacrifice myself for it. If something was said that was disrespectful toward me or loved ones, I would keep my mouth shut because the fear of speaking up and causing conflict was stronger than my ability to step into my personal power—to be assertive and speak my mind in a respectful way. And so I'd go along with the crowd and dishonor my deep intuition and truth, again and again. *What would I say? What would it feel like to finally speak up? What would it look like if I started to define what behaviors I was going to allow in my close relationships? What would happen if I asked for the treatment and respect that I felt I deserved but had kept silent about for so long?*

Then my anxiety would strike with vengeance. I would feel anxious again—about having to fulfill all the expectations I had complied with doing. I would be anxious about all the time that I would need to spend. Anxious about all of the precious energy I would need to expend to help with something that I didn't even want to do in the first place. Anxious about the emotional burdens I would carry for others, feeling so invested emotionally in their problems. Anxious about betraying my own truth and beliefs, my own values, and not standing up for what I believed in. I would feel ashamed that I wasn't brave enough or courageous enough to speak up for myself, for what I knew was right. It was a vicious cycle. But it was one that taught me just how intimately connected passivity and anxiety are. Passivity is fuel for anxiety and leaves us without any way to control the flames.

The sad reality of the majority of women who struggle with anxiety is that we often silence ourselves on a regular basis, martyring ourselves to the needs of others. We are killing ourselves in trying to be "nice." We often hide it behind honorable phrases such as "I'm a people-pleaser" or "I like to make people happy" or "They need me."

Sometimes it can be hard to understand the connection between your relationships with others and your own anxiety, but I can promise you, as you work through this section and implement some of the strategies I recommend, you'll learn how to identify your passivity and unravel these patterns for good.

chapter 24

ASSERTIVENESS MEANS SPEAKING FROM YOUR PERSONAL POWER

The most common response I hear when I talk to women about being assertive is that they think it means "being a bitch all of the time." In fact, it's the total opposite. It doesn't mean being harsh, manipulative, or sneaky. Being assertive doesn't even mean you'll always get your way. In fact, if you don't get your way in a certain situation, being assertive means you are in control of your own emotional reaction to that. Being assertive means that you are aware of what you are responsible for and not responsible for in a conversation and in a relationship. It means understanding that you cannot control others or how they respond to you, you can only control how you speak and respond to them. To become more assertive, you need to harness your personal power.

Speaking from within your personal power means that you can communicate calmly, respectfully, and confidently from a place separate from emotional activation. You have radical responsibility for your own thoughts, emotions, and actions. You understand that you alone are responsible for managing your own emotional state so that you may have respectful and constructive conversations. You maintain high standards of behavior for yourself, from boundary setting to interpersonal communication. You do not submit to the will of others merely out of a fear of being disliked or of conflict. You expect and project respect, confidence, and ruthless compassion. You are unshakable.

Reacting and behaving from an emotional inner state is what causes many women to communicate passively in their lives. When we are in a conversation and sense a potential conflict arising, our emotions (anxiety and sometimes anger) are triggered almost automatically. Many of us respond from this emotionally activated place rather than pausing to manage our emotional reaction first. It's important to remember that the time between feeling emotionally triggered and us reacting with behavior tends to be very short—the reaction is automatic—so we need to be on alert and strengthen our emotional intelligence to avoid doing it.

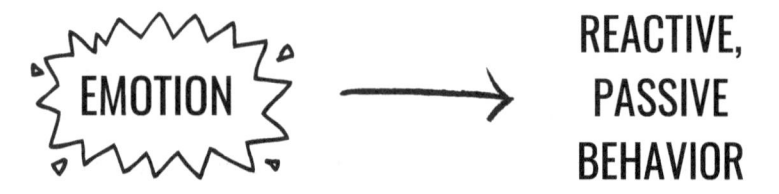

EMOTION ⟶ REACTIVE, PASSIVE BEHAVIOR

One of the most important things I teach to women who are trying to be more assertive and speak from their personal power more often is to work within the space between being emotionally triggered and responding. The fact that you are triggered and experiencing an emotion is not the problem. It is when we react and behave from an emotionally compromised and activated place that we tend to be passive, or in some cases, speak disrespectfully or say things we later wish we hadn't. By working in this space, we take radical responsibility for how we behave.

We can take this responsibility by employing the strategies of Elevated Communication, which is a communication framework I teach to clients to help them feel more empowered to have positive and constructive conversations with their loved ones. When we practice and master Elevated Communication strategies, we help ourselves avoid acting out of emotion. We avoid saying things we regret and, in turn, damaging our relationships. By using Elevated Communication, we also become more aware of our tendencies to react in a passive or people-pleasing way and can work to intervene in this behavior loop. To many of us, our relationships are sacred and we do not want to be the reason that the strength of a relationship is threatened. However, so many of us also have such powerful emotions that we react first and feel guilty after.

A central concept to understand when you are learning how to use Elevated Communication is that our ability to respond from our personal power assertively, respectfully, and constructively is compromised in an emotionally charged situation or conversation. It is especially challenging in those relationships when the person we are communicating with knows exactly how to rile us up or generate emotion in us (like our partners, our children, our parents, or other close relatives). When we react out of anger, we say things we don't mean. When we are very sad, we might make rash decisions or lash out in retribution for who hurt us. When we react with anxiety, we behave passively and self-sacrifice. These reactions are often not in alignment with the true highest version of ourselves or the value that we place on our relationships. Furthermore, hostile or angry responses only serve to disrespect the person to whom we are talking. To make matters even worse, we often find ourselves feeling ashamed about how we reacted in the moment.

It's from this situation that I created this framework. When you employ Elevated Communication strategies, you are more intentional about how you respond in any given moment. Using these strategies takes a lot of practice and awareness to allow them to become automatic. It's important to be patient and compassionate with yourself as you work to integrate these into your own life.

There are three components to Elevated Communication: Emotional Intelligence, Self-Regulation Skills, and Assertive Space-Making Statements. Let's break it down.

Emotional Intelligence: One of the most powerful skills we can have in our lives and in our interpersonal relationships is a finely tuned ability to detect changes in our own inner emotional state.
- Emotional intelligence is your ability to detect and identify your own emotions as they happen to you and recognize that you have become emotionally compromised in that moment. I think of it as your ability to detect when your emotions are activated.

- It often means paying close attention to how your physical body feels and changes while you're in a conversation or situation. When you detect there's been a shift in your emotional state (i.e., you feel angry or detect anxiety due to a conflict), this moment is a critical time at which you recognize that you are now emotionally compromised. Sometimes you may feel an urge to control someone else, comply, or submit to their preferences to please them or because you feel guilty. You are emotionally activated and emotionally compromised, no longer in your personal power.

Self-Regulation Skills are those skills that allow you to process and regulate your own emotions, such as anger, sadness, etc.
- Note that I did not say that self-regulation skills help you stop feeling emotions or bury them away. The ability to self-regulate is the ability to master your emotions by taking yourself in an emotionally activated state, processing the emotions that surface in a healthy way, and returning to an emotionally neutral state.
- In the sequence of steps in Elevated Communication, self-regulation skills come in when you have identified that you are emotionally compromised. While it's sometimes easier and gratifying to act on your emotions, the skill of self-regulation requires us to take radical responsibility for our own emotional state and manage it on our own.
- Self-regulation skills may look like somatic skills such as deep breathing, tapping (EFT), yoga, or going out for a heart-pumping walk. They also may look like more cognitive

and distracting skills like journaling or a body-scan meditation. These skills are essentially the strategies you call on to help you sit with and process your emotions as well as diffuse the energy that is coursing through your body and making you feel reactive. You may need to experiment with different skills to determine what is most effective for returning you to your neutral state.
- If your emotional activation is one of anxiety, which then triggers your passive response, it may mean reflecting on some sections in this book, labeling, or replacing your anxious thoughts.

Assertive Space-Making Statements are critical in-the-moment statements that you can use to request space to process and regulate yourself in the middle of a conversation.
- I recommend having a number of statements in your mind that you can use when you identify yourself as being emotionally compromised in a situation. It looks like asking for space in a kind and respectful way that allows you to express your awareness of being emotionally compromised in the conversation so you can regulate your emotions.
- Some examples:
    - "I really want to finish this conversation with you, but I'm having a lot of emotions right now. I'm going to step away for a few moments and rebalance myself, but I'll be back."
    - "I sense I'm getting emotional about this situation, and I know that I won't make the best choices in how I speak when that happens. I'm going to go for a walk and clear

my head and then I'll come back so we can continue this conversation."

The four key characteristics of Assertive Space-Making Statements are:

1. **Acknowledging your own emotional state.** This acknowledgment allows you to bring what is happening inside of you out into the space between the two of you and may help the other individual to also recognize their own emotional state.
2. **Expressing your need for space to process it.** Note that you are not requesting space but assertively stating your need for it. It doesn't sound like "Do you mind if . . ." but rather "I'm going to take a few minutes . . ."
3. **Reassurance that the situation is important to you and that you'll return.** Using these statements does not look like screaming, "I'm not talking to you about this anymore!" and slamming the door behind you. No, they involve ensuring the person is aware that this situation is important to you and that you intend to return once you are neutral.
4. **Respect and ruthless compassion toward yourself and the other person.** When using these statements, it's important to do so from a place of respect and compassion for both of you. You are both human beings having human emotions, and there is no shame in it.

To use Elevated Communication, you have to be motivated. While it may sound simple as you read this chapter, it's an entirely different ballgame when you are in the midst of a heated argument with your partner. Note that Elevated Communication does not involve any form of controlling the other person; that is, you cannot use this strategy to control the entire conversation. You can only use it to control your part of the conversation.

The important thing to remember is that you are doing it for the goodness of your own relationship and to strengthen your own assertiveness skills. By doing so, you are lessening your anxiety and reclaiming your personal power. Your desire for a constructive, positive relationship-preserving conversation needs to be greater than your need to act out of emotion and react in a way that you might regret. It takes considerable practice—be gentle with yourself as you assert yourself in any charged situation. When you use Elevated Communication consistently, you will begin to develop a high standard for your own behavior and communication with others, which is critical. Called emotional mastery, it is the ability to detect when you are emotionally compromised and intentionally choose to not communicate from a reactive place, something that is life changing and powerful for every area of your life, not just your personal relationships. Imagine what your work relationships could look like if you were able to use this strategy there as well.

EMOTIONS → EMOTIONAL INTELLIGENCE + RETURNING TO POWER → ASSERTIVE BEHAVIOR FROM PERSONAL POWER

Self-Check:
1. Take a moment now and consider the use of Elevated Communication in your relationships.
2. What do you think about using this framework? In what relationships do you feel it would be the most helpful for you?
3. What signals does your body give you when you are becoming emotionally compromised?
4. How will using Elevated Communication strategies help you to achieve regarding your anxiety?
5. What do you feel are some obstacles to using this form of communication, and what can you do to overcome them?
6. Write down some Assertive Space-Making Statements you can use in your next heated conversation when you become emotionally compromised. What are some activities you can use to self-regulate your emotions so you can return to the conversation naturally?

chapter 25

YOU NEED TO STOP BEING SO INVESTED IN THE LIVES OF OTHERS

It is not enough to simply learn how to communicate more assertively in our conversations. We often need to also closely examine how we are showing up in our relationships as well. In my experience, women have a natural tendency to become very emotionally invested in the lives of others around them. I believe that if women spent half as much energy that they spend on others and redirected it toward caring for themselves, as a population, we would all be doing better. Rather than maintaining strong, kind, and healthy emotional boundaries and only owning what is theirs to own, many women allow their own emotions to be held hostage by the situations and problems of other people. It may look like becoming angry when your brother yet again makes another bad financial decision, even though you've told him how to do better. It may look like you becoming frustrated when your parents can't seem to make the decision that you believe is best for them. We become invested in the lives of others. We have a hard time staying on our own side of the street. I believe there are a few reasons why this behavior happens.

First of all, you are not a bad person for becoming emotionally invested in the lives of your loved ones. You are not a bad person, but you are making your life more difficult. You love them, and you don't want to see your loved ones hurt, make bad decisions, or fall on hard times. You have a big heart, and that's good. The problem is that many women with big beautiful hearts allow those same hearts to be dragged through the mud by becoming emotionally wrapped up in situations they cannot control. They also often allow their family members and friends to dump all their emotional baggage on their front step. Placing boundaries around their own energy and emotions often doesn't even occur to them because they live in fear of the backlash from others. After all, what will *they* say? Let's build a privacy fence (at least) around your big beautiful heart.

So, other than having a big and loving heart, why else do we become so emotionally invested in the lives and decisions of others? Once more for the folks in the back, let's recall that your anxiety serves to reduce any form of distress. When you love someone and they are making what you believe to be a straight-up stupid decision, the fear that you feel about their situation becomes a source of distress for you. No one wants to see their family member in dire straits, in a terrible relationship, or unable to speak up to their abusive boss. It's frustrating and can be devastating to witness someone's downturn or poor situation. I get it; *bleeding hearts of the world unite.* Anxiety seeks to control things that cause discomfort and distress, so we become so neurotically focused on controlling the lives of our loved ones so as to minimize our own discomfort. When we feel responsible FOR someone, we set ourselves up for inevitable pain and discomfort because ultimately, we cannot control the decisions or life choices and situations of another human being.

The third reason we become so emotionally invested in the lives of our loved ones is a lack of healthy boundaries within that particular relationship. There are people in life who believe that you are their emotional dumping ground and they visit regularly to make deposits. That has got to stop, for your own good. When someone regularly offloads their emotional baggage on you or tells you too many intimate details about their lives and then fails to take any action to make things better for themselves, we often begin to develop some sense of responsibility for that baggage and fixing those problems. Most of us by nature are problem-solvers. The mere knowledge that a problem exists can make us feel like we need to fix it. Not true. **The fact that you are aware of a problem of a loved one does not mean you're responsible for it.** Write that down. Seriously.

I've often had clients ask me, "How do you listen to people's struggles all day and not feel burdened?" and I explain, "When I'm on a call with you, I am responsible to you as a therapist to listen, mirror, and help you find solutions. When you get off the call with me, it is your responsibility to put those things in place. I do not own your problems or take them on after our call. I am not responsible for your problems, even though I am aware of them." When you find yourself feeling burdened by someone's problems and are looking for solutions to fix it for them, take a moment to consider if you're feeling responsible FOR them or TO them.

Finally, the fourth reason we become so invested in the lives and decisions of others is because we feel that we are helping them. It gives us a sense of purpose. Who doesn't want to be helpful? In fact, it's usually this excuse that comes up when we're criticized for being "too controlling" over someone's life. Have you ever responded to such an accusation with something like "I am just trying to help?" Yes, you. I am looking at you.

Listen, you may think you're helping someone by solving their problems for them—be it your mother, your brother, your spouse, or even a friend, but you're not. The truth is solving problems for other people prevents them from learning skills and challenging themselves. It hinders their growth and doesn't help them build self-trust within their ability to resolve it themselves, something that applies to both practical problems as well as emotional ones. Whether it's answering their calls when they're distraught about how their crappy boyfriend treats them so horribly (again), driving them around like a chauffeur because they don't have "anyone else" to do it, or providing unending amounts of advice in hopes they will make the right decision for themselves—if you are constantly swooping in to save or fix things for them, they are not learning the skills they need to fix it themself. Plain and simple. To develop skills necessary to be emotionally stable, independent adults who can meet our own needs, we need to experience some form of struggle in order to adapt, learn, and grow. It is through falling on their skates over and over again that children learn how to get their balance. It's by experiencing challenge or failure in school that we learn how to study, be resourceful, and develop skills to be successful. Similarly, struggles in interpersonal relationships are necessary for humans to learn skills to navigate these hurdles. For example, when we struggle with resentment, it's likely because we haven't yet learned how to communicate our needs effectively and assertively. When we struggle with inappropriate guilt, it's because we haven't learned how to define our boundaries, evaluate the validity of our emotions, and regulate them. When we struggle with loneliness, we need to learn how to reach out and ask for support and connection. The reason you've picked up this book is likely because you're experiencing some sort of struggle with anxiety in your life and have experienced enough pressure from this struggle to seek new knowledge and ultimately develop new skills. The struggle is real, no doubt, and necessary for us to grow and learn.

It's common that many women actually derive their own value and validity as a person from being able to help others, which is honorable. The problem with this belief, however, is that you are often unable to see how your chronic self-sacrifice for the benefit of helping others both hurts you and your self-esteem and doesn't help the person you believe it's helping. When someone you love is angry, lonely, or defeated, going to bat for them like the superwoman you are does not encourage them to learn the skills required to fix that problem; it handicaps them. You take away their opportunity for learning.

For example, one of my clients had a sister who was quite emotionally demanding. She expected my client to answer her texts immediately and be available for her emotional breakdown calls at any time. She depended so heavily on my client and had no friendships to lean on outside of her. My client was desperate to figure out how to put a boundary in place in this relationship, as it was taking a serious toll on her own mental and emotional health. Understandably, she feared that her sister would be completely alone and unable to cope if she set some boundaries around the support she was willing to offer her. We explored together what sorts of support she felt were healthy and appropriate for her—what she was able and willing to provide without sacrificing her own needs and values. We discussed how she would explicitly explain these new boundaries and planned for the anticipated backlash. Although it was challenging and emotional, my client was able to successfully (albeit uncomfortably) communicate her boundaries with her sister. As expected, the inevitable backlash ensued. While it was indeed uncomfortable for my client, she also felt a massive amount of relief that she was able to free herself of the burden of being her sister's only emotional support. It was also incredibly interesting to observe that within weeks of these boundaries being put in place, my client's sister was starting to reach out and develop more local friendships in her community to serve as supports. What my client was now realizing so saliently was that by continually being the sole support for her sister and trying to solve all of her problems, she had prevented her sister from learning the skills of reaching out and making more connections.

The important thing to realize is that sometimes the healthiest way to help someone is to not help them. Now, this advice may sound cold-hearted, and I'm not suggesting you not be loving, supportive, and present for them in their time of need. It means instead of doing something for them to solve their problem, you encourage them to do it for themselves. It also essentially means understanding to a deep level that you are ultimately not responsible for someone else's problems or their struggles and being okay with it.

Instead of sacrificing ourselves so everyone else is happy, we need to model being responsible for our own happiness and give the responsibility of their happiness back to them. We need to model being in our personal power and taking radical responsibility for ourselves, our mental health, and our lives. It then allows others to step into their own personal power. By doing so, we release the pressure on ourselves to make everyone happy. Imagine what it would feel like to no longer feel responsible for ensuring everyone around you was happy? What if you didn't have to be everyone's emotional dumping ground? Yeah, feel that for a hot minute. Feels good, doesn't it?

chapter 26

YOU DON'T OWN THAT

Now, I am a passionate advocate for setting boundaries, empowering your loved ones to be their own problem-solvers, etc., but I don't want you to walk around being a cold-hearted rock who doesn't help anyone with anything. **There is a fine line between being responsible to someone as an empathetic support and being responsible for someone.** Through my anxiety recovery journey, I've become very good at putting boundaries around who I am responsible *to* and what I am responsible *for* in my interpersonal relationships. Doing so is a critical step in overcoming chronic people-pleasing and thereby taking your power back. Let's break it down a bit.

I am responsible to my family to be loving, compassionate, patient, and kind. I am responsible to my patients to be knowledgeable, professional, evidence-based, and safe. I am responsible to my clients to be supportive, responsive, and to help them get results.

I am not, however, responsible FOR anyone's happiness.

I am not responsible FOR anyone's loneliness.

I am not responsible FOR anyone's health.

I am not responsible FOR anyone's recovery.

I am not responsible FOR solving anyone's problems.

And neither are you.

When you are responsible to someone, you are enough by being who you are. You don't have to give up any of your personal power or sacrifice yourself for them. You do not need to sacrifice your own energy, values, or beliefs to support them (unless you assertively and willingly do so). You are enough by supporting your loved one to do things for themselves rather than doing what they should be doing for themselves. When you behave as though you are responsible for someone, you sacrifice yourself and your integrity to fix them or fix their problems for them. When you are responsible for someone, you feel the burden of their emotional baggage and their problems as if they were your own.

Do you see the difference? Being responsible FOR something is an ownership position. We are responsible FOR things we own. For example, my dog—I own my dog and am responsible for his health, his veterinary care, his food. When there is a problem with his health, I am responsible for taking him to the vet, paying the bill, and making sure he gets his medicine.

On the flip side, I am not responsible FOR my husband. As a perfectly capable adult, he is responsible for himself. I am not responsible for ensuring he is fed, he is happy, or he is taking good care of himself. I am responsible TO my husband—I am responsible to be loving, honest, trustworthy, and kind—all qualities I have within myself already. By being helpful and encouraging to my husband, I empower and support him to make the correct decisions and take the correct actions for himself.

While drawing the lines of responsibility in some relationships is straightforward, when it comes to the parent–child relationship, the line is a little less clear. Many parents feel very responsible for their children (even when they are young adults) because it has been part of their role since their children were babies. When our children are young, we are indeed responsible for them, but that doesn't remain the case as they grow up. Just as we are not helping others to develop valuable problem-solving skills when we help them, this applies to our children as well (once they are young adults). There is no hard-and-fast rule about when the transition from *responsible for* to *responsible to* occurs when it comes to our children, but a reasonable guide is the following: If your child is considered an adult in the eyes of the law, you are no longer responsible for them (barring any unique cognitive disabilities, etc.). If your child is living independently, maintaining a job (or trying to), managing their own finances, and making their own decisions, you are no longer responsible for them. It's time to let them fall (and learn) on their own.

When you feel responsible FOR someone, you fix, change, persuade. You smother, do things for them, and feel that their happiness is your responsibility. When you're responsible TO someone, you support, love, and give them the room to be responsible for themselves.

> *Self-Check:*
> Responsibility *To* versus Responsibility *For*
> 1. Consider now the relationships you have in your life. Where are you responsible to others?
> 2. Where are you behaving as though you are responsible for others?
> 3. What differences exist in these relationships? How do you feel about relationships with people in which you feel responsible for them?

Boundaries

It may sound dramatic, but I really believe that having boundaries are one of the most fundamental mental health strategies I teach. It is one of the most important strategies to keep your relationships healthy and maintain control of your anxiety. Now, the term "boundaries" is very clichéd and often used in the online space and in personal development, and thus, it can have a lot of misinterpretations or misunderstandings around it. There may be many different definitions of what boundaries are, but for me, they're cognitive concepts that allow you to define limits in your life. These limits may be related to what you engage in physically, energetically, or emotionally. They may be related to things that you allow to be around you or things you permit to be in your space. Understanding the concept and applying it to your life implies that you are fully taking responsibility for your life and how you feel in it.

For many women I have worked with in the past, the concept

of boundaries is elusive. Admittedly, the concept can seem vague, especially if boundaries are nonexistent in your life. To simplify, I will call upon our friend Mr. Webster to share his definitions.

> **Boundary (n):** something (such as a river, a fence, or an imaginary line) that shows where an area ends and another area begins; a point or limit that indicates where two things become different; unofficial rules about what should not be done; limits that define acceptable behavior.

I feel that for the purposes of our discussion, the third and fourth definitions are the most helpful. Boundaries serve as cognitive constructs, unofficial rules that define acceptable behavior in the context of a relationship. They help establish an understanding about personal responsibility in a particular relationship. I often conceptualize boundaries as imaginary limits or barriers that define what is my responsibility in a relationship and what is not. They help us define the limit beyond which we will no longer tolerate certain behaviors. They are basic rules that define how you treat yourself and how you will allow others to treat you.

How we define and structure boundaries varies widely. You may have very strict boundaries or ones with which you are more flexible. Depending on the relationship or setting, your boundary may be negotiable or firm. You may have closer boundaries or more spacious boundaries. It's up to you to define your boundaries in your relationships in such a way that protects your peace and comes from your personal power.

One of my favorite ways to conceptualize boundaries is to think of your front lawn and your neighbor's. There is usually some dividing line between the two properties, whether it's a hedge or a fence, and it denotes where your lawn ends and your neighbor's lawn begins. It also defines where you are responsible for mowing your grass, and where your neighbor is responsible for mowing theirs. It's not that you don't care about what occurs on the other side of the fence or with your neighbor, but you don't believe it's your responsibility to mow their lawn. They may ask you to mow their lawn, and you may agree once, but that doesn't mean that you will forever mow their lawn. Similarly, if you somehow end up mowing their lawn all the time, they may stop mowing their own lawn completely or even forget how to run the lawnmower. As a result of mowing their lawn constantly, you don't have any energy to mow or take care of your own lawn. They don't help you with your lawn, so you may begin to feel resentment toward them. If this behavior continues, they might get quite comfortable with you doing their part for them because it doesn't require their energy anymore. When you learn about boundaries and begin learning to only mow your own lawn and leave their lawn untouched for a time, they will not like it. They are used to you mowing their lawn and them not doing it. It might be frustrating for them or make them angry, but at the end of the day, their lawn is actually not your responsibility, and now you've realized it.

Good interpersonal boundaries help foster healthy relationships and are critical to our anxiety management efforts. Without healthy emotional boundaries, you may take on too much of someone else's emotional burdens, worsening your own mental health in the process. Without good energetic boundaries, you may find yourself spending a lot of time and energy on relationships that no longer serve you.

It can be helpful to further expand the discussion of boundaries into the different categories of boundaries that you can have. As you read through these different types of boundaries, reflect on your own boundaries and whether they need a tune-up.

Internal versus external boundaries

For ease of understanding, I separate boundaries into those you use to regulate your relationship with yourself and those you use to regulate your relationship with others.

Internal boundaries are imaginary rules that define how you regulate your own behavior, your self-talk, how you control what you worry or think about, and your self-discipline. If you set up a constraint in a habit, you are essentially setting up an internal boundary about that behavior. By using internal boundaries and being diligent to follow them, you can help yourself avoid self-sabotaging behavior, overcome bad habits, and protect your own health and happiness.

External or interpersonal boundaries are boundaries that you use to regulate your relationships with others in your life. There are a variety of different interpersonal boundaries that we will review now.

Types of interpersonal (external) boundaries:

Informational boundaries are essentially rules that dictate who knows what about you and your life. These are often the most intuitive and simple types to understand. Basically, an informational boundary is a limit that you set on what information is shared with whom and in what settings in your life. When you have poor information boundaries, you tend to overshare too much of your life with people who shouldn't be privy to such information. Similarly, poor informational boundaries on your side may invite a lot of oversharing from others who also have weak informational boundaries.

Information boundaries often fluctuate or change depending on setting, group of people, or content of the information. For example, you may be someone who only shares intimate details about your life in the context of your closest relationships and who maintains a tighter and more rigid boundary around personal information with only those closest to you being privy to it. Work colleagues or acquaintances may be outside of that informational boundary and therefore, such intimate details are not shared with them much, if at all. Alternatively, you may also be "an open book" type of person who shares lots of intimate details with anyone with whom you come in contact, and you would be considered to have a very loose or nonexistent informational boundary.

An important thing to note about information boundaries (and all boundaries really) is that simply because a boundary was set in a particular way at one time does not mean it cannot be changed. Boundaries are not set in stone (until you choose them to be). If new developments happen in a relationship, you are completely entitled and *encouraged* to adjust your boundaries as you feel appropriate. For example, someone who originally was allowed a looser informational boundary (i.e., they knew more about your life) and did not respect or protect that information may need a stricter boundary about information sharing. You are in control, you make the boundary, and you can change it how you see fit.

Physical boundaries define who you allow into your physical space or interact with your body. Your physical boundaries should guide others on how you allow yourself to be touched, whether you give a handshake or hug, etc. These are very important boundaries to create and often can be a challenge when women have young children at home who seem to climb all over them all of the time. Creating and communicating healthy physical boundaries can be incredibly helpful if you're often experiencing sensory overload from being constantly touched by children. Physical boundaries also refer to your sexual boundaries—how often you want to have sex, who you have sex with, etc. in the context of your romantic relationships.

Material boundaries define how you manage your own possessions. Your material boundaries may also define whether you lend money, who you lend money to, or who you let borrow your favorite book or shirt.

Energetic boundaries refer not only to the energy that you expend but also the energy you allow to enter into your space. We cannot explore the concept of boundaries without discussing energetic boundaries. It is incredibly empowering when you realize that you are in complete control of where energy flows in your life by establishing energetic boundaries.

When I speak about energy, I'm referring to your physical energy (your actual presence or bodily effort), your emotional energy (what you choose to become emotional about), and your mental energy (thinking about something, problem solving, planning, etc.). It is imperative that we are intentional and responsible managers of all our energies, as we all have limited amounts of energy, and we have the ability to manage energy, meaning that if something feels unaligned with your goals, your mission, your values, or your personal standards, you do not put your energy toward it. Poor energetic boundaries may look like giving away too much of your time or energy than what is right for you.

When I discuss managing the energy coming into your space, I'm referring to the types of people you spend time with or the relationships that you spend energy in. Sometimes when I speak out about energy, women become a bit freaked out and feel like the concept is too esoteric for them. However, many women can acknowledge that certain relationships feel different. For example, when you spend time with someone who is always negative and complaining or never has anything good to talk about, you may often feel like your energy is being drained or that their negative energy is seeping into your space and making you feel down or sad. In contrast, spending time with people who are positive, grateful, and motivated to see the best in every situation can cause you to feel energized, happy, and positive as well. We have the power to curate the energy in our lives by being intentional about who we spend our time and energy with on an ongoing basis. If you feel compelled to leave a situation that feels energetically misaligned or negative to you, honor that instinct. It's okay and safe to do so.

> *Self-Check:*
> Let's reflect on your boundaries.
> 1. Reviewing the different types of boundaries explained, write a list of the boundaries that you feel could need improvement in your life.

> 2. Where in your life are your boundaries (or lack of boundaries) making an impact on your mental health?
> 3. What is preventing you from creating new, more healthy boundaries in your life?

Emotional boundaries are the messiest of interpersonal boundaries and the cause of so much distress and strife in relationships. These boundaries define who is responsible for managing what emotions in a relationship. If you have poor emotional boundaries, you feel responsible for everyone else's emotions, or you may put the responsibility for your emotions onto others and expect them to manage your emotions. You often feel guilty if someone is sad or disappointed, or you may constantly feel like the victim.

Happiness, guilt, shame, anger, and sadness are all emotions that can occur within the context of a relationship. The key is understanding that there is a very clear line of responsibility regarding emotions. A healthy emotional boundary is one in which neither individual feels responsible for managing, "dealing with," or "fixing" the other's emotional experience. It involves having a genuine understanding and acceptance that someone else's emotional experience is not your responsibility.

If you are someone who has loose or nonexistent emotional boundaries, it's likely that you assume it is your responsibility to "mow others' emotional lawns," so to speak. Women lacking emotional boundaries can often feel like "emotional garbage dumps," where everyone dumps their emotional baggage onto you—to deal, feel, and heal. I once had a female patient in my office who was exhausted, emotional, and depleted from the daily calls she would receive between feuding family members. Her daughter and granddaughter were forever at odds, and she was their go-between, the mediator and emotional support for the both of them. She would receive about a dozen calls each day from them, complaining, venting, and dumping their emotional baggage on her throughout the day. This behavior went on for months and months. By the time she came to see me, her mental and physical health were in shambles. She had zero self-confidence, cried at the drop of a hat, and no longer could tell me what she loved or spent time doing that she actually enjoyed. She had no time in her life for her own enjoyment or health-promoting behaviors. Her emotional and cognitive resources were constantly demanded and taken up by this emotional warfare between her family members. She no longer wanted to be a part of it and wished they would simply stop calling her. Her physical health and chronic medical conditions continued to worsen, and she struggled to get out of the house to do the things she loved the most. Exasperated, it was clear she genuinely felt deeply all the pain of her family members along with an obligation to help fix the problem or create reconciliation between these two adults.

The unfortunate reality of this story and of so many stories I hear from women regularly is that trying to fix and solve problems for family members is the opposite of what our family members need, and it's certainly the opposite of what we need for our own mental health. When she finally realized that being their emotional doormat was hurting her and that she lacked a healthy emotional boundary with these family members, we took time together to explore what sort of emotional baggage and information she was going to allow to cross her boundaries in these relationships. We practiced how to assertively and explicitly explain these new boundaries to her family members.

This example is just one of numerous women I see in my office who have poor or nonexistent boundaries and, as a result, incredible anxiety in their life. The truth is that we play a central role in choosing whether we are someone's emotional dumping ground. We are often oblivious to the fact that we have any choice at all about our involvement in this emotional reality TV show. In fact, one patient told me that she couldn't even fathom not answering the calls when they came in. It had never occurred to her that she could simply not answer the phone or choose to direct the conversation away from things that she didn't want to discuss. When we discussed what creating healthier emotional boundaries in her relationships would look like, we came face-to-face with her fear of being shamed or her family members assuming she "didn't love them anymore." She genuinely believed that taking on their emotional baggage daily was how she was helping solve their situation.

If you often feel obligated to do things (like answering phone calls, running errands, etc.) that you don't want to do, I want you to pause. The next time you find yourself feeling this way or that you "don't have a choice," I want you to use it as a red flag to stop and realize it in that moment—you DO have a choice of how to respond or whether you participate in behaviors that do not serve you. It requires a mindset shift to begin to change your behavior, and it might feel terrifying at first, which is why I often recommend setting boundaries with the support of a good therapist.

It takes an awful lot of emotional work to become not only aware of what you're responsible for but ultimately accept what you are not responsible for. Many of us have been raised or taught the perception that we are responsible for more than what we actually are, which is why it requires mindful awareness and work to deprogram these beliefs.

It's normal for boundaries to feel hard or uncomfortable

It's also okay if you don't feel very familiar with the concept of boundary setting. Having healthy boundaries is a learned behavior, something that many of us have not been taught. Many of us have been raised to have very poor personal boundaries that require self-sacrifice for the greater good while drowning out our inner voice. We are taught that by asking or advocating for ourselves, we will inconvenience someone else, jeopardize a relationship, or make someone angry, which brings me to a critical mindset shift that you need to have in order to set healthy boundaries in relationships: Many of us have been raised to disappoint or sacrifice ourselves first rather than risk disappointing someone else. We have been raised or conditioned to believe that the happiness or satisfaction of others is more important than our own. At the root of it, we've been conditioned to believe we are not as worthy as others. By carrying this belief, we continue to allow ourselves to be in relationships that are not healthy—these relationships may be abusive or disrespectful. When we fail to see ourselves as worthy as everyone else, we continue to allow ourselves to be treated poorly in relationships.

Quite often one of the biggest barriers to creating healthy boundaries is the belief that people with boundaries are harsh or unloving. Admittedly, if not done properly and not from a place of love, it can feel that way. It can feel like you are excluding people from your life or being a control freak about what you will allow. However, when done properly, from a place of wanting to maintain a healthy relationship rather than sustain an unhealthy one, boundaries allow relationships to be healthy, free, and spacious. So, although it may seem uncomfortable, I've got you. Let's take it one step at a time.

chapter 27

YOU NEED BETTER BOUNDARIES

So, how can we identify the relationships that are unhealthy or could use better boundaries? There are many different ways to do it. I will walk through some of my own strategies for you so you can apply them to relationships in your life and begin to set better boundaries. There are a few red flag features of relationships that I have identified as those needing better boundaries. I have seen these red flags pop up consistently in relationships, and I could likely be adding to this list long after this book is finished.

Some of the first red flag features are emotions. I have stated before that emotions are helpful messengers and an important part of being human. We need to develop an emotional awareness and strengthen our emotional intelligence so that we can identify our emotions and use them as the tools they are—signals of how to act in certain situations. In the case of interpersonal boundaries, here is a list of some of the red flag emotions that I want you to watch for in your own relationships, as it may signal a need for healthier boundaries.

Resentment

Resentment is a feeling of bitter indignation—a feeling of being treated unfairly. Most often, resentment in personal relationships comes from feeling like you have given something to a relationship and it has not been reciprocated when you felt like it should have been. When we over-give of ourselves to others or take on too much of what is not ours to own, it can happen that the other person doesn't do the same for us. When they don't reciprocate, we often feel resentful toward them. We feel as though the balance in the relationship isn't equal in effort or energy. We feel resentful that the other person doesn't give as much as we give in a relationship. We feel as if that person has taken advantage of us.

The problem here is that we tend to get resentful because others don't give as much as we do, but we fail to realize that how much we give or take on in a relationship is completely our own responsibility. We make the decision. However, when we have poor emotional boundaries, we tend to feel that the other person is taking too much from us and pass the responsibility for our resentment to them. We fail to recognize that we are in control of how much we give, which is a clear sign of a lack of boundaries. If you find yourself feeling resentful toward anyone in your life, check your emotional boundaries with that person.

Now, resentment doesn't always mean you have poor boundaries, as it may have been that you have put in effort that you feel is appropriate and it is not being reciprocated. It may not have been that you overstepped or mowed someone else's lawn, it may be that you have appropriately mowed your own but now feel resentful that the other person is not mowing theirs and making the neighborhood neat like you had agreed. In this case (and you feel that your giving was appropriate), it's time to flex your assertiveness muscles and express yourself. If you don't, the resentment will stick around and make you bitter.

Guilt

Guilt is the feeling that we have done something wrong. If you spend time in a relationship and feel guilty about how another person is feeling, unless you did something actually wrong in that situation, this response is considered inappropriate guilt. Guilt about not mowing someone else's lawn is inappropriate because you were never responsible for their lawn care.

Many women feel guilty about saying no or refusing to help someone with something. You are entitled (and I would hazard to say that it is imperative) to say no to things that are not right for you. The outcome of what transpires after saying no, whether it results in someone being disappointed, sad, or angry, is actually not your responsibility.

I could write many chapters on the experience of guilt for women, as it is one of the most common and most powerful emotions with which my patients struggle. If you struggle with chronic feelings of guilt, one of the first steps is to realize that simply feeling an emotion does not mean it's a valid or appropriate response to the situation. For example, saying no to something that isn't right for you is not doing anything wrong, so any guilt that follows is simply conditioned inappropriate guilt. Feelings are not facts, and not all feelings are accurate or appropriate for the situation you feel them in. Understanding that feeling guilt does not actually mean you have done something bad is the first step to reclaiming control over inappropriate feelings of guilt.

Obligation

Obligation is similar to guilt, meaning that we feel we *must* do something, even though we don't want to. I often tell my clients that if they can identify feeling obligated in a certain relationship, I would closely examine the boundaries in it. In many instances, we feel a sense of obligation when others emotionally manipulate us because we feel that if we don't do something, they will experience a negative emotion or behave in a negative way. Typically, women with no boundaries tend to feel that someone feeling sad or having negative emotions is their responsibility, hence feeling obligated to do whatever is asked of them to avoid the person feeling that negative emotion.

Here are some other common signs of a relationship that needs healthier boundaries:
- It always feels like you are putting in more effort than the other person to maintain the relationship. It feels very one-sided—the benefits are always going to the other person.

- After spending time with that person, you feel drained. You might feel resentful, annoyed, or angry after being with them.
- It feels like you are on edge when you spend time with someone. You feel that if you make a mistake or do something they don't approve of, they will dismiss you or treat you badly. You feel like you have to be "on" all the time and say just the right thing.
- Someone doesn't take no for an answer and continually asks you for something, even though you have clearly stated you are unavailable or unwilling.
- You constantly sacrifice yourself for someone else's emotional wellness. It may look like doing extra work so they are not overwhelmed or doing more than you want to so you don't upset them.
- You feel like you need to help people feel better or are responsible for their emotional experiences or problems.
- You feel guilty if you cannot help someone with something or when you advocate for yourself.

Self-Check:
Reflect now on the relationships in your life.
1. Reflect on the aforementioned list of emotions and characteristics. Do you identify with any of these types of situations or relationships?
2. Who in your life makes you feel guilty, resentful, or uncomfortable when you're around them?

3. What would happen in that relationship if you were to behave in a way that upset that person or if you were not available to them?

Information boundaries

When it comes to information boundaries (basically, who gets to know what about my life), I use a set of rules to make these decisions. I call these rules the Good News Criteria and Bad News Criteria. Both rules help you decide those people in your life you should have close or distant boundaries with, and with whom you can safely share your good and bad news.

First of all, can you think of anyone in your life with whom you hesitate sharing good news? Imagine: You've finally scored your dream job. You've saved enough to buy that new car you've been wanting. You finally meet that goal you've been working toward. You win something or come into some good fortune. Who do you rush to tell? Who do you know will be excited for you?

When we share good news with our loved ones, those of us who have healthy relationships established will most often be met with genuine happiness or pride for our good fortune and success. These people understand that your good fortune does not mean less for them because they see your value and respect your worth. They understand and believe that you are deserving of the good things that happen to you and are genuinely happy for you.

On the other side of the coin is the friend who doesn't seem to feel the same way. There are some "friends" in our lives who, no matter what happens to us, cannot seem to be happy for our good fortune. These friends often respond to hearing about our good news with phrases like "Of course that happened to you," or "Good things always happen for you," or my favorite, "Must be nice!" This person attempts to make your good fortune mean less for you because it makes them feel bad about themselves; it is someone who cannot be genuinely happy for you because there are messy emotional boundaries—they feel that you are responsible in some way for their happiness. They feel that in some way your good fortune reduces their happiness. It's also common that you may feel the need to minimize or shrink your accomplishments because you know that they will feel bad when they hear of them, and because you feel responsible for their happiness (messy emotional boundary), you avoid sharing your good news in all of its glory.

I'm going to tell it to you straight: If you have someone in your life around whom you feel the need to shrink yourself or your accomplishments and good news, you need to set some serious boundaries around this relationship. A healthy relationship is one in which each individual is genuinely happy for the other because they understand that each person is inherently valuable and responsible for their own happiness. When good things happen to you, a healthy relationship is one in which that individual celebrates you and feels excited and happy for you. Identify those people in your life and share your good news with them.

The Good News Criteria defines who gets to know your good news. If the person you are telling cannot handle the news and be genuinely happy for you, they do not meet the criteria. To prevent yourself from being treated negatively or being made to feel bad about your positive events, the boundary you need to create is to simply stop telling this person about your good things. You may initially feel sad about it, which is completely understandable. The truth is, however, that even though we feel we should be able to tell our loved ones about the good things in our lives, some people simply cannot handle that information in a loving and healthy way. If we keep telling them our good news when we know that they cannot handle it, whose fault is it when they repeatedly make us feel bad about it? It's ours. So, we can use the Good News Criteria to guide our behavior in this situation.

To explain this concept, I often use the example of a well. Imagine you have a well on your property, and you frequently go to that well for water. Despite going multiple times, it has never given you any, yet you continue to go to the well even though you feel disappointed each time. Whose fault is it that you are disappointed? Yours or the well's? This example is analogous to a relationship in which you are not provided with the support or feedback that you need. I see this situation often with my patients. They have a person in their life they want a certain type of support from, and despite trying multiple times to get it, that person doesn't seem capable of giving it. The person is the well that doesn't give water. So, whose fault is it if you continue to return to the well, even when you know it doesn't give you water? Perhaps it's time to find someone else (a new well) who can give you the support you need.

The second way to identify relationships that may require stronger boundaries is to use the Bad News Criteria. There are two components to this particular criterion. First of all, can you think of someone in your life who has your back, no matter what? This person likely knows all of your weaknesses, your mess-ups, and the flaws that you're most self-conscious about and still believes in you 100 percent. Can you think of someone who knows something about you that's one of your soft spots, or something that you're not proud of or that makes you uncomfortable? How do they handle this information? Do they protect you if that comes up in conversation? Do they perhaps change the subject? Do they protect and defend you if you're feeling attacked or sensitive? Can you think of someone who, when you share your darkest pains or mistakes, always sees the best in you and encourages you rather than shames you? This relationship is a healthy one with good boundaries.

Now, can you think of someone who instead of protecting your weak spots uses them against you? Someone who exploits your mistakes or pokes fun at your soft spots? Someone who brings up uncomfortable topics in conversation and makes fun of you or jokes about things that they know are sensitive for you? Imagine a friend who knew that you were anxious when talking about your recent job loss and that it was painful for you to discuss it but continued to bring it up in social settings? Can you think of anyone who fits these descriptions? This someone needs a firmer, more distant boundary.

If there is negative or more sensitive information in your life that you are worried someone might use against you or take joy in, this relationship does not meet the Bad News Criteria. Someone who uses your weaknesses or flaws as ammunition against you is not someone who should be privy to your deepest and most sacred parts. Whether it be good things, bad things, successes, or struggles, these are the relationships that need some of the most rigid and distant boundaries.

Think back to the last time something bad happened to you. Perhaps you had a mess-up at work, an argument with your partner, or a setback on a goal. Think of who you'd go to in these situations and how they'd make you feel. Do you feel better or worse? Do you feel supported or belittled? We often have someone in our lives who seems to derive joy from our misery and misfortune. This person breaks the Bad News Rule. This rule helps define who gets to know the "bad news" in your life, who gets to know your mistakes and your insecurities.

You deserve to have people around you who are rooting for you all the time. Choose to surround yourself with people who are safe havens for your information, your insecurities, and your good news. Most of all, be responsible for who you share your information with rather than expecting everyone else to hold it in the right way. If you have identified that someone cannot handle your information properly (they do not meet the Good News or Bad News Criteria), stop sharing it with them. Full stop. Sometimes putting this practice into place is easier said than done, but with effort and support, it is possible and empowering.

The truth is that we often feel that we must share everything with everyone in our lives. We don't. In fact, we would serve ourselves better by being intentional managers of who knows what about our lives.

> **Self-Check:**
> 1. Reflect on the Good News Criteria. Do you have anyone in your life who doesn't meet these criteria?

> 2. Do you ever run to tell someone something positive about your life and leave feeling bad or as if you have to shrink the good news?
> 3. Consider the Bad News Criteria. Who in your life protects your soft and vulnerable spots? Who exploits them or makes fun of them? Who in your life needs firmer information boundaries?

The sad and brutal reality is that many women actually believe that there are relationships in their lives in which they simply cannot speak up. I was once asked in a podcast interview, "Carly, when you speak about putting boundaries in your relationships and being more assertive, what if the person who you need to be more assertive with is a loved one or a family member who you have to see all the time?" She was referencing her mother-in-law, but it could have been her mother, her father, her sibling, or even her spouse. It's the relationships that you feel like you "have to put up with" the behavior because you're bound to these people by blood or marriage that are the hardest ones to set boundaries in and assert yourself. And it makes sense. It's often these relationships that can disrupt the entire dynamic of a family unit, so we often just silence ourselves and continue to comply with the crowd despite not wanting to. We don't want to ruffle feathers, "ruin Christmas," or "make anyone mad."

So, what if the people that drain you *are your family*? What if the people who make you feel "less than" or who won't celebrate your successes are your closest relatives? What if the ones you need to protect your peace from are actually family members? These people are exactly who you need to put boundaries in place for, something I tell women all the time. One reality of boundaries is that they are not as hard to set with people who don't need them the most. I've had many women tell me, "I have no problems setting boundaries in my work relationships, but when it comes to my family, I can't."

This inability to set boundaries in the relationships that need them the most is due to what I refer to as the "Care Factor." Let's first consider work relationships or relationships with acquaintances. In a relationship of this category, you can simply choose to not engage with that person. You don't really care if you have a relationship with them. If you have an annoying colleague, you don't have to talk to them. You can choose to sit elsewhere in the lunchroom, avoid them at meetings, etc., and no one will likely care or even notice. It's easy to set boundaries in that relationship because it's not important in your life. You don't have an emotional attachment to having a relationship with that person. You don't really care all that much that they don't like you or that you aren't friends with them. The Care Factor is pretty low.

In a friendship relationship, depending on how long or deep that relationship has been going on, the Care Factor varies. It's likely that if someone you just met treated you in an crappy way, you'd just not spend time with them anymore. You would likely consider that person a jerk, cut ties, and move on. In a relationship between two friends, you can just choose to not be friends with someone who treats you poorly (although it depends on how long you have been friends, obviously). There are no blood or marital ties forcing you to be friends with anyone, so it's usually easier to set boundaries and limits around that relationship. You may choose to limit the time you spend with that person, or you may choose to not be friends with them at all. In a deeper, long-lasting friendship, there tends to be a bigger emotional investment. The Care Factor is higher, and thus, putting boundaries into this relationship may be more challenging (depending on the relationship). The longer and more invested you are in the relationship, the deeper the behavioral patterns and interpersonal routines have been established in that relationship. If you are in a friendship with someone who tends to behave in a passive-aggressive or narcissistic way, and you've developed into the passive partner, it will almost certainly be harder to put in a boundary or be more assertive.

When it comes to family members, however, we (women especially) typically place a heavy emotional investment in maintaining the relationship. Whether it be our parents, our siblings, or our in-laws, we feel as though we "must" maintain the relationship. We also care a lot about these relationships—whether they support us and what they think about us. The Care Factor is high. If this relationship became threatened, we would feel sadness and despair. Due to our dependence on the relationship and our fear of conflict within it, we often feel like we can't speak up or voice our own opinions if contrary to others, as it can cause conflict and threaten the relationship.

I hate to say this to you, but I'm going to call BULLSHIT on this thinking.

This way of thinking is exactly what passivity is: believing that because we are legally or blood-bound to another individual and because that individual is close to us so we merely HAVE to put up with behavior that is unhealthy or negative. Stop it, ladies.

Nobody has the right to manipulate or demean you—no matter if they are your mother, your sister, or your spouse. I know the mere thought of putting boundaries in those relationships makes your stomach do flips, and if you're feeling those flips—the time is now. That person you're thinking about and feeling as if you could never establish a boundary with is EXACTLY who we are talking about right now. We have been taught that we should merely accept the poor treatment or disrespect that we are given from family members "because they are family." Wrong. No matter what role someone plays or place they hold in your life, they do not have the right or permission to treat you in ways that make you feel bad, demeaned, guilty, ashamed, or obligated. They do not have the right to take your personal power away.

The reality is that it takes a lot of bravery and strength to be assertive and to put boundaries in place with family members. What keeps most of us silent rather than assertive is the fear of conflict, making others angry, or creating tension within our family units. What will Thanksgiving look like if you speak up? What will this holiday or that gathering be like if you assert yourself? It would be superhuman to not fear these consequences of assertiveness. It's only natural to fear these things.

> ***Self-Check:***
> Here are a few questions to ask yourself when you are deciding how you want to participate in a relationship with a toxic family member.
> 1. If this person were a stranger, would I spend time with them?

2. What would I advise my best friend to do if someone spoke to them this way?
3. Would I behave differently around this person if I didn't believe that I had to have a relationship with them?

chapter 28

AN UNHEALTHY RELATIONSHIP IS NOT A RELATIONSHIP YOU NEED

Relationships are precarious. When they're great, they can bring us so much joy, but when they're not, they can bring misery. And sometimes the mere thought of dealing with them can cause anxiety.

> "But it's my mother, I can't cut her out of my life."
> "It's my sister, I should have a relationship with her."
> "I need to have a relationship with them."
> "I will feel so bad if I don't have a relationship with him."

If you resonate with these statements and they bring to mind a relationship that you are currently participating in that feels negative or needs better boundaries, I want you to ask yourself a few very important questions:

- If someone is treating you badly and making you feel ashamed/coerced/guilty for the majority of the relationship, is that a relationship that you want to continue?
- If every single time you are with someone you leave the interaction feeling negative or drained, do you want to continue spending time with them?
- What do you gain from remaining in this relationship? Really, what are you getting out of it that is good and fulfilling?
- How do you feel when you think about this person? Do you dread spending time with them? Why do you continue to spend time with them?

Now, let me be clear: I am not advocating for you to cut every single person out of your life who has ever been mean or negative. I am asking you to evaluate your relationships critically. I'm asking you to consider if you ever feel good in that person's energy or if you are often wondering why you make the effort to spend time with them at all.

So many of us fear losing the relationships in our lives that are the most toxic, when perhaps that is exactly what we need. In some cases, we may cut ties and go our separate ways. We need to let that relationship die so we can start to build a new one that is healthier. It doesn't mean we can't ever have another relationship with that person but that the current one is not healthy and should cease to exist. We need to start stepping into our personal power and defining what relationships we actually want to have in our lives and stop allowing the relationships that are not healthy for us.

In my work with women, it never ceases to astound me the degree of emotional coercion and manipulation that they allow to exist in their lives. Sometimes the coercion is so subtle that they don't even recognize it as such, and therefore, an enlightening chat with a therapist or best friend or coach can be incredibly helpful. Women will allow their in-laws to say terrible things to them, to disregard their requests, or to go behind their backs without even a word or complaint. They will bend over backward to accommodate the wishes of a friend or sister who threatens, coerces, or manipulates them into doing things they don't want. They will allow their partners to mistreat them or not help out around the house because they believe that "it's just the way they were raised." This behavior has got to stop. Yes, we may have been conditioned to be silent and to let ourselves be disrespected or emotionally manipulated because we lived in a household where our mothers catered to the whim of every friend and family member who asked. That buck stops here, with us. With you. With me. It may be how it has always been but that does not mean it is how it must continue.

But, Carly, what if they get mad at me? Here's the truth: When you start setting boundaries in place in your close relationships, especially in the ones that need it most, they will not like it. We train people how to treat us, and failing to set healthy emotional boundaries allows others to take advantage of our time, energy, and emotions. It's almost a certainty that they will be angry or try to shame you more into silence and passivity.

I read an anonymous quote once that said, "The only people who get upset when you set boundaries are the ones who benefited from you having none." And it is so true. When we adopt a more assertive mindset and speak up for ourselves, the people with whom we've behaved passively will not appreciate it. Unfortunately, people are most comfortable when others in their lives are predictable, and many of your family members or friends are likely very comfortable with you being passive and submitting to their demands. When you begin to assert yourself more often and set boundaries in your relationships, you have to expect there to be a backlash. And I'm telling you: THAT IS TOTALLY FINE.

Here are a few things to be aware of when you begin setting boundaries in your life:

People won't like it.
- We can't expect to set boundaries and have people just agree with them; we must be prepared for some pushback. People are used to having a certain amount of freedom. Whenever you set a personal boundary, others will usually struggle against it. The important thing to realize in this situation is that because others are getting angry or unhappy does NOT mean you're doing something wrong.

Your boundaries won't be followed right away.
- Your boundaries might not be followed right away. It's human nature to challenge boundaries. I think of it like when you get on a roller coaster and the chest piece and bars come down over you—what do you do? Every single person pushes

back on the support to make sure that it will hold them in. We test it, which is exactly what will happen when you begin to set boundaries.

- For example, perhaps you have a child who insists on staying up watching television after their bedtime. You become assertive and tell them, "If you're not in bed by your bedtime, I will turn off the television and you will not be able to watch TV tomorrow." At first your child may not believe you and may respond with outrage if you follow through on your promise. If you are able to keep to this new plan, they will eventually adapt to the new rule and abide by it.

People will think you are mad at them or something is wrong with you.

- Sometimes when passive people begin to set boundaries, those around them may think that they're angry with them. It is key, therefore, to set your boundaries in a clear and assertive way. I like to explain to someone that I am implementing a new boundary and why. Sometimes these conversations get heated, and that's okay. You are not responsible for reassuring someone that you're not angry or for helping them navigate their reaction to your boundary setting.

You will feel the need to overexplain yourself.

- If you find yourself scrambling to explain why you're setting a boundary, pause. We often feel that if we give the other person enough information about why the boundary is being placed, they will understand, and their feelings won't be hurt.

This overexplaining is simply a passive way to avoid conflict. It's fine to provide some simple information around your boundary, but realize that explanation is a courtesy, not a requirement. Try to be aware of why you feel compelled to explain yourself.

- When we constantly explain ourselves, it may seem to the other person that we are not very confident in what we are stating, or that with some negotiation, they can change our minds. Be confident in your boundary setting and come prepared with how much you plan to explain. Know that at the end of the day, "no" is a complete sentence. You are entitled to healthy boundaries and do not need to validate or explain yourself.

Here are some guidelines about creating boundaries in your life that can help you handle the backlash:

1. Expect that people won't like it. If you can expect some backlash, you can be more emotionally and strategically prepared.
2. Understand that someone reacting negatively to you setting boundaries does not mean you're doing the wrong thing. In fact, their reaction to your boundary setting reinforces that you are doing the exact correct thing in that relationship.
3. Don't try to set boundaries with every single person in your life at one time. Start small with a relationship that is not the worst one; strengthen your skills there first.
4. When you set a boundary, hold it like your life depends on it. Wishy-washy boundaries are not good for anyone. For a

boundary to be effective, it needs to be firm, clear, and fixed.
5. Therefore, only set boundaries you know you can uphold 100 percent. If you go back on your boundary setting and behave in a passive way even one time, you provide the other person an opportunity to manipulate you out of creating the boundary.
6. Don't decide to set boundaries when you are emotionally activated and compromised. You need to be in an emotionally neutral space to make clear decisions about what boundaries you want to create and how you want to create them.

Self-Check:
Let's talk about your boundaries.
1. What is one relationship in your life that is the most important for setting healthy boundaries right now?
2. What about that person or relationship feels icky to you?
3. What would a boundary look like in that relationship?
4. Where can you go to for support if this person reacts negatively to your boundary setting? Who can you rehearse boundary setting with?

How to set healthy boundaries [a script]

Anxiety and our own emotions are often the biggest obstacles to our setting clear and healthy boundaries. More often than not, women feel embarrassed about crying or becoming emotional when they set boundaries. This emotional reaction may happen when you first start this practice, but I promise you that if you're diligent with your practice and learn to work through the fear, boundary setting will become easier and easier. Before you know it, you will be setting boundaries like the badass you are and won't give a second thought about it.

However, many women I work with struggle to find the right words when setting boundaries, and then when the emotions start to overwhelm them, they panic and abort the boundary-setting mission. The strategy I recommend in this situation is to become as prepared as possible and even to rehearse what you will say with someone you trust ahead of time. I do this script work quite often with my patients and clients.

To get the juices flowing and help you think up some ways to set assertive boundaries in the relationships in your life, I've provided a few scripts for you to consider. Feel free to use my sample scripts word for word if you need to in the beginning. It doesn't matter if you have rehearsed what you will say 100 times before saying it. The important thing is that you no longer allow toxic relationships to go on without setting some healthy boundaries for the sake of your own mental health.

I will use an example to illustrate this practice. Let's imagine that your mother-in-law, without fail, brings up your weight or how much food is on your plate at family meals. Her comments make you feel insecure, embarrassed, and anxious. You don't even want to go to meals with her, but she insists on family dinner every Sunday, so you've been going and keeping your mouth shut because you don't want to "ruffle her feathers" and make dinner awkward.

However, you have decided enough is enough. After reading this book and realizing the importance of boundaries, you decide this relationship is one in which you would like to set one.

First things first: Let's get prepared. It's likely the mere thought of addressing this issue with your mother-in-law is making you sweat. It's okay and is totally understandable. Your initial attempts at boundary setting are very uncomfortable, but it doesn't mean it is wrong. It simply means you are challenging your anxiety and stepping out of your comfort zone.

To get prepared for this conversation, you might rehearse something like the following:

> "I wanted to talk to you about your tendency to make comments about my weight and how much I'm eating at meals. They make me feel very uncomfortable, and I am now asking that you stop making those comments. I like spending time with you at family dinner, but those comments make me not want to come. In fact, I'm creating a boundary around discussing my weight and my food, in general. I hope you can respect this boundary."

This script likely feels very uncomfortable to you at this moment. You are likely thinking to yourself, *I could never say that.* Again, like all anxiety triggers, the more often we expose ourselves to them, the more often we face them and survive it, the less they will trigger us. Take some time to read over the script a few times and consider how you could make it work in your own situation.

There are a few things about this script I want to draw your attention to:

- It prepares the other person for what is to come: "I want to talk to you about . . ."
- It clearly addresses the problem behavior: "your tendency to make comments about . . ."
- It finds common ground: "I like spending time with you, but . . ."
- It asserts a boundary: "I am now asking that you stop making those comments."
- It uses the word "boundary": "I'm creating a boundary around . . ."
- It expresses an expectation: "I hope that you can respect this boundary."

In some relationships, it may be necessary to assertively state the consequence if the boundary is violated. It is not required in all situations and depends on the relationship. If you have tried to set a certain boundary with someone already in the past, I would likely add on a statement that expresses what will happen if they fail to comply with the boundary you have set:

> "If you cannot honor the boundary I have set in asking you to not make comments about my weight when we come for family dinner, I won't be attending anymore."

The important thing about expressing the consequence of someone not honoring your boundary is to ensure that the consequence is something you will be able to actually do. It will not do much good if you state a consequence and then not actually follow through if the boundary is violated. Your inability to follow through will simply demonstrate that your boundary was not as important as you said it was, and it will teach the other person that your boundaries are things that can be crossed without any fear of consequences.

Remember that you are setting these boundaries from a place of love and wanting to preserve the relationship. You are not setting boundaries to be nasty or mean. You are setting them because you have identified that this relationship is detrimental to your anxiety, your mental health, and happiness. It's important to find a good balance between kindness and firmness when setting boundaries. If you state them too kindly or gently, people will not take you seriously. If you are rude and harsh, or say them out of anger or in the heat of an argument, you will not communicate them in a clear and loving way.

part 4

SELF-CARE IS MENTAL HEALTH CARE

Now, before you skip over this section because you feel as though you know enough about self-care and don't want to hear another lecture, don't. Trust me, you need to read this section and think twice about neglecting your self-care any longer. There is no way around the fact that without some regular attention paid to your mental health and your self-care, your anxiety will not get better. In fact, if you continue to ignore what's going on in your mind and act like everything is fine, your anxiety and overall mood will likely get worse.

Now, if your self-care game is already on point, I still think this section is important because you likely have never considered your self-care from the perspective of managing your anxiety or stepping back into your personal power. I have helped hundreds of women get their anxiety under control, and I believe to my depths that a solid intentional ritual for self-care is one of the most important strategies that helps them. **It is truly incredible what happens to our mental health when we begin to care for it like it is important.** In fact, it is truly unbelievable how much more of our personal power we can harness and step into when we dedicate time each day to realigning with it.

chapter 29

SELF-CARE IS NOT MASSAGES AND BUBBLE BATHS

I have often read criticisms of self-care in popular and social media, claiming that self-care is a superficial bandage and not what anxious and overwhelmed women really need. I'll admit that I both agree and disagree with this statement. As our evolution goes on and women become more and more involved in activities and jobs outside of what has been considered traditional for our gender, there have been staggering increases in the level of overwhelm, exhaustion, and anxiety among women. We are being expected to do it all, be it all, and have it all. From a beautiful, well-adjusted family and a spotless and flawlessly decorated home to a fit and healthy body, perfect relationship, and successful career, the expectations that society places on women (and that women place on themselves) are unending. We have taken on more responsibilities without shedding many of the older ones, and women still do more housework and childcare than men do, even if they continue to work outside of the home. Women are chronically exhausted and burned out, and it's easy to understand why.

And because of this draining existence, self-help gurus, coaches, and personal development experts alike are espousing the benefits of "self-care" (sheepishly raises hand). Being that I have been one of these mothers, burned out and resentful at the never-ending pile of expectations on me, someone suggesting I spend a "little time on myself" does seem like a slap in the face. I believe to scratch the surface of this burnout epidemic among women, we don't need to spend more time on ourselves, we need more support. We need more devaluing of perfectionism and productivity in society and more emphasis on women's wellness. Instead of women feeling as though they need to be it all and do it all, they need to hear that they need to rest more often. They need to hear that time for themselves is the most important way to spend their time. They need societal structures and systems that allow them to take the time off they need without fear of loss of income and stability. They need longer, more financially and emotionally supported leaves from work for childbearing and parenting. They need asking for help to be normalized and seen as a sign of strength rather than weakness. Women need to hear that the most sacred and productive thing a woman can do in our society is to look inward, take care of, and heal herself first. Society has a long way to go to help mothers, and self-care can, at times, seem like a very easy and superficial cop-out to the problem of widespread burnout.

Now, while I do believe all of that, I also believe that we have a role to play in helping ourselves. We are not merely victims of a society prioritizing perfectionism and productivity, selflessness, and the mother-martyr paradigm. Let's not throw the whole self-care baby out with the bathwater. There is another piece to this self-care puzzle when it comes to why self-care in itself is not a "fix" for anxiety and overwhelm. We have also let ourselves slip to the bottom of the to-do list, and I believe it's due to a pervasive disease among women: lack of self-worth.

First, let's get some definitions out of the way so we're all on the same page. In my opinion, self-care is not massages, manicures, and long luxurious bubble baths with wine and candles. These activities create a superficial and bastardized version of what I believe self-care really is and the way I describe it to my clients and patients. In fact, the term "self-care" is so overused and over-suggested these days that I have even gone so far as to consider using a different word to describe the concept, as women often either don't have a clue what I'm talking about, or they shut me down entirely when I bring it up as they assume they have no time for self-care. To be honest, the way that self-care is portrayed in society, we actually don't have time for self-care that looks *like that*. If a woman in a hair wrap with cucumbers on her eyes and relaxing in a soothing bubble bath is how you think of self-care, that is not at all what I'm referring to as self-care.

In fact, I would hazard to say that this sort of imagery and messaging about self-care is not only unrealistic and unhelpful to women today, but it can also be quite damaging to the already frail self-esteem and sense of competency that women have as well. I honestly can't remember the last time I had time for a bubble bath and candles, but

I can tell you that every single morning I meditate and journal. I may not take long shopping and coffee dates with girlfriends often, but I exercise regularly for both my physical and mental health. While the former activities are certainly lovely and nice to have, they are not really what I define as self-care. Not only that, expecting mothers to be able to leisurely engage in activities like that regularly is unrealistic and damaging. In fact, it might be fair to say that by recommending this type of "self-care" to women, we only set them up for failure and shame as they work to achieve yet another unrealistic ideal of what a "good" woman or mother does. If you're not doing these things and are feeling like a failure at your self-care, I'm here to assure you that you can stop. We don't need more massages and bubble baths, we need to cultivate a genuine belief of our worth and validity. Self-care is less about what you do and more about what you believe.

Now, I cannot talk about self-care activities and creating a self-care routine without discussing buffering activities. As a rule, human beings have a very low tolerance for distress and discomfort. We don't like feeling uncomfortable, and we automatically (and usually subconsciously) seek and engage in behaviors that serve to reduce that distress. Remember, our anxiety's sole mission is to keep us alive while avoiding discomfort and pain. This knowledge alone helps explain so much about human behavior and why we develop patterns of negative, self-harming behaviors. In my experience, nearly any negative behavior that someone engages in is a means to reducing discomfort of some sort. The human brain is incredibly adept at creating habits and behavior loops, so if a behavior is effective at mitigating or reducing discomfort in the moment, it quickly becomes strongly reinforced. The longer and more often that behavior is relied on to mitigate the distress, the stronger and more automatic the behavioral loop becomes. This simplistic definition is one reason why many of us have a hard time breaking habits such as smoking cigarettes or eating sweets. It also explains why we develop incredible anxiety or behave in chronically passive ways.

I refer to these behaviors that we engage in and that help us reduce discomfort in the moment as buffering activities. Developing an awareness of the activities that you tend to buffer with is an enlightening and powerful step in your anxiety management journey. Your buffering activities and tendency to lean on them will be an additional helpful sort of intel in understanding your anxiety.

Buffering, by definition, is any behavior that we engage in so that we don't have to feel our emotions or get lost in stories. Typically, any behavior that reduces our experience of pain, distress, or discomfort will be reinforced, whether it's a positive healthy behavior or a negative one. How often we engage in buffering activities will fluctuate, and more often they will increase in response to stress or anxiety. It's important to note that the majority of buffering behaviors are not inherently "bad" habits or behaviors. When done in moderation and with intention, there is absolutely nothing wrong with binge-watching Netflix or eating ice cream. It's when these behaviors become our coping strategies and the way that we numb ourselves to avoid feeling painful internal experiences that they become maladaptive. Therefore, to discriminate between normal behaviors and buffering activities, it can be helpful to think of them as the "over" behaviors: overeating, overdrinking, oversleeping, over-scrolling, over-shopping, over-Netflixing, etc.

> *Self-Check:*
>
> Before we go on, I encourage you to take some time to reflect on your own behavior. I've provided some questions to help you identify what behaviors you rely on when you're buffering.
>
> - When you find yourself in discomfort, whether it be sadness, anger, or resentment, what behaviors do you engage in?
> - Do you numb out with video games or binge-watch TV?
> - Do you eat when you're feeling emotional or hurt?
> - Do you spend mindless hours on social media, scrolling and forgetting your own life?
> - What do you feel you "need" when things are getting stressful? Do you reach for the bottle of wine or grab a bag of chips or box of cookies?
> - Do you find yourself stress-shopping online in the evenings after a stressful day or napping more often to "get away from everything"?

Realistically, it may take some time and self-reflection to really identify what behaviors you use to mitigate your own distress, as many of them are automatic and subconscious behaviors. When I have worked with women in coaching, many of them are shocked to realize how many buffering activities they've been relying on to numb their emotions and help themselves cope. Admittedly, it was months before I made the connection between my anxiety and finding myself locked in the pantry eating chocolate chips out of the jar.

The sugary rush of the chips was enough to temporarily reduce my distress in the moment, and before I knew it, almost anytime I felt anxiety or increased stress, there I was again with my hand in the jar.

Not all buffering behaviors are obvious. While many of the most common buffering activities are overt external behaviors such as those mentioned above, some of them are subtler internal patterns. Self-sabotage, chronic indecisiveness, and passive behavior are all forms of buffering activities.

An important point to make about identifying your buffering habits is not to use them against yourself or as fuel for more negative self-talk or shame. The idea is that if you can develop an awareness of all the activities you use to buffer your own emotions, all the negative habits you fall into when you're feeling uncomfortable, you can use them as clues and triggers for action. As in all aspects of this anxiety management journey, it is critical that we take the objective observer approach to monitoring and tracking our buffering activities. Rather than shame and guilt, it's important to view these behaviors with curiosity and compassion. It serves no one to blame yourself for using the coping strategies that have become habitual over years and years of using them. Buffering activities are often automatic, reactive responses to stressful moments or painful emotions.

The reality is that it takes a lot of effort and motivation to engage in self-care intentionally in those moments when you really want to buffer. When you've had a long day and your kids are tired and you're feeling exhausted trying to get dinner ready, having a glass or two of wine feels like a really good idea. It's times like this that it's critical to become aware of your emotional experience and your urge to buffer. A mindfulness practice is so important in these instances so that you can become an objective observer of your experience and work to be more intentional about your response to the situation. If you can be more aware and intentional in those moments (rather than try to numb yourself from your experience), perhaps you can see the experience as a sign to change something in your life to allow more time, more space, or more calmness in your day.

To be honest, many women I work with lean on buffering activities and call them self-care. Whether it's genuine confusion or simply not wanting to do self-care when a glass of wine is quicker and easier, we do cheat ourselves when we call something self-care that isn't. If you are genuinely not sure if a behavior is self-care or buffering, I would encourage you to examine the intention behind the behavior as well as the outcome. Recall that the definition of self-care activity is that the intention behind the behavior is to improve or enhance your well-being. The next time you're wondering if an activity counts as self-care, ask yourself, "Why am I engaging in this task?" Consider whether it's an automatic reaction to the situation you're in or a task that you've chosen to engage in because it makes you feel genuinely positive, healthier, or more at peace.

A final note about buffering behaviors: I am not saying it isn't nice to have a glass of wine every now and then or to binge-watch a cheesy show on a rainy Sunday afternoon. However, there is a difference between the results of meditation and the impact of drinking a few glasses of wine. There is a difference between regular exercise and checking out for thirty minutes on your phone to "get some alone time." There is a difference between doing a gratitude practice and scrolling mindlessly on social media. I would hazard a guess that you know there is a difference too. Activities designed to numb our feelings or shut us off from the world are not health-promoting ones, and the intention is not typically for the preservation or enhancement of our health. When was the last time you grabbed that bottle of wine for your health? Your sanity in the moment perhaps, but how many times have you felt worse after it?

When we engage in buffering activities and call them self-care, we cut ourselves short and miss out on the genuine benefits of true self-care. These activities can also take up a lot of valuable time, a resource that many women already find is in short supply. If you spend three hours a night watching TV to forget about your day, you're spending twenty-one hours each week on something that is neither a health-promoting activity nor a productive one. Imagine what you could do in those hours. Could you read a personal development book? Could you spend even seventy minutes of those twenty-one hours practicing meditation for ten minutes a day to calm your active mind? Even drinking that glass of wine is a time-suck, as I consider myself pretty useless after a glass of wine. I often feel tired and go to bed with a headache, only to wake up late the next day feeling foggy and sluggish. It's clear how these activities are not self-care, but many women continue to call it their "self-care time" and buffer their emotions away.

I also think the issue of self-care runs so much deeper than not having the time or desire to do it. When I think about self-care and why so many women avoid it, I feel as though that avoidance of it or failure to prioritize it actually comes from a pervasive lack of women believing themselves as inherently valuable. It's a lack of belief in our worthiness and wholeness that prevents us from making a point to care for ourselves and realign with our power. In my opinion, to authentically prioritize and intentionally commit to mindfully taking care of your body and mind every single day, you must have a strong belief in your own value and self-worth. Yet how many of us were raised to believe that women are caregivers first? How often do you feel as though someone else's needs are more important than your own? Where has that belief come from? Have you been conditioned to believe that you are not worthy of taking time for yourself?

If you do not believe you are valid and important as a human being and equal in importance to others around you, no number of massages or pedicures will change that. Whether resulting from our strict upbringing, self-defeating perfectionism, or even an abusive relationship that has stripped us of our belief in our own value, women today think far too little of themselves. This damaging narrative comes from a different place for all of us, and each story is worthy of being heard, acknowledged, and healed. After we become mothers, we then learn that being a "good mother" means being self-sacrificing and caring for everyone else before ourselves, which only further serves to reinforce our beliefs of our unimportance and unworthiness. As all behavior and habit follow from underlying beliefs, we begin to live our lives in congruence with these beliefs and treat ourselves as unimportant. Before we know it, we're last on our to-do list (if we're even on it at all) and are more anxious, depressed, unhealthy, and overwhelmed than ever. Our negative self-talk and beliefs about our unimportance only serve to reinforce our habits of putting others before ourselves, our silence when we are mistreated, and our feelings of being victims to a life we should love.

The truth is that self-care is as much of a belief in your own value as it is the behaviors in which you engage. In fact, without a strong belief in your validity and worthiness, it won't matter what activities you do and slap them with a label of self-care. Instead of doing self-care "because you are supposed to," I encourage you to look inward at the beliefs you have about your own worthiness and value. We should not be engaging in "self-care" activities from a place of expectation from society (or even because I recommend you to), but rather from a place of ourselves being worthy and important, and that conscious and intentional care of the being we inhabit is so vitally important.

In order to genuinely do self-care in the way that heals and helps in the way it's intended, we need to work on our deep beliefs about ourselves. Put simply, **self-care is both a mindset of self-worth and a pattern of behavior that is congruent with and supports that belief.** When you genuinely believe that your worth as a human is equal to that of any other human, you put your own needs on the same level of importance as everyone else. When I use the word self-care with clients and patients, I use it intentionally to encourage women to examine the narrative they carry around their self-worth and value. Most often I am met with blank stares when I ask the pointed question, "What does your self-care look like right now?"

If doing self-care is painful for you, if it's difficult to find the time or if you become plagued with guilt after caring for yourself, your beliefs about your own inherent value are either nonexistent or in desperate need of repair. I use it intentionally to encourage awareness of our deep beliefs about ourselves and how worthy we are. Explaining it in this way, I encourage them to acknowledge themselves as valuable and important, to heal old wounds that taught them otherwise, and to cultivate a deep, genuine belief of their worthiness. As this practice is so counter to what so many women naturally feel, it can make many feel deeply uncomfortable. As they have become accustomed to the beliefs they carry of themselves being of little importance, working to shift these beliefs about themselves often comes with an intense flooding of guilt, shame, and anxiety. Taking the time to heal these wounds and to redesign and foster new beliefs about our self-worth is the embodiment of self-care.

When we believe we are truly worthy, taking care of ourselves naturally becomes a priority. When we believe something is truly important and valuable, we care for it. Many mothers have no difficulty viewing their children or spouses as valid and deserving of care, compassion, and protection, and they easily find themselves doing these things on autopilot. These activities feel aligned with their beliefs and follow naturally from the belief. Similar to how mothers are naturally protective of their children's well-being, as we shift our internal beliefs of ourselves being truly worthy, we become equally as protective of our own. We begin to embody the belief that we are critical in the ecosystem of our family and that the regular maintenance of ourselves is vital to the balance and harmony of that unit. And when we begin to believe it to the depth of our soul, the natural translation of that is a drive to honor ourselves with intentional and meaningful self-care practices. Just as aligning with your spiritual and religious beliefs brings forth the urge to pray, cultivating the mindset of self-care (I am worthy of care) and believing it to the deepest part of your being naturally translates into a desire to act on this belief structure.

When you believe your mental health is important and valuable, you prioritize activities and practices that preserve or enhance it, such as journaling, meditation, and silence. When you believe your spiritual health is critical to your well-being, you naturally incorporate time for prayer and alignment with your chosen Source. When you believe your physical health is a gift, you view it as more important than housework or chores, and you intentionally care for your body with the reverence and honor it deserves to keep it healthy and functioning well. When you genuinely believe you are worthy of joy, you make it an intentional practice to seek more of it and create it. When you view your emotional health and wellness as sacred, you understand the importance of healthy limits and assertive communication, and you work to maintain relationships that nurture you rather than make you feel resentful, guilty, or ashamed. Self-care means that you understand your health and mental health are a priority and take intentional action each day to preserve and enhance them.

When we begin to put ourselves first from a place of deep belief of our worthiness, an incredible transformation begins. Intentional time taken each day for your own self is no longer viewed as a chore or something to feel guilty about but rather something that is vital to your survival, your well-being, and the survival and well-being of your family. The positive feelings that come from prioritizing yourself serve to strengthen the budding beliefs in yourself of being worthy and valid, and so begins a cycle of reinforcing beliefs and behaviors. We harness the power of the behavior loop and the magic of compounding habits.

With purposeful time set aside for yourself, your healing takes priority, and you begin to look deep inside for those parts of you that remain dormant or unexpressed. They are given light and love, brought into the world, and before you know it, you're a fuller version of yourself, feeling empowered and abundant in your role as mother, woman, and human. Those dreams once buried under the burdens of expectation and conditioning are given room to breathe and space to grow. The habits you have cultivated become a lifestyle, and you become the walking embodiment of self-care. It is this metamorphosis from burden to open and free that awaits all of us when we can work to face the beliefs about ourselves that keep us from taking the care of ourselves that we truly need to thrive. So, when you see a social media post claiming mothers need more than self-care, consider it from this place. Self-care is not simply the behavior you engage in; it's the thoughts, intentions, and belief from which those behaviors come that matters.

> *Self-Check:*
> What does your self-care look like right now? Let's take some time now to reflect on your own beliefs and feelings toward yourself and how you take care of yourself. It is important that you reflect on these questions honestly, no matter how painful it might be for you to realize your feelings.
> 1. What does my self-care look like right now? (It's okay if it doesn't look like much right now.)
> 2. What does self-care mean to me?
> 3. What do I do every single day to take care of myself?
> 4. If I don't do anything, what keeps me from doing it?
> 5. Do I genuinely believe that my worth is equal to those around me? If not, why not? What experiences in my life have led me to feel less worthy than others? What do I gain from continuing to carry those beliefs?

6. Am I willing to adopt new beliefs around my self-worth and the value of my self-care?

chapter 30

BEHAVIORAL ACTIVATION: SOMETIMES YOU HAVE TO FAKE IT TO MAKE IT

If you are like many women and have identified that you don't believe you are genuinely as worthy or valuable as others around you, take a breath. Many women before you and around you likely feel the same way. In fact, I believe a lack of belief in our own self-worth is a pervasive disease among modern-day women. It's important for you to realize that you are not broken because you have this belief but rather that you've been subjected to years of society's conditioning to teach and instill this belief in you. Identifying this belief is the first step to changing it. As in all things, awareness is the first step.

It's okay if you do not yet carry the belief that you are worthy of self-care. The good news is that behavioral habits are easier to create than beliefs are to change, and we can lean on the theories of cognitive behavioral therapy (CBT) to help us. Recall that the CBT triangle states that our thoughts/beliefs, behavior, and feelings all influence one another. While traditional CBT focuses on addressing flawed thoughts that are causing distressing emotions and behaviors, we can also harness the triangle in a different way. This concept, referred to as behavioral activation, is what I think of as "hijacking" the mind. Basically, if your thoughts influence how you feel and act, the reverse is also true. How you behave and the activities you engage in also have an impact on how you feel and what you think.

Let's take a day when you're in a crappy mood, for example. When you are in a low-mood/emotional state, these feelings are typically the product of negative thoughts and beliefs. On these days, it's common that your behavior reflects your emotional state: you might lie around all day, be unproductive, or find yourself engaging in buffering activities to help ease your distress. You feel depressed and become inactive, which only strengthens and furthers your low mood. How you feel affects how you act; it's a reinforcing cycle.

When it comes to self-care and the underlying beliefs around your worth and value, being deserving of self-care and feeling good about yourself, sometimes the behavior has to come first so we can birth and nurture the positive beliefs around our self-worth and validity. While it initially takes considerable effort to do something you don't feel like doing, when you are engaging in self-care behaviors that feel good to you and cause you to have positive emotions and thoughts about yourself, the cycle becomes reinforcing. It's this premise that I often use to explain to women that waiting until you "feel like" doing something is actually a bad idea. How many times have you known that doing something would be good for you (exercising, for example), but you didn't do it because you just didn't feel like it? Further to that, how many times have you sucked it up and did it anyway and then felt much better afterward? You went for a run, did a yoga DVD, or just got out for a walk in the sunshine and then your mood was noticeably better? This phenomenon is behavioral activation in action. By engaging in a positive, mood-enhancing behavior, even when we don't want to (or I'd hazard to say, exactly when we don't feel like doing it), we directly improve the way we're feeling.

The reason this premise can be easier than trying to first improve our thoughts about self-worth and value is because we have more control over our own behavior than we do over our thoughts and emotions, especially early in the process of anxiety recovery. When we are anxious and overwhelmed, our low-vibe emotions do not directly encourage positive self-care behaviors, so sometimes we have to simply force ourselves to engage in those behaviors and trust that the positive, self-affirming emotions and thoughts will follow.

I've often referred to this idea as "parenting your own mind," as it reminds me of how a parent enforces a rule or behavior on a child because it "will be good for them," even though the child doesn't want to do it. In this scenario, you are the parent and your mind is the child. Your mind is telling you that you absolutely do not want to do self-care (and likely is very creative about finding reasons why it won't work), but the objective "you" also knows deep down that it will be good for you. We need to think about starting our self-care routine in this way initially: I don't want to do it, I don't feel like doing it, but I know it's good for me so I will do it anyway. While your self-care may feel like a chore at first, it won't feel that way for long. I often encourage women to take even a mere ten minutes each day to engage in behaviors that feel good to them as their self-care routine. It's common that within two to three weeks (sometimes less), these women return to me and express how pivotal those ten minutes were in their day, and how they had increased the time to twenty and then to thirty minutes. These behaviors are self-reinforcing. When you behave in ways that make you feel good, you feel better about yourself and want to engage in the behavior again and again, which is the premise of behavioral activation and why it can play a helpful role in our self-care habits.

chapter 31

LET'S DO THIS THING: CREATING A SELF-CARE RITUAL

Now that we've explored the importance of regular self-care to your anxiety management and mental health and how you might have to start the habit without initially having the supporting beliefs, we are ready to explore how to actually create a self-care ritual that helps to manage anxiety. So, let's break it down, shall we?

It's important for you to know that there is not a single correct or "right way" to do self-care. The very nature of self-care is that it is individualized and serves the need of whoever is doing it, the "self." That being said, if you are totally stuck on how to create a self-care routine, or if you want to follow the structure I prescribe to my patients and clients, I will share it in this chapter, but do understand that it is merely a guideline. While the suggestions I make are what I find help the majority of women with whom I work, it's important to do what is best for you and what works for you. We are all different, both inherently and in our external lives, from work schedules and home responsibilities to childcare availability and resources.

Here are a few simple guidelines regarding self-care routines or rituals. I will break these down into more detail in the next few chapters.

Dr. Crewe's No-Bullshit Self-Care Guidelines for Anxiety Management

1. What you do in your self-care routine should make you feel good, lift you up, and help you connect with your mind and body. A self-care ritual or routine should be designed to prepare you for experiencing your day and its emotions and to help you process your day and your emotions. Prepare and process.
2. At minimum, I suggest a self-care ritual that includes an activity that stills your mind (mindfulness), moves your body (movement), and helps you process emotions and connect with and express yourself (expressive self-care).
3. While it is best if your self-care ritual happens on a daily basis, it doesn't have to happen in the exact same way or at the exact same time each day. For the purposes of habit formation, doing it at the same time each day is helpful to make it easier to build into your schedule.
4. It's important to be flexible with your self-care ritual as it should be dynamic and responsive to how you're feeling each day. Perfectionism will not help here.

5. I've often recommended creating two versions of your self-care routine: a more full-length comprehensive one and a shorter, bare-minimum routine for those days that are simply bananas.
6. While I encourage tracking your self-care ritual and mood regularly in the next section, it's not required on a long-term basis and should be done *mindfully* to avoid self-shame and the perfectionism trap.

Sound solid? Great. Let's dig into these a bit deeper.

To do self-care, you actually have to do a self-care activity.

There are about a million different activities that you can do in a self-care ritual. However, as I do sometimes see confusion regarding what constitutes a true "self-care activity," we can look to the dictionary for the technical definition. **A self-care activity is one that you intentionally engage in for the purpose of maintaining or enhancing your mental and physical health**. I like this definition as it breaks down a few very important requirements for a self-care activity.

Put in simple terms, self-care activities are those things that we do because they make us feel good and because we feel good after doing them. We want to do them for the sake of our own enjoyment and well-being, and they are good for us. A self-care activity is not for anyone else's benefit, and it is not intended for any other purpose than your own wellness and enjoyment. A self-care activity could also be defined as something that not only feels good and brings joy but also makes you feel calm, happy, and refreshed after doing it. For some of my clients, this care can be listening to music and tuning out the world, getting outside for a walk with the dog, going for a sweaty run regularly, or journaling and meditation.

If you're stuck on finding activities that feel like self-care for you, I would encourage you to consider activities that bring you genuine joy and a sense of happiness. If you've struggled with your mental health for some time, I recognize that it may be a challenge to identify something that brings you joy. It may be something as small as a walk in the woods among nature, taking some time to sip a delicious cup of coffee, or playing with your pet. Most people can bring to mind an activity or experience that conjures feelings of enjoyment and joy. These positive feelings are clues and helpful guides to showing us what activities actually make us feel good (not numb, but good). Finding these activities may take some time or practice, and you may need to be a bit experimental about trying some new things before you find something that really fits and feels good.

The other important part of the definition is that the activity is "intentionally engaged in." So, what does that mean? Frankly, self-care does not have to be fancy or complicated (in fact, it shouldn't be), but it should be intentional. As our lives get busier, it is more and more challenging to fit in time reserved strictly for taking care of ourselves, and I have noticed women haphazardly denoting a naturally occurring event in their day as self-care in an attempt to check off the "self-care" to-do box. Nah, this won't do. Self-care is best when it is planned and intentional. However, what it doesn't mean is that it has to be rigid or look the exact same every single day. I often encourage women to create a "regular" self-care ritual that they can use most days, and a flexible "bare minimum" self-care routine for those days when life is hectic. The point, however, is that the activities and time you devote to them are done so with the intention of caring for and monitoring your own anxiety and mental health.

So, what do I mean by intentional? Well, it may require you to take a few moments in the morning to look ahead at your day and decide what period of time is going to be devoted to your own self-care and mental health. It may mean that you head to the school fifteen minutes early and do a quick meditation in your car prior to after-school pickup as a bare minimum. It may mean that you wake up early to fit in a quick yoga routine, mindfulness practice, and some time with your journal before your family wakes. It may also mean that you reserve twenty minutes after dinnertime to get out for a heart-pumping walk with your dog. If it's easier for you, mapping out your entire week ahead might be helpful as well. I like to spend time on Sunday evenings with my agenda, blocking out time each morning for my self-care. With that time intentionally planned on my schedule, I'm sure to avoid scheduling other things in that space. Voilà, intentional.

You only think you don't have the time for yourself

When I first begin working with women to manage their mental health, I recommend starting small with just ten to thirty minutes of self-care each day. That doesn't sound like too much, does it? Sometimes I've even referred to these little micro moments of self-care as "mental health first aid" when things are really bad for a patient and they're struggling to get through each day. A little can go so far in these times. Now, I'd love for you to have more like thirty to sixty minutes for your self-care routine each day, but I understand that these chunks of time can be a hard place to start.

Finding the time is usually the biggest obstacle that comes up when women begin a self-care routine, so let's get that out of the way right now. As a woman who often has a very full schedule in running an online business, being a practicing physician, and being a mother to twin girls, I can assure you that I do not have more time than you do. I can also tell you that fitting in my self-care is not optional. I have been intentional about making it a priority. "Not having enough time" is an excuse that women often lean on when they lack the belief that they are worthy or don't believe that their needs are as important as everything else on their to-do list. The women who cannot find time to spend ten minutes on themselves each day are the ones who struggle to see their own worth and value. There is no way around it: when you value something, you make it a priority to maintain it. If you're struggling to fit in even ten minutes of self-care on a daily basis, it is not a time-management problem, it is a priority problem.

It's also possible that if you can't seem to find any time to spend on your self-care that you have become acclimated to being busy and need to take a step back to objectively ask yourself some hard questions. Many times we have taken on responsibilities and soldier on with them even when they are no longer serving us or are in our best interest. We fear letting others down if we back out on commitments or feel guilty saying no. Take some time now to consider everything with which you fill your schedule and time. Is everything that you commit to really more important than your own health? You need to make yourself a priority in your own life.

If you are trying to fit in your self-care for ten to thirty minutes a day and still cannot seem to find the time for it, it's high time for you to review your current schedule, workload, and the expectations you put on yourself. It is absolutely imperative that you honestly evaluate how you're spending your time and whether it's sustainable. As women, we tend to believe that rushing around being everything for everyone is what we are supposed to be doing, but it's not. We take on so many extra responsibilities (often out of obligation or fear of disappointing others) or hold ourselves to such high expectations that we do not realize that we are burning ourselves out. A wise person once said, "If you don't make time for your wellness, you will be forced to make time for your illness." The speaker is unknown, but the sentiment is true.

No matter how much time you can carve out for your self-care routine, there are a few guidelines I usually recommend so this practice is beneficial, and your time is used in the most worthwhile way.

You don't have to do your self-care first thing in the morning, but it's helpful

The most common and (typically) most effective time to do your self-care routine is in the morning before the day begins and everyone else in your household wakes. That's when I'm writing this chapter right now, in fact. I believe that starting off your morning with a delicious cup of coffee (or tea), a mindfulness practice, some quiet reflection, and designated time to focus on your passion or listen to an audiobook is just the best damn way to start a day (the silence alone is worth it, to be honest). I know there are fierce advocates both for and against morning routines, as they have become quite a hot topic in the past five years in the personal development space. If you look up morning routines, you will find that many famous and successful individuals were known to have a morning routine, and you can find limitless books and blogs espousing the benefits of the same. I firmly believe that the benefits of doing my self-care first thing in the morning far exceed any benefit I get from that extra hour of sleep. However, waking up early is not always best for everyone, and I acknowledge that it doesn't work with everyone's biological clock. So, while morning might be an excellent time to do a self-care routine for many women, it might not be for you, and that's okay. If you're interested in exploring more insights and tips on starting a morning routine, I've included some of my favorite resources on the subject at the end of the book.

If early morning doesn't work for your morning routine, take some time to reflect on when in your day you can carve out time to focus on your self-care activities. The evening before bed is another commonly enjoyed time, as it gives you a chance to reflect on and process your day. In fact, some women do combine a morning routine with exercise and then meditation with a journaling and gratitude practice before bed as a means of bookending their day. While this routine may seem like a lot of work to fit into your day, remember you can always start small and begin with just one habit at a time.

With your time set aside and your activities chosen, it's time to start your self-care ritual. But it's important that we work to create it in such a way that it doesn't increase our anxiety. Too often women tell me that they feel "stressed" about having to fit in their self-care each day, which is completely counter to the purpose of this exercise. It is not imperative that your self-care happens every single day at the exact same time or exactly how you plan it out. That expectation is your anxiety wearing a perfectionism mask.

Take some time to write the answers to these questions in your journal before moving on to the next chapter.

1. Is there a time each day that you can block out for your intentional self-care time?
2. If your schedule is constant (i.e., you work set hours each day), will you do your self-care at the same time each day?
3. If your schedule is variable, can you take some time to look at the overview of your week and ensure you're putting self-care on your schedule once each day?
4. How much time do you want to start spending on self-care?
5. What activities will you use for self-care?

chapter 32

THE THREE COMPONENTS OF A SELF-CARE ROUTINE

Remember, what exact activities you do are less important than putting time aside each day to intentionally care for and check in on your own mental health. However, I have noticed a trend in the self-care rituals that women find most helpful, and they reliably include Mindfulness, Movement, and Expressive Self-Care.

Meditation and Mindfulness: Calm the Mind

You need to get over your damn self and learn how to meditate already

Smartphone apps and websites such as Balance, Calm, HeadSpace, and Insight Timer all offer beginner courses in meditation to help a newbie get a sense of what it means to observe their thoughts.

These courses are often a seven- or ten-day series of brief practices, where a voice describes what to do while you sit quietly in whatever position that is comfortable for you and listen to the instructions. There are many simple and less intimidating ways for you to explore meditation and experience the benefits of being a quiet observer of your mind.

For meditation beginners, the simplest and least intimidating way to begin is with guided meditation. In a guided meditation, an instructor provides guidance on focusing the attention on a particular focus. The "goal" (if there is one) is to try to effortlessly direct the attention to a particular focus for a defined period of time. There are innumerable options for guided meditations, and it may take some trial and error to find an instructor, platform, or style that you prefer. Depending on the meditation, the focus of attention may be something subtle such as the inflow and outflow of our breath, although for many of my patients, this sensation is likely too subtle for the very activated and anxious mind.

One particularly helpful modality that I find useful for my patients who are very anxious is a body-scan meditation, as it provides a source of focus that changes frequently and requires more "active" involvement of the mind, which is helpful for maintaining focus. Chants or mantras are also common focuses during meditation. The important thing to remember is that the mind drifting off or becoming distracted is actually the point of the practice, and it's inevitable. When your mind drifts off from the focal point to thinking about thoughts of your day, worries of the future, or regrets of the past, the practice of meditation asks that we simply and gently redirect the mind back to the focal point.

One of the most important parts of meditation is remaining emotionally objective; that is, to avoid judgment of the mind drifting or becoming emotionally caught up in whatever story the mind starts spinning. It's right here that a lot of people feel that they "fail" at meditation because they're unable to be nonjudgmental about their practice. When their mind drifts off, they chastise themselves and layer on negative self-talk about their perceived failure. However, that is *so not* the point. When your mind drifts away to another thought, meditation instructs us to catch it in the distant thought and objectively and compassionately reorient the attention, bringing the mind back to the "task" at hand, whether it be focusing on or counting the breath (depending on your meditation). It's this process of the mind drifting off, us catching our minds off in another place, and lovingly and intentionally returning our attention to the focal point that is the practice of meditation. Our minds have to drift off for us to catch them and learn how to bring them back. It's this same skill that we can use when we have anxious thoughts; it helps us learn how to emotionally detach and remain objective about them.

Your power to manage your own anxious thoughts lies in your ability to observe your thoughts objectively and remain emotionally neutral to them. When we can step back from our thought process and observe where our mind goes, mindfully catch ourselves in certain thoughts, and reorient it back to a focus, we can learn to do the same with anxious thoughts. When our mind begins to ruminate about our particular anxiety trigger or something in the future, we can use our skills of thought awareness to identify we are in that thought and purposefully, lovingly, and intentionally return our mind to the task at hand or a more reassuring thought. We can also more objectively evaluate that thought for validity rather than being swept up automatically in the emotional vortex that comes with those anxious thoughts. This practice is how we reclaim the power from our anxious thoughts.

It's important to start small

As you begin your meditation and mindfulness practices, it's important to start small. No one is expecting you to carve out thirty minutes in your day to meditate every day right from the start. In fact, both meditation and daily mindfulness are skills that must be learned, and that learning takes time, commitment, and practice. Many of the apps I suggested provide practice opportunities in as little as five minutes a day. These are great places to start.

For an easy and manageable start, begin with just five to ten minutes a day of a meditation and commit to your practice for one week. You may try early morning for your meditation sessions, or in the evening to help you settle before bed. Before you know it, with diligence and compassionate commitment, your meditation sessions will be something you look forward to, and you will begin to experience the myriad of benefits from this ancient practice.

As with meditation, it's important to understand that incorporating daily mindfulness is a lifestyle change that is called a "practice" for a reason. It is not a skill to be mastered but rather an ongoing practice that will strengthen over time. In my clinical and personal experience (and this experience is supported by research as well), there is a negative correlation between the frequency of one's mindfulness practice and level of anxiety. That is, the more often you practice mindfulness and reorient yourself in your present-moment experience, the less often you will experience anxiety. The truth is that anxiety lives in the stories in our minds, whether of the past or future, and by reorienting ourselves in the moment (no matter how challenging that is), we take back our power from anxiety.

Exercise: Move your body

Important preface to this section: The following section encourages the addition of movement in your self-care routine as being important to your mental health. It is critical to me that I make it clear that I am aware that movement and exercise are not possible for everybody. If you are disabled or chronically ill and movement is not an option for you, please know that I see the unique challenges you experience. I encourage you to skip over this section if you feel like it. I'm aware of the fact that the majority of self-help and mental health advice is ableist and that those who are disabled or otherwise unable to move their bodies are at a disadvantage in that there are little to no accessible resources available that acknowledge their unique experience.

Now that we have explored the practice of meditation and how valuable it is in your anxiety management and self-care routine, I want to explore the second most important activity: movement. At least one of the activities you include in your self-care ritual should be moving your body in some way. Whether it's a heart-pumping jog or some gentle stretching and yoga, exercise is absolutely invaluable to mental health and anxiety management.

Now, let's be clear: By no means am I prescribing that you begin training for a marathon or doing an hour's worth of weight training tomorrow. Like meditation (and all things really), starting slow and steady is key to habit formation. I also want to clarify that exercise or movement doesn't have to look the same for all of us, and it doesn't have to look the same from day to day. When I encourage my patients to get regular exercise as one of their self-care activities, it may look like a brisk after-dinner walk, a quick twenty minutes of YouTube yoga, or some time on a stationary bike while reading a book. To be frank, I don't care how you move your body regularly as long as you do something (and no, your "active job" doesn't count—I wasn't born yesterday).

I've often compared the brain to a dog. If you have a dog in your house, it's likely you can attest to your dog getting a bit squirrely when he doesn't have a walk. The same thing occurs with your brain, especially an anxious brain. Just as anxious energy manifests itself as physical sensations, I believe that we need to exercise anxious energy *out* regularly to avoid it causing more problems. Anxious minds often have an excess of mental energy that benefits from a sweaty workout or heart-pumping hike. *Move the body, still the mind.*

If you seriously want to get your anxiety under control, you are going to have to exercise

There are few situations in my career as a family physician that bring up more resistance in patients than when I suggest increasing their physical activity. It would seem that people either love being active and consistently do some sort of exercise, or they hate it, avoid it completely, and pretend it doesn't exist. If you fall in the latter group, I see you. Some of us just hate exercising. It's a lot of work and requires a lot of motivation and self-discipline to do it regularly, especially when you're anxious and chronically tired because of it. I get it.

But exercise is important. Moving your body is important. I have worked long enough in my job to notice a clear and stark difference between the aging and health of a body and mind that exercises regularly and one that does not. Trust me, the difference between an eighty-year-old who exercises regularly and one who does not is startling. Furthermore, aside from my personal observations, the research is very clear that regular exercise is vitally important to our health, both physically and mentally. In fact, some research suggests that exercise may be as effective as medication for the treatment of anxiety and depression. (If you are someone reading this book who actually loves exercise and doesn't have any difficulty doing it, then you can skip over the next few paragraphs.)

For all my exercise-resisters: This moment may be one of the first during your anxiety management and recovery journey that you come up against a recommendation that you really don't agree with or want to comply with, and that is fine. Acknowledging your resistance is important. I believe when we experience internal resistance about something in our lives that we know to be good for us that it is important to explore that resistance and dig deep. I often ask my patients to reflect on their beliefs and options in a given situation when it comes to not wanting to participate in well-known health-promoting recommendations.

For example, you may really want your anxiety to get better and you also may really not like exercising. You also may believe and appreciate that exercise is important for mental health and understand that research shows how important it is. However, you may also *really hate* exercising. You may have all sorts of reasons and excuses and stories why exercising will not help you or why you can't do it (your beliefs) and therefore, alas, we are at a crossroad, which is why realizing our power of choosing our beliefs is so important.

Consider the following: While it may be possible to "get better" or manage your anxiety without regular exercise as part of your treatment plan, it's likely going to be harder to fully get better. You may not reach the level of healing and recovery that you could have if you started to exercise regularly. You may get about 70 percent better but always wonder if you could achieve just a bit more control over your anxiety if you had just started exercising, which may or may not be acceptable to you, and the reality is, you are the one who gets to choose.

You also get to choose if you want to continue carrying your beliefs around exercising. Perhaps you believe it's awful or you don't like it, that it isn't fun, or that your body isn't meant for it. You get to choose these beliefs, but you need to acknowledge that they are in direct conflict with your desire to get better. Ah, the power of choice.

So, which is more important to you? Your anxiety getting better or your beliefs about hating exercise? Which of these do you want to keep or choose? While they may not be totally mutually exclusive, which one is more important to you? It is okay if you're willing to sacrifice your full anxiety recovery to hold onto those beliefs about exercising because exercising for your own health is just too damn hard or too terrible for you. That is totally fine. That is your choice, but understand it that way.

There is no denying that exercising regularly is important for your mental health. I would suspect that if you have read this far into a book about anxiety management that your mental health is important to you. So, are you willing to put in the hard work to get what you want?

Expressive Self-Care: You have to get the ick in your brain out.

The third and final type of activity that I recommend to include in your self-care routine is some form of expression. Expression (in my simplified view) refers to getting what is inside your mind out of your mind in some way.

We are not meant to keep our anxious thoughts (or energy) inside forever. Have you ever experienced relief after you were able to share your thoughts with a friend or therapist? Have you ever felt better writing down how you feel about something and seeing it on paper? Or perhaps you're an artist, and you "create" your emotions out.

Journaling is likely the simplest and most common means of including expressive self-care in your daily ritual. It is the most common expressive self-care activity I see women doing, and it is one that I recommend. Many people find journaling transformational, while others find it awkward and unhelpful writing to themselves in a "dear diary" sort of way. Personally, I find journaling helpful when I need to work through a complex situation, as I believe seeing emotions, thoughts, and beliefs on paper can help me see them more objectively. If you are like many of my patients and struggle to find things to write about in your journal, I have provided some ideas. Like any self-care activity or habit already discussed, it's important to start small and introduce habits in a manageable way to avoid overwhelm.

Here are a few suggestions to help you get the journal juices flowing:

- **Self-Love Journaling:** Each evening, write down three separate things you loved about yourself that day. Were you particularly patient with your child during a meltdown? Were you assertive with your sister-in-law? Did you use self-care instead of buffering? Did you take time to rest?
- **Gratitude Journaling:** Gratitude practices are incredibly powerful for helping to shift our lens to the more positive aspects to our lives, and it has great research supporting its benefits for rewiring our brains. Try writing down three things you were grateful for each evening and watch how your brain begins to seek out more moments to be grateful.
- **Morning Pages:** Morning pages are a practice of stream-of-consciousness journaling intended to be done first thing in the morning. It's a practice of downloading all of the thoughts, emotions, and noise that pop up in your brain first thing. It's intended for you to write two or three pages nonstop right when you wake up.
- **Brain Dumping:** If you're a more visual thinker or have many scattered and disconnected thoughts spiraling around in your brain, you can write them all down and see how they connect. Try mind-mapping to see where the connections lie that you haven't seen yet.
- **Journaling Prompts:** The internet is a goldmine of journaling prompts related to almost anything you can think of to write about.

Again, your form of expressive self-care does not have to only be journaling. The main principle of expressive self-care is to do what feels best to you to get your emotions, thoughts, and beliefs out of your mind for a time. It's important to find the activity that feels good to you and do it regularly. Whether it's painting, sculpting, journaling, or singing, we are expressive beings and not meant to keep our emotions and thoughts bottled up.

Self-Check:

Reflect now on some ways that you could include expressive self-care in your ritual. I have included some questions for you to explore this concept.

1. What creative or expressive activity have you done in the past that makes you feel good?
2. Is there any activity that you used to do and that you loved but has since been buried under adult responsibilities or having too much to do?
3. What creative activity do you miss doing?
4. How do you feel about journaling?

chapter 33

TRACKING AND MONITORING YOUR ANXIETY: THE EASY WAY

We have now reviewed the three most important types of activities to include in your (preferably daily) self-care ritual. We have discussed buffering and how buffering activities can sometimes be disguised as self-care activities and why it is so important to distinguish between the two and develop an awareness of your buffering activities. The final strategy I want to discuss regarding self-care routines is Tracking. Tracking is very important for your awareness of your anxiety so that you can develop a proactive approach to managing your anxiety when it flares up rather than hiding from it and then panicking when it's going haywire.

Many people panic at the thought of having to track anything in their lives, and tracking their mood and anxiety is no different. However, there is so much valuable insight to gain from regularly keeping track of and documenting your mood and level of anxiety from day to day and comparing it to the frequency of other habits, behaviors, and tendencies you have in your life (i.e., exercising, drinking alcohol, meditation, etc.). For one, tracking something prevents you from avoiding it, and that is one thing that many of my patients try to do a lot of the time (and in quite creative ways, I might add). Second, by tracking your anxiety and behavior on a daily basis in a little square chart in a fancy-looking journal or notebook, you will not only probably feel more responsible and scientific about the whole thing, you'll also be a bit more objective about your emotional days when you can see the facts down on paper. Finally, it is only by observing ourselves and our minds for a period of time that we can develop the critical emotional awareness we need to make true change in our mental health.

So, what exactly will you be tracking? When I begin working with a new client or patient on their anxiety, I ask them to track three basic things each day: anxiety/mood, self-care activities, and buffering habits. Typically, tracking is most easily done in the evening so that you can reflect on the entire day (rather than in the morning when you will be tracking the previous day and it may not be as accurate).

I have included a basic Mood Tracker system in the Resources section for this book. You can use it or any other form of tracking chart or system you prefer, as the important thing is that you actually track rather than specifically how you track. Feel free to adapt the tracker to fit your lifestyle and habits. I've included an example here for you to get an idea of how to set up your tracker.

	M	T	W	T	F	S	S
Mood	5	6	4	5	8	9	9
Anxiety	9	7	7	8	4	3	4
Meditation	X			X	X	X	X
Yoga					X	X	X
Netflix	X	X					

Tracking your mood and activity does not and will not need to be a lifelong, never-ending practice starting from today. In my clinical and personal experience, tracking for eight to twelve weeks is typically more than sufficient for patients to gain considerable clarity and insight into their own anxiety and how they can make an impact on it with behavior change. So, rest assured, you will not need to track your anxiety and self-care for the rest of your life (unless you want to). Many of my patients do find the insights gained from tracking to be invaluable, and they develop a fondness for the practice as it allows them to remain intentional and focused on their mental health, which is helpful for relapse prevention and long-term mood stability. Personally, I have found that when my anxiety or mood begins to worsen over the course of a few weeks, I will lean back on my tracking practice to gain more clarity into what may be contributing to my feelings.

So, let's break down tracking using the example chart I provided. In this example, you can see how mood and anxiety were both rated out of 10 (10 being high and 0 being low). For the case of anxiety, 10 equates to very high anxiety/distress and 0 is no distress or anxiety at all. It is also important to track your overall mood, or how positive or negative you felt overall throughout the day. You will also track it on a scale out of 10, with 10 being very positive and 0 being very depressed. The practice of tracking both your anxiety/distress and your mood is important for a few reasons.

First of all, consider that your mood and anxiety are like two ends of a teeter-totter. You will notice (if you haven't yet) that when one of these things is up, the other is down. When your anxiety is higher, your mood is typically lower. When your anxiety improves and is lower, your mood goes up. Learning to notice this pattern between your mood and anxiety provides more insight into your own mind.

The second important reason for this purposeful daily tracking of your mood is so that your "mood glasses" do not cloud your ability to notice improvement in your anxiety and mood. Think back to a day that you were in a positive emotional state, everything felt good, and your anxiety was low. From this place, everything in your life is rosy and positive. Everything that once felt negative suddenly doesn't feel so bad. Your worries seem smaller, your kids seem to get along better, and you handle upsets with more ease. The lens with which you view the world is positive and "rose-colored" because of your good mood.

Now, consider the last time you were in a low-mood state. The world seemed very dark, your goals seemed unattainable, your kids seemed to misbehave more, your diet was terrible, and you were lost in a vortex of negative self-talk and thoughts. The entire world was tainted with a dark lens of sadness.

It is this shifting lens through which we see the world that is defined by our mood, which is precisely the reason why I encourage my patients to track their mood and anxiety on a nightly basis for a period of time. When you can track how you were feeling as you reflect on your day, you have a more accurate assessment of how that day went. I see it often in the office between appointments with my patients who are struggling with anxiety and depression. If their appointment is on a day that they're feeling down or worse than usual, it seems like the entire period between appointments has been "bad" and nothing we are doing is working. In contrast, they can also have an exaggerated sense of things improving if they happen to be in a positive mood that day. Tracking is the only way to have an accurate and objective sense of the trend of your mood and anxiety.

Note that a few other things are tracked on the example chart. Two self-care activities (meditation and yoga) are also tracked with a simple X on the day they were completed. You may also notice that on the days that yoga is checked off, the anxiety is rated a bit lower and the mood a bit higher. While I created this rating as an intentional example for the purposes of illustrating this concept, it is common that many women find this same trend in their own charts. The more self-care that is done in a given day, the more likely we are to feel calmer and happier.

The final item tracked on our example chart is Netflix. In this example, my fictional patient has realized that on her particularly bad days, she immerses herself in movies or a series to completely numb her emotions and buffer. Interestingly, tracking buffering activities has been one of the more surprisingly powerful practices I recommend to my patients and clients.

I remember when one of my early clients realized that she buffered her emotions in one way or another nearly seven days a week. While that is not necessarily a bad thing, she recognized it as a sign that her anxiety was indeed not under control. It's important to become aware of what we do when we're not "paying attention," as it can often help us understand what is going on deeper in our minds and can give us insights into where we need to go next. To track, if you happen to find yourself in a buffering activity (say, overeating chocolate chips in the pantry like *yours truly*), you would simply put an X in the row for that day and that activity. At the end of the week, you can then reflect on the frequency of your buffering activities and pay attention to patterns. It's often that on days when our anxiety level or distress level is higher, our buffering activities will show a correlational increase in frequency as well, as our subconscious mind tries to reduce our own discomfort through these activities. By tracking and becoming more aware of our buffering activities, we can use it to identify periods of increased anxiety when we may benefit from increased dedicated self-care time to compensate.

Take a few moments to consider how you might incorporate tracking into your self-care routine and into your life. I love doing my tracking during my self-care routine, as it helps me refocus on how my mind is feeling, what my mood has been like, what triggers came up for me during the day, and what buffering activities I engaged in. This tracking and awareness allows us to notice patterns and increase our understanding of our particular anxiety monster. It's this awareness that is power and will help us maximize our efforts doing all of the other hard work, for when we can anticipate our anxiety will get worse, we can plan for it and be more proactive.

chapter 34

LET'S GO DEEPER: ANXIETY, ALIGNMENT, AND TRUST

I remember when I reached the point in my postpartum mental health journey that I realized I had finally come out the other side. I had been working hard with a therapist, uncovering all my hidden cognogens, unpacking my perfectionism, and mindfully caring for myself with a regular self-care ritual. I remember feeling so proud of how far I had come, realizing that I had overcome what had held me back for so long.

For quite a few months, my anxiety was controlled. I knew that as long as I continued keeping track of how I was feeling, adjusting my self-care practices to support myself when it began to increase, and being proactive about working with my thoughts, the anxiety I had been so consumed by was now under my control. I felt almost limitless.

I have come to realize through both my own experience and through working with hundreds of women with anxiety that there are actually two different "types" of anxiety. There is the superficial anxiety that bothers us most of the time, the day-to-day fears and worries. This anxiety may be about driving on icy roads, worrying about whether your child will do well on their math test, or the anxiety that comes with running a chaotic household. It's this superficial anxiety that overwhelms the majority of us and is likely what brought you to buying this book in the first place.

There is also a deeper, more buried type of anxiety. This anxiety is often unnoticed under the day-to-day busyness. In myself and in many women with whom I work, it is not until the more superficial anxiety is under control that this sneakier, subtler anxiety surfaces.

I began to notice a different sort of anxiety was beginning to bubble up to the surface in my own life after I had been well for a time. I initially panicked, fearing that my anxiety was back (which is a very common response in most women). However, as I had learned and practiced being mindful of my reactions, I instead approached this increasing anxiety with curiosity. Instead of frantically wondering if I had done something wrong, I took to my self-care ritual with a vengeance. Without a clear trigger for why my anxiety seemed to be returning, I spent time with my journal in quiet reflection, asking myself (as I often do), "What does my anxiety need me to realize right now?" I meditated and allowed for my mind to work through whatever it was dealing with at that time. I trusted that no matter what my anxiety did or what it was coming back for, I would be prepared and could handle it.

I began noticing patterns around when my anxiety would surface. When I was doing my monthly finances and reviewing the progress made toward paying down our household mortgage, my gut was in knots. When I was making a trip to the hardware store to buy more tools and supplies to do a repair in the house, my heart was beating fast and my hands were sweating. When we were stuck in the yard on a beautiful summer day, pulling dreaded weeds out of the garden beds and wasting valuable time that we could spend playing with our girls, I was resenting the fact that we had our house. That was when I realized it. I was living my life out of alignment.

What happened next is what I identify as likely the second most stark and uncomfortable realization of my life: I didn't want my beautiful big house. I had worked so hard for it and had set goals to own my own home. Although I was grateful for it and loved the beauty of it, I realized I didn't really want it anymore. When my husband and I first viewed the house, I remember feeling like it was our "dream home"—the one everyone dreams their whole lives for owning, and we were living in it. But I realized that while it was (and still is) our "dream home," it was that living in a home wasn't actually ever my dream. I had fallen victim to the script that so many of us follow without questioning that buying a beautiful home would mean that you had made it and would live happily ever after.

I realized I was working so hard all the time to pay for a home that we rarely had time to do what we really loved, which was travel, explore, and spend time as a family. Instead of spending Sunday afternoons exploring the woods with my girls, I was cleaning floors and bathrooms of a house that was much too big for us. I realized that I had been living inside someone else's dream and doing so was preventing me from fully realizing what was really our true dream. It was an overwhelming and complicated time.

My husband and I began to have some difficult conversations. I shared with him that my anxiety was telling me that there was something else we should be doing, another way we should be spending our lives. He expressed that he, too, found the upkeep and maintenance of our dream home tiring and unfulfilling. We shared bigger aspirations of wanting to travel more, show our children the world, and make the most of our time as a family. We began exploring ways that we could do just that and came across exciting ideas like tiny homes and full-time RV living. When I imagined selling our house and being free of the responsibility, both my anxiety and I felt a sigh of relief.

For once, I realized that instead of being my enemy as I had always assumed it had been, my anxiety was actually my ally. I reflected on when I was very sick postpartum and my anxiety pushed me to learn how to become more assertive and set healthy boundaries. I remembered when my anxiety reminded me that I should exercise to keep it under control and encouraged me to cleanse my calendar and to-do list of things that no longer served me. I realized that perhaps there had been a method to the madness of my anxiety all this time. My anxiety had been telling me where I was out of alignment with my truth and my soul.

I have seen this same pattern in so many women as well. After we have worked together to get their anxiety under control for a few months, they will often return puzzled. They say things like, "I was doing so well, and now I am having weird anxiety again. I'm not sure what it's coming from." Together, we go through all the healthy habits and mindset shifts she has made. We review how often she is working with her thoughts and if there has been some sort of change in her life. When we come up empty-handed, I often say, "There is something your anxiety is telling you, and I suspect it has something to do with what you're not seeing. Whether it's a dream that you've put on the back burner, a relationship you're continuing to tolerate, or a situation you are in, there is something out of alignment in your life."

What if we began to view our anxiety as a superpower instead of a weakness? What if instead of a chink in our armor, it was our armor? What if instead of forcing it away, we learned to embrace it and lean in? What would it look like if you saw your anxiety as a clue of what you needed to focus on in your life to truly live in alignment? If every single time you had anxiety about conflict in an unhealthy relationship, is it possible that your anxiety was encouraging you to set healthy boundaries?

It takes a certain level of self-awareness and anxiety management to reach this point, however. When you are in the vortex and so anxious you can barely think straight, it's not easy to see the forest for the trees. We need to first learn about our anxiety, learn how to turn down the volume and regain our control. Once we have become agents over our anxiety and are no longer being controlled by it, once we have demonstrated our willingness to do hard things and face dark corners in our minds, only then can we see the truth of our anxiety. Only then can we see that it has been trying to help us all along. This awareness is why taking care of your physical body, working with your anxious thoughts, improving your self-worth, and setting healthy boundaries in toxic relationships improves anxiety. When we do something that brings us closer to our truth, when we advocate for ourselves, when we start exercising and meditating, when we develop a greater sense of confidence and set healthy boundaries, our anxiety reduces and rewards us. It has been giving us clues the entire time.

So, what does it mean to truly be in alignment? For many women, alignment is a vague, murky concept. In our modern age of personal development, alignment is sometimes used as a way to get out of something, almost a cop-out from doing hard things. "It doesn't feel aligned," some of my previous clients have said when they felt the next right step was too challenging for them to take. Deciphering between the discomfort of superficial anxiety and the discomfort of being out of alignment is not easy. It's the difference between "I'm scared I will fail" and "This is 100 percent not right for me." It's the difference between your mind spewing anxious warnings at you to retreat or abandon a project and your gut feeling of "nope." I wish I could tell you there was a simple step-by-step process to learn how to fine-tune this knowledge, but the reality is that it takes time and learning by trial and error. If you have ever said yes to something and had that gut feeling it wasn't right for you and then were kicking yourself afterward because you knew it wasn't aligned, this awareness is how you learn to listen to yourself. I know I can think of at least ten times in my life that although my gut was saying no (or maybe even hell no), I said yes and later regretted it, wondering why I didn't listen to myself when I knew better. Whether you refer to it as intuition, a gut feeling, or alignment, being able to listen and trust yourself and trust in forces greater than you is the ultimate anxiety management strategy.

When you reach the point in your anxiety management journey that you feel a sense of true agency over your worried thoughts and are confident in your ability to manage it, it's common to think that your anxiety will never become severe or incapacitating again. How I wish that were true. If you are diligent with everything I have shared and taught in this book, I am confident that your anxiety will be better managed and will cause you less trouble, but as I've reiterated multiple times, your anxiety will never completely go away. Let's be honest: There is literally zero chance that you will never have anything happen in your life that you will not be worried about. You now have the skills and mindset to handle it, but you need more than that. At the end of the day, one of the most important and fundamental strategies you need is leaning in to a deep sense of trust that no matter what happens, you will be okay. Trust is such a fundamental and foundational part of managing anxiety and being mentally well. However, it seems esoteric and nebulous to most women who are right in the thick of anxiety and looking for help with managing it. If I were to talk to a woman who is having daily panic attacks or is constantly overwhelmed with her life about cultivating a deep sense of trust in herself and the universe (or God, Spirit, what-have-you), it would seem insensitive and shallow. I have done this work long enough to know where a woman's head is at different places in her mental health journey. In the early days, not only will this recommendation fall flat, but it could be borderline offensive to a woman who has no time to waste and needs to feel better today. However, as you become more and more aware of how to manage your anxiety, and your ability to detect it, manage it, and interpret it becomes more advanced, it is often this strategy that I recommend to incorporate into your life.

Realistically, all of the tools, self-care, and mindset shifts aside, having a deep and genuine sense of trust is the fundamental antithesis of anxiety. Anxiety tells us nothing is safe, and trust tells us it will all be okay. When your child is starting school and you're wrought with worry about their first days, you have to trust that you have done everything you can for them up until then. When your relationship seems to be rocky or you're feeling less than confident about it, you have to trust that even if it ends, you will be okay, and everything will work out. Cultivating a deep sense of trust that there are forces outside of you that are influencing your life in ways that you cannot see is invaluable. When you lose your job or get sick, although it seems insurmountable at the time, a sense of trust will carry you through. Whether you are religious or spiritual or not, whether you believe in Spirit, God, the Universe, Allah, or Mother Nature, at the end of the day, you have to believe that things will be okay and that forces outside of your control are working in your favor. In the words of one of my favorite spiritual guides, Gabrielle Bernstein, you have to believe "The Universe has your back."

I recall when we listed one of our rental properties for sale. Although it had a few views, there was minimal interest and zero offers. I was so frustrated. I was impatient. I was anxious about it. I didn't know what would happen if it didn't sell. I would have to carry the mortgage longer than I wanted to. We would have to keep maintaining it when we were out of town. All the "what ifs" caused me to have anxiety, and my sleep became affected. Luckily, I was aware of what was happening in my mind, and I applied all my proactive skills to manage the anxiety in the moment, increased my self-care appropriately, and worked with my thoughts. But it didn't take away the reality that if the house didn't sell, all those things would happen, and I would still have to deal with them. All those fears were legitimate and could realistically occur. So, while I felt better overall about my experience of the anxiety and was able to help it bother me less, it still hung around. The house didn't sell.

Fast-forward eighteen months in the future. When our plans for parking our RV on our planned lot fell through at the last minute, we were stuck with quite literally nowhere to live. We ended up moving into our rental property that hadn't sold. It was then that it hit me. The universe had had this figured out the whole time. I realized that had our rental house sold when I had so desperately wanted it to, we would have essentially had nowhere to live or park our RV. Although I had planned in my mind how things were supposed to go, the universe had alternate plans for how things would work out, and they did work out.

I wish I could say that this experience was the only time something like it has happened, and I don't believe it is because I am simply lucky. In 2020, when the government in my province made sweeping changes to healthcare and made devastating impacts on my career in unexpected ways, leaning on a deep belief that it was happening for a reason allowed me to stay resilient, bounce back from sadness, and be more open to new opportunities. Without those changes happening, I would never have stepped fully into my zone of genius in mental health, opened my virtual mental health clinic, or launched my online membership program. My life would literally not be what it is today had those negative things not happened. In the thick of it, I remember feeling like the world was ending until I realized that even the chaos of 2020 was happening for a reason. I surrendered to a plan greater than I was aware of and trusted I would be okay. There are at least a handful of other times this type of trust and surrender have happened in my life.

Can you think of any time in your life that you realized that things worked out exactly as they were meant to, even though it seemed awful in the moment? Has there ever been something you were so worried about but then realized that in hindsight, it made perfect sense? Maybe a relationship you thought was "the one" went up in flames, then afterward you met the true love of your life and had the experience to make the relationship even more solid? Or maybe losing that job you loved actually put you toward a path of finding your true calling and more joy than you imagined was available for you? While it can be so hard to trust in those scary and uncertain moments that there is a greater plan you are not aware of, it's experiences like these that can help reinforce your ability to trust. Trust yourself, trust the universe, and trust that you will be okay.

Integration

We have covered a lot in this book and you have made it to the end. Congratulations! I am so excited for you. You now have the knowledge, awareness, and strategy to truly create a lifelong approach to anxiety (and other mental health symptoms). It may seem overwhelming to reflect on everything I have taught you. You may be wondering, *How the heck am I supposed to do it all and remember it all?* Don't panic; you've got this. Here's a basic review of what we have covered and some guidance on where to begin.

I recommend starting with your self-care routine and making it really solid. Consistently carving out time in your day to intentionally focus on your mental health will go so far toward you integrating these habits and strategies into your life. Begin tracking your mood and buffering behaviors. Start putting in an earnest effort to journal and begin opening your mind so the emotions, thoughts, and beliefs can start coming up and out. Spend time with them, write them out, read them over, and watch for patterns. There is so much to learn that is within those thoughts, and spending the time with yourself is the way to begin.

When your anxiety spikes and you are overwhelmed with anxious thoughts, fall back onto your thought management skills. Label your thoughts, write them down, challenge them, and replace them. Be mindful of what you are making your thoughts and emotions mean about you, and remember that your thoughts are not facts. Use meditation to help you view your anxious thoughts in an objective way. Exercise to relieve anxious energy building up. It will help clear your mind and strengthen your body.

Consider the meaning you have assigned to your anxiety in your life. Remember that it is separate from you; it is a force that you can learn about and gain mastery over. Spend time evaluating your relationships and pay attention to how your body feels when you are with people in your life. Begin to desensitize yourself to speaking up and being more assertive by saying no or setting healthy boundaries in small ways. You will realize in time that your fears of conflict are usually unfounded and simply that—fears, not facts. Continue practicing and know that you only fear what you have not yet lived through and survived. Strengthen your assertiveness muscles and you will feel a new sense of empowerment and agency, realizing that you can reclaim your personal power and stop letting others cause you to feel small, resentful, obligated, or guilty. When you begin to place healthy boundaries, you will realize that not only are you helping yourself, but you are also helping others develop their own skills and autonomy as well. You will realize the incredible power of releasing yourself of the obligation to maintain toxic relationships and instead begin to choose yourself and your own happiness at the risk of disappointing others (because that risk won't bother you so much anymore).

As your anxiety ebbs and flows, you will begin to notice the patterns that it follows. By tracking your anxiety and mood, you will become aware of different triggers, how often you are buffering, and how you feel when you take care of yourself, all which will help reinforce your self-care habits. You will begin to develop a deep understanding of the importance of maintaining consistent self-care habits rather than riding the roller coaster of crisis management. When you can maintain a consistent self-care routine, you will develop a deeper sense of awareness and be more proactive rather than reactive in your approach to your mental health.

Find a community of supportive people that can help you stay accountable and provide a healthy sounding board for your thoughts and anxieties. Get out of your own echo chamber regularly. Embrace others who understand what anxiety is like and are motivated to face it with agency rather than apathy. Dismiss recommendations of quick fixes and reach for those who love you despite your struggles because being human means to have struggles sometimes, and that's okay. Know that support is always available, whether it be from me, another professional, or a group setting, in person or online.

Sometimes it takes trying a few different things before you find your fit, but when you do, the searching will be all worth it. Within that community, be vulnerable about your thoughts and experiences. You will be shocked at how similar your false thoughts and anxieties are to others around you, and you will learn that you truly are not alone. The commonalities I find between those women with whom I work are startling. In fact, that's one reason I knew that each one of the concepts in this book needed to be shared widely. Although our lives are all so different, our fears, anxieties, habits, and conditioning are remarkably the same.

Understand that anxiety management is a lifelong journey rather than a quick fix. Know that nearly each and every time you let your good habits slip away, your anxiety will remind you to restart them. You might kick yourself a few times for stopping (because you know better), but know that each time this happens, it will serve to reinforce your habits over and over again. Understand that you are a work in progress that is always learning, and sometimes we need to learn things a few times before we really absorb them. That is the process. That is how it goes.

Finally, cultivate a deep sense of trust that no matter what, you will be okay and that there are forces outside of you supporting you and your mission. If you are religious or spiritual, incorporate practices into your self-care ritual that help you connect with your source, your spirit, and the energy of the universe on a regular basis. This connection will help support you when you're feeling unsure and have tried everything you can to feel better.

Continue to learn and expand your knowledge about mental health. Be open to exploring new approaches and be willing to try new things, then sift through what works and what doesn't. I have provided a list of books and resources at the back of this book for you to follow what interests you so you can dive deeper.

I wish you all of the strength, motivation, and positive energy you need to truly love yourself. Believe you are worthy and take these exhilarating and scary steps toward your one beautiful and expansive life. Welcome to the next chapter of you.

acknowledgments

I quite literally could not have created this book without the support and love of so many souls I am blessed to have in my life. To my publishing team at YGTMedia Co., thank you for calling me up to share my story and being unfailingly confident in my message and how important it is to share it with the world. To Sabrina Greer, thank you for your patience with all my questions, for your expertise and experience in publishing, and for always wanting what is best for me. To Kelly and Christine, your ability to transform my scattered ideas and concepts into a beautiful, effective, and soul-filled journey for my readers has been truly divine.

To my daughters, who patiently waited while Mommy finished one more chapter when they really wanted to read a book or go outside and play with me, you are truly my why. It's my hope that I can help create a world where women are no longer taught to value others over themselves. I hope that in my writing this book, you will know that I have committed to instilling these beliefs in you as well as that my dream for you is to be the first of a new generation of women. I hope you know that even though it was so hard to be away from you while I was working and writing, chasing my dreams and helping women, that all that time away was so you had a model of what a passionate, soul-filled, and dynamic woman was. I believe children learn most effectively through what they observe. In order to help you believe in your own inherent worthiness, I need to believe in my own. For you to learn healthy boundaries, I need to learn them first. For you to truly chase your dreams without fear of disappointing others, I must as well. You are my inspiration. Thank you for making me a mom.

To my husband, Ryan, you are my rock and will always be. The passionate and independent woman in me has always needed a man who was equally as passionate and independent to support me when I feel weak and lift me up when I fall down. You have been unfailingly confident in my success, even when I wasn't. You have trusted me with all of my wild ideas and new plans and embraced my insatiable desire for personal growth with reckless abandon. Together we are creating the future of our dreams as we love hard on our girls and continue to grow as individuals and in our union. I could not think of a better partner to share my life with, and I am so grateful for you.

And finally, to all of the women who have entrusted me with their stories, their struggles, and their hearts, I would not have learned or mastered my craft without you. You are the reason why I have written this book and why I continue to show up day after day to help share these tools with more women. I genuinely believe that, as women, we have the power to change and heal the world, but we must first be well ourselves. I hope that this book will be the start of a revolution in how women care for their mental health, a manifesto for women no longer willing to carry the passive, self-sacrificing beliefs of our previous generations and our social conditioning. I hope that by reading the words on these pages that you will see how truly valuable you are and that you'll put in the hard work to help yourself feel truly well. We need you. The world needs you. You need you.

resources, works cited, and next steps

I have created a diverse collection of resources, worksheets, and templates for you to accompany this book and help consolidate and integrate your learning.

Download them for free today at CarlyCrewe.com/anxietybook

If you're looking for more support, whether 1:1 or in a group format, you can also explore courses and group programs at CarlyCrewe.com, all based on The Eunoia Approach to mental health.

Meditation Apps

Calm
HeadSpace
Insight Timer
MindShift

Community

The Eunoia Collective, a monthly mental health membership for women at CarlyCrewe.com/membership/

Reading List

Looking to dive deeper into a certain topic? I have included a list of some of my favorite books related to anxiety management. These are books I have found personally and professionally helpful, and ones I have often recommended to my patients and clients.

Starting a morning routine
- *The Mind Over Motherhood* Podcast, Season 1, Episodes 1–3
- *The Miracle Morning* by Hal Elrod (2012)

Postpartum mental health
- *Dropping the Baby and Other Scary Thoughts* by Karen Kleiman (2015)

Eating for mental health
- *Eat Complete* by Dr. Drew Ramsey, MD (2016)
- *Eat to Beat Depression and Anxiety: Nourish Your Way to Better Mental Health in Six Weeks* by Dr. Drew Ramsey, MD (2021)

Exercising for mental health
- *Exercise for Mood and Anxiety: Proven Strategies for Overcoming Depression and Enhancing Well-Being* by Michael W. Otto, PhD and Jasper A.J. Smits, PhD (2011)

Cognitive Behavioral Therapy
- *Mind Over Mood: Change the Way You Feel by Changing the Way You Think* by Dennis Greenberger and Christine A. Padesky (2015)
- *White Bears and Other Unwanted Thoughts: Suppression, Obsession, and the Psychology of Mental Control*, Daniel M. Wegner, PhD (1994)
- CBT: Canada, http://cbt.ca/
- *Rewire Your Anxious Brain: How to Use the Neuroscience of Fear to End Anxiety, Panic, and Worry* by Catherine Pittman, PhD (2015)

Cultivating trust
- *The Universe Has Your Back* by Gabrielle Bernstein (2018)
- *The Surrender Experiment* by Michael A. Singer (2015)
- *Women Who Run With the Wolves* by Clarissa Pinkola Estés, PhD (2017)
- *A New Earth: Awakening to Your Life's Purpose* by Eckhart Tolle (2008)

Emotional intelligence
- *Choose Wonder Over Worry: Move Beyond Fear and Doubt to Unlock Your Full Potential* by Amber Rae (2020)
- *Emotional Agility: Get Unstuck, Embrace Change, and Thrive in Work and Life* by Susan David, PhD (2016)

Identity
- *Untamed* by Glennon Doyle (2020)

YGTMedia Co. is a blended boutique publishing house for mission-driven humans. We help seasoned and emerging authors "birth their brain babies" through a supportive and collaborative approach. Specializing in narrative nonfiction and adult and children's empowerment books, we believe that words can change the world, and we intend to do so one book at a time.

ygtmama.com/publishing
@ygtmama.media.co
@ygtmama.media.co

Made in United States
Troutdale, OR
08/15/2023